AF412818

For Sonia Stern,
With warmest wishes from
Mary Lensky Friedman
1-24-90

THE EMPEROR'S KITES

A Morphology of Borges' Tales

MARY LUSKY FRIEDMAN

DUKE UNIVERSITY PRESS   *Durham 1987*

Permission to quote from the following selections is gratefully acknowledged.

From *The Aleph and Other Stories, 1933–1969*, by Jorge Luis Borges, edited and translated by Norman Thomas di Giovanni in collaboration with the author. English translation, copyright © 1968, 1969, 1970 by Emecé Editores, S.A., and Norman Thomas di Giovanni; copyright © 1970 by Jorge Luis Borges, Adolfo Bioy-Casares, and Norman Thomas di Giovanni. Reprinted by permission of the publisher, E. P. Dutton, a division of New American Library.

From *Borges: A Reader*, by Jorge Luis Borges, edited by Emir Rodríguez Monegal and Alastair Reid. Copyright © 1981 by Jorge Luis Borges, Alastair Reid, and Emir Rodríguez Monegal. Reprinted by permission of the publisher, E. P. Dutton, a division of New American Library.

From *A Universal History of Infamy*, by Jorge Luis Borges, translated by Norman Thomas di Giovanni. Copyright © 1970, 1971, 1972 by Emecé Editores, S.A., and Norman Thomas di Giovanni. Reprinted by permission of the publisher, E. P. Dutton, a division of New American Library. For the British edition (London: Allen Lane, 1973), permission by Penguin Books Ltd.

Ralph Waldo Emerson, "The Past," in *The Complete Works of Ralph Waldo Emerson*, 9:257–58, Cambridge: The Riverside Press, 1904; reprinted by AMS Press, Inc., New York, 1979.

Contents

The death of Jorge Luis Borges in June 1986 brings home to us how much we are his heirs. His idiosyncrasies of mind, startling four decades ago, no longer shock us. Rather, they are the accepted premises of literary theory in the 1980s. Borges' view of literature as the work not of individual men but of literature itself—or writing, as we now say—has firmly taken root as the notion of intertextuality. His idea that a reader alters a text, and in a sense creates it, forms the basis of reader criticism. And his taste for paradox and ever-deferred meaning anticipates Derrida. Critics have taken seriously and pushed to their logical extremes ideas that must have charmed Borges, at least in part, because of their very whimsicality. Be that as it may, in defining our intellectual stance toward literature we have chosen Borges as a precursor.

Precisely because this is so, my study will, to some, seem anachronistic and even un-Borgean. Its subject is Borges the man and his relationship to his work. The thesis I propose is that Borges builds each of his tales around a single narrative paradigm, and that this Borgean ur text expresses aspects of his psychic life. I argue that Borges returns again and again to his paradigm, with the tenacity of obsession, because each time he rehearses it he attempts to resolve conflicts arising from his ambivalence for his father. And I try to account for certain changes Borges makes in his paradigm after his father's death—changes crucial to his coming of age as a writer of tales—by explaining how they express Borges' mourning for his lost parent.

Necessarily, I rely on biography—and on biography conceived of not as the "rereading" of a life but in more stolid terms, as the accumulated store of more or less provable facts about a person. And I regard Borges' work as the product not of *écriture* but of one man's consciousness. For those who think of writers as the products of cultural codes, functions rather than people, my study may seem naive. Yet for anyone interested in why Borges' stories move us, I hope to open a new path of understanding. To speculate about the unconscious impulses that drive a great writer to create his art may shed light on the qualities in his work that compel our response.

I do owe a debt to structuralism, or at least to one of its thinkers. Vladimir Propp, in his 1928 work *The Morphology of the Folktale*, approaches fairy tales just as I do Borges' stories. Abstracting from a hundred Russian fairy tales a uniform sequence of functions—in my terms a paradigm—Propp claims to have discovered the basic structure of the fairy tale. In a similar way, I aim to isolate a structural pattern that informs each of Borges' fictional works. It is no accident, then, that my title echoes that of the great Russian formalist. Unlike Propp, however, I study texts produced by a single writer, not by an entire culture. And unlike him, I try to interpret the paradigm, to understand, from Borges' perspective if not from that of his reader, the psychic function the paradigm fulfills.

I am concerned here with exploring the psychic freight of certain key elements in Borges' tales that seem powerfully to affect us. Chief among these is Borgean *irrealidad*. I should explain at the outset that in translating the Spanish term I have stretched English usage and chosen "irreality"—by which I mean distorted reality—over "unreality." The latter term denotes frank non-existence, not the mysteriousness with which Borges suffuses many of his tales.

The study that follows does not, in any strict sense, interpret Borges' works. Nor does it attempt to descry any specific effect that Borges' paradigm may exert on a reader. Other critics, I hope, will take up where I leave off and study how the paradigm shapes a reader's response to Borges' work. To understand better how Borges' unconscious conflicts impinge on a reader might make us better understand how the pleasure of reading a great work of literature is born.

Acknowledgments

The generosity and friendship of many people have supported my work on this study and given indispensable help in its preparation. My warmest thanks go to everyone who volunteered good will, time and pains to facilitate my research, improve the manuscript or make possible its publication. I am particularly indebted to Ana María Barrenechea, whose guidance and example lie behind this book.

A research grant from Wellesley College in 1980–81 and a 1981 Summer Stipend from the National Endowment for the Humanities enabled me to carry out the research. Rutgers University also greatly furthered my work by relieving me of teaching duties during the fall of 1981. A more recent grant from the Archer M. Huntington Fund, administered by the Spanish Department of Wellesley College, has helped to meet the book's publication costs. I am grateful to these institutions for their support, and to the many colleagues there who have encouraged me. Justina Ruiz-de-Conde, Elena Gascón-Vera, and Tino Villanueva at Wellesley and Phyllis Zatlin and Margaret Persin at Rutgers deserve special mention.

Many people have in one way or another guided my research and given me invaluable advice. Martin S. Willick spent hours discussing with me many aspects of this study, and his tact in applying psychoanalysis to literature did much to shape many parts of the manuscript. Laura Jarett and George O. Papanek also helped to orient me in the psychoanalytic literature to which I refer, and Gerald E. Warshaver recommended anthropological studies germane to my subject.

To gain access to research materials, I relied on the help of librarians and friends. Ripon College extended me every courtesy of its library during 1980 and 1981, and Peter Chobanian, research librarian there, used every resource at his command to procure for me hard-to-find documents. The Argentine National Library and the Instituto de Literatura Argentina opened their collections to me. And the family of Sergio Provenzano allowed me to consult their private collection of Argentine periodicals during my visit to Buenos Aires. C. Jared Loewenstein, curator of the Borges collection at the University of Virginia Library, was helpful and prompt in answering my inquiries. And Norman Thomas di Giovanni, the principal translator of Borges' fiction into English, made some of his own scholarship available to me in manuscript form.

My trip to Buenos Aires depended for its success on the kindness of Ana María Barrenechea, Gene Bell-Villada, and Ronald Christ. Largely through their auspices I was able to meet a great many *porteños* who shared their ideas with me, among them Gloria Autino, Josefina Ludmer, Martha Mercader, Enrique Molina, Enrique Pezzoni, and Raúl Santana. The Fulbright Commission in Buenos Aires found me lodgings with Nélida Fratantoni, who treated me as a friend, not a tenant, during my stay with her.

Those who patiently read and commented on the manuscript include Joanne Ferguson and Pam Morrison at Duke University Press, as well as Gene Bell-Villada, Ronald Christ, Joseph Schraibman, and my father Louis Lusky. Any grace the study has is probably due to them, any awkwardness to my own intransigence.

As for the people who kept me from discouragement as I worked on the study, they are many and I am particularly indebted to them. My students at Rutgers University deserve mention here, as do my parents, all of my friends and my colleagues. My husband Michael H. Friedman has served untiringly as patient listener, ruthless editor, and loving friend. His judgment and ideas have surely affected my work in ways of which not even I am aware.

Borges' work is cited by page references within the text. Nearly all references to Borges' books appear in parentheses, immediately after the passage quoted. When two page references are given, the first refers to the original Spanish text, the second to the English translation on which I have relied. When I have modified another translator's work, a notation appears. In cases where no attribution of an English translator is given, the translation is my own.

Borges' following in the English-speaking world is so considerable, and good English translations of his work are so easily had, that I have thought best to make this study accessible to those who know Borges' writings chiefly in English translation. I have therefore chosen to give all quotations in English. When there is a reason for including the original text as well as the translation, I have done so. As for titles, I have chosen to use English translations of the titles of Borges' own works, since by now standard titles for so many of them have come into general use. In most other cases, I have left titles in their original language.

Two lists of abbreviations follow: the first of works in Spanish, the second of works in English translation.

ABBREVIATIONS FOR WORKS IN SPANISH

FBA *Fervor de Buenos Aires.* Buenos Aires: privately printed, 1923.
I *Inquisiciones.* Buenos Aires: Editorial Proa, 1925.
IA *El idioma de los argentinos.* Buenos Aires: Gleizer Editor, 1928.
OC *Obras completas.* Buenos Aires: Emecé Editores, 1974.
LA *El libro de arena.* Buenos Aires: Emecé Editores, 1975.
OCC *Obras completas en colaboración.* Buenos Aires: Emecé Editores, 1979.

ABBREVIATIONS FOR WORKS IN ENGLISH

A *The Aleph and Other Stories, 1933–1969.* Translated by Norman Thomas di Giovanni in collaboration with the author. New York: E. P. Dutton, 1970.
BR *Borges, A Reader: A Selection from the Writings of Jorge Luis Borges.* Edited by Emir Rodríguez Monegal and Alastair Reid. New York: E. P. Dutton, 1981.
BS *The Book of Sand.* Translated by Norman Thomas di Giovanni. New York: E. P. Dutton, 1977.
DBR *Doctor Brodie's Report.* Translated by Norman Thomas di Giovanni in collaboration with the author. New York: E. P. Dutton, 1970.
F *Ficciones.* Translated by Anthony Kerrigan. New York: Grove Press, 1962.
L *Labyrinths.* Edited by James Irby and Donald Yates. New York: New Directions, 1962.
OI *Other Inquisitions, 1937–1952.* Translated by Ruth L. C. Simms. Austin, Texas: University of Texas Press, 1964.
SP (with Adolfo Bioy Casares). *Six Problems for Don Isidro Parodi.* Translated by Norman Thomas di Giovanni. New York: E. P. Dutton, 1980.
UHI *A Universal History of Infamy.* Translated by Norman Thomas di Giovanni. New York: E. P. Dutton, 1970.

The Borgean Paradigm

Each evening, high, shiftless flocks of airy dragons rose from the ships of the imperial squadron and came gently to rest on the enemy decks and surrounding waters. They were lightweight constructions of rice paper and strips of reed, akin to comets, and their silvery or reddish sides repeated identical characters. The widow anxiously studied this regular stream of meteors and read in them the long and perplexing fable of a dragon which had always given protection to a fox, despite the fox's long ingratitude and repeated transgressions. The moon grew slender in the sky, and each evening the paper and reed figures brought the same story, with almost imperceptible variants. . . . The widow came to an understanding. She threw her two short swords into the river, kneeled in the bottom of a small boat, and ordered herself rowed to the imperial flagship.

. . . On climbing aboard, the widow murmured a brief sentence: "The fox seeks the dragon's wing."
—*Jorge Luis Borges*, "The Widow Ching, Lady Pirate"

So ends the pirate career of the marauding Widow Ching, nineteenth century scourge of the Manchurian coast. She succumbs, as Borges' retelling of her story would have it, not to cannon fire from the Chinese emperor's ships but to the silent salvos of kites that the ruler sends forth. Each of these delicate missiles carries a version, slightly different from other variants of the same tale, of a single story, the fable of a she-fox who defies a benevolent dragon. The emperor's beautiful, mysterious weapons achieve their effect; the widow, troubled by the fable and persuaded by its message, consigns herself to the emperor's protection. By deploying a collection of texts, texts that greatly resemble one another, the youthful Chinese leader restores order to his realm.

The ending to the widow's tale that Borges invents seems emblematically his own. The very idea that multiple versions exist of a single concept or story is one that recurs in many guises in Borges' writings. The works of fiction on Borges' imaginary planet Tlön, for example, explore a plot and all of its permutations. And Herbert Quain's eccentric novel *April March* includes nine variants of its basic argument. What is more, Borges structures many of his essays by examining one by one several manifestations of an image or idea as it recurs in the course of history, its meaning subtly skewed by changing cultural circumstance.

Yet as far as Borges' own stories are concerned, we are not accustomed to think of them as variants of a single fictional text. The seventy-odd tales that comprise most of the canon of Borges' narrative art do not seem to recapitulate the same story again and again. If the Chinese emperor's kites tell and retell the same exemplum, Borges' own short stories do not appear to do so. Certainly, they make no uniform impression on a reader. The high good humor of "Pierre Menard, Author of the Quixote" or of the comic tales of H. Bustos Domecq seems far removed from the darkness of a study in masochism like *"Deutsches Requiem."* And the luminous mystery of "Averroes' Search" is nothing at all like the equally oneiric greyness of "The Circular Ruins." Borges' fantastic tales bear little obvious likeness to those of his stories that are realistic psychological works, or even to a horror story like "There Are More Things." And the affectlessness of a tale like "The Immortals" seems scarcely akin to the harsh anger of a tale like "The Disk" or the sad affection that colors a story like "The Other."

What is more, the plots of Borges' tales vary a good deal. Some of his narratives seem more like essays than tales and can scarcely be said to have any plot at all other than the act of their narration. Others are short stories after the traditional manner and follow characters who act and are acted upon. And even within this latter group of tales Borges' plots appear quite diverse. The fate of Jaromir Hladík seems very different from that of, say, Emma Zunz or John Vincent Moon.

And still another reason exists to dissuade us from the idea that Borges' stories are all variants of a single tale. Borges has talked a good deal about the experiences that inspired his stories. It is clear that, to Borges' perception at any rate, each tale was born out of a specific experience—"The South," for example, out of his bout with blood poisoning, "Funes the Memorious" out of the experience of insomnia, and so forth.

Nevertheless, there is a sense in which each one of Borges' works of short fiction doubles every other. Imbedded in each of Borges' tales lies the same structuring ur narrative, a story that coexists with the plot but does not necessarily coincide with it. Like the Chinese emperor sending forth on his beautiful kites multiple, variant versions of a single text, Borges casts in tale after tale one basic narrative. The purpose of this study will be to locate in Borges' fiction this paradigmatic plot-beneath-the-plot around which the argument of each tale is spun and to account for its presence in Borges' short stories.

Before investigating the presence of a single narrative paradigm, it is necessary to distinguish between the texts themselves—the stories on the page—and Borges' narrative paradigm or ur text. The difference between these two modes of narrative is analogous to the distinction Sigmund Freud draws between the manifest and latent content of a dream. A dream's manifest content, the images and impressions that flash before the dreamer's sleeping mind and often form a more or less coherent plot, expresses but is no literal transcription of a latent content of thoughts and fantasies. These latent thoughts strive for expression in the dream but are debarred from the dream's manifest content insofar as they affront the dreamer's moral sense, a moral sense to some extent relaxed by sleep but nonetheless still in force. Debarred, that is, in their undistorted form. Disguised, though, by devices of representation that conceal their forbidden message, latent fantasies do elude repression's censorship and come to be cast in the narrative of the dream. Elaborated in ways that considerably distort their form, these threatening thoughts are, in the radical sense of the word, *masked* by the manifest content of the dream.

A dream, then, has two faces. The manifest content presents, in disguised form, an underlying set of unconscious fantasies. In a similar way Borges' stories, as all works of literature do, elaborate underlying fantasies. Yet Borges' tales are assuredly not dreams. Consciously conceived and consciously, painstakingly wrought, they have public meaning in a way that dreams do not. What relationship obtains between the form of one of Borges' tales and the latent fantasies it elaborates? Norman Holland, in his 1968 book *The Dynamics of Literary Response*, approaches aesthetics from a psychoanalytic point of view. He tries to see how the form of a literary work renders tolerable and, what is more, pleasurable the fantasies it contains. "All stories—and all literature—," he writes, "have this basic way of meaning; they transform the unconscious fantasy discoverable through psychoanalysis into the conscious meanings discovered by conventional interpretation."[1]

It makes sense to think of Borges' short stories as publicly effective elaborations of private fantasy. As Holland suggests, one can discriminate between the surface of a literary text and the fantasies out of which it emerges and to which it gives form. Sometimes it is illuminating to develop this distinction. In this study I shall explore the nature of the fantasy material that Borges, with quite remarkable consistency, recasts in each of his tales. Borges' narrative paradigm, a text-beneath-the-text, is in some ways analogous to the latent content of a dream. Although considerably better organized than the welter of wishes and associations that press to find expression in a dream, this ur narrative stands behind his short stories much as latent thoughts stand behind dreams, endowing each tale with one kind of structure. If, as Holland asserts, it is the interrelationship between fantasy and literary form that shapes a reader's response to a work of literature, it will be meaningful to identify Borges' narrative paradigm and to understand how it functions in his tales.

But what would persuade a reader to believe that works as different from one another as are Borges' tales embody a single paradigmatic story? The most visible evidence lies in the stories' smallest details. Borges' stories reuse, more than any interpretation of them has yet explained, not only the same large themes but the same minutiae. Some of these details—mirrors, masks, labyrinths and the like—serve as images that convey predictable connotations, and these constitute what amounts to Borges' personal lexicon of symbols and motifs. That is to say, they function as vehicles of public meaning. Others, however, seem opaque to interpretation. Adduced to different effect in different tales, they sometimes seem arbitrary or trivial. Few readers would miss the dog that barks at Emma Zunz had Borges chosen to omit it, and few would care if Funes were eighteen and not nineteen years old. Yet dogs—or other less than human creatures—and numbers that include the digit 9 appear in virtually every one of Borges' tales, as do bricks and iron and the color red and one form or another of text. The intriguing presence of some twenty of these details in each of Borges' stories leads one to wonder why they are there, and to wonder, too, what function they might serve, for it seems legitimate to suppose that Borges includes them to some purpose—whether conscious or not—and, what is more, that this purpose may well go beyond the narrow, particular role of each one of the details as it appears in a given narrative.

True, whenever he uses one of these details, Borges provides it with a plausible context. The iron staircase up which the Moslem student flees in "The Approach to Al-Mu'tasim" is iron as outdoor staircases often are, and Yu Tsun's iron bedstead and the iron bars through which Juan Dahlmann glimpses the deepening night call no particular attention to themselves. So insistently, though, does Borges accommodate iron objects in the fictive scenes he invents that one is led to ask whether the "iron windowblinds" (*OC*, 1049) that screen an old lady's apartment windows in a late Borges tale might bear some relationship to the "stones and iron" that, in one of Borges' earliest narratives, the people along the Mississippi River collect (*OC*, 296). Quite clearly, insofar as Borges' use of iron affects the reader, it does so in a different way in each new tale. The "hierro candente" ("white-hot iron") (*OC*, 457) that brands thieves in "The Babylon Lottery" is a horrifying engine of punishment, while the "ferretería" ("hardware store") in whose vicinity Alejandro Villari finds a room in "The Waiting" is evidence that the neighborhood is lower middle class. Yet Borges' sundry allusions to iron—his use of the word "hierro" and of compounds containing the root "ferr-"—may nonetheless have, if not a common function vis-à-vis the reader, a common source in a paradigmatic fantasy beneath the tales.

Anatomists, comparing organisms in the natural world, distinguish between analogous and homologous structures. Analogous structures—for example, a fish's gills and a mammal's lungs, or quills and hair—serve the same function in different animals but have evolved from unlike kinds of tissue. Homologous structures, in contrast, may accomplish different functions in different creatures, yet they bear the same relationship to an original or fundamental morphological type. A penguin's flippers and an eagle's wings are thus related through homology although they serve their owners in markedly different ways. In a similar way, the many small details that recur so insistently in Borges' tales may prove to be textual homologies whose relationship to an underlying narrative type needs to be understood.

If such a Borgean paradigm does exist, what are its features? How can it be recognized? Reduced to its most schematic outline, the fantasy that informs each of Borges' tales tells the following story: A mishap sets in motion a protagonist, who responds to the calamity by setting out on a journey. In the course of this journey Borges' hero travels through surroundings that are progressively more impoverished and irreal until at last he arrives at a structure that walls him in. Immured there, he is privy to a marvelous but blighting experience, an experience that blasts his selfhood and annihilates him.

This is a bare-bones version of Borges' narrative paradigm. To locate it easily in individual tales, one must flesh it out by pointing to some of the themes and images that Borges regularly invokes in connection with different stages in his ur story. Because Borges' fancy adheres quite faithfully to particular habits of representation, one can learn to recognize many of the characteristic ways in which he figures four phases of the paradigm: motivating mishap, impoverishing journey, enclaustration, and annihilation of selfhood.

Let us consider the motivating mishap, the mischance that befalls Borges' protagonist and incites him to act. Both the outbreak of fire (as in "The Theologians") and the purloining of a valuable thing (as in "Death and the Compass" and "Tai An's Search") may occasionally serve as the Borgean mishap. But by far the most common form the initial mishap takes is the death of a character. The death may either take place within the tale, as does the stoning of a Hindu in "The Approach to Al-Mu'tasim," or have occurred before the actual narration begins. Borges mines the opening paragraphs of many of his tales, where the first phase of the paradigmatic story is often found, with allusions to those who have died and whose death is bound up with the action that the narrative depicts. Emma Zunz, for example, receives word at the beginning of one tale that her father has killed himself, and the rest of the tale describes her complex reaction to the news. And Viktor Runeberg's murder inspires his fellow spy to conceive the bizarre crime that unfolds in "The Garden of Forking Paths." While sometimes the action of a story explicitly devolves from the death alluded to at the outset of the tale, at times the reader is left to supply the link between the death at a story's inception and the protagonist's course of action. "The Zahir," for example, portrays a narrator bereaved, at the beginning of the tale, by the death of the woman he loves. Emerging from her wake, he at once receives in change the mysterious coin that will, in the remainder of the tale, drive him insane. The reader is left to infer a relationship between the obolus the narrator acquires and the bewitching woman he has lost.

There is one group of Borges' tales that deserves to be singled out, even at this early stage in my analysis: the group of stories whose principal action is the act of narration itself. (Some would argue that all of Borges' first-person narratives—and they are by far the majority of his tales—fall into this category.) The mishap that regularly motivates the crucial act of recounting in Borges' tales is the death of someone the speaker has once known. The narrators of "Pierre Menard, Author of the Quixote," "An Examination of the Work of Herbert Quain," "Funes the Memorious" and "The Other Death," to cite only a few of this important set of tales, take up the task of storytelling as a response to the death of someone they wish to memorialize.

However Borges depicts the catalyzing misfortune that sets in motion a given tale, that mishap is colored by issues of loyalty and betrayal. In fact, the motif of allegiance forsworn so regularly attaches to the initial Borgean mishap that questions of fealty and treason serve as indicators of the first phase of Borges' paradigm. Often the victim of the original mishap belongs to some sort of confraternity—it may be a heretical sect or unusual religion, an exotic nationality, a utopian secret society, a band of smugglers or a gang of urban thugs, or even, in some tales, a scholarly elite. The activities of these confraternities run counter to—that is to say, traduce—the commonly embraced orthodoxies of their fictive worlds. One kind of betrayal, then, is the subversiveness of the Borgean sect to which the protagonist nearly always belongs. Another is the protagonist's disloyalty to someone who is his fellow or his leader in one of these subversive groups. The victim of the Borgean mishap often enjoys a privileged position in these fellowships, while Borges' protagonists, complicitous in apostasy, tend to occupy more menial stations in these same proscribed bands.

In spite of the original alliance of victim and protagonist, Borges often hints that his heroes have helped to bring about the downfall of the mentors they are sworn to defend. To cite a single example, John Vincent Moon, in "The Shape of the Sword," both joins the conspiracy to overthrow English control of Ireland and double-crosses the steadier corevolutionary who protects him. In this story and in many others, then, Borges invokes the motif of loyalty and betrayal in two ways: the seditious group in which victim and protagonist collude works to subvert society's norms, and, directly or indirectly, the hero betrays a leader to whom he has pledged fealty.

The theme of loyalty and betrayal may appear incidentally at every stage of the Borgean paradigm; however, it is an invariable attribute of the paradigm's initial phase, the account of the motivating mishap. The second phase of the paradigm, too, has its characteristic motifs. In the part of his tales that represents this second phase, Borges' protagonists embark upon an impoverishing journey. Fugitive and pilgrim, exile and vacationer, missionary and troubadour, they travel, in body or in mind, beyond the pale of the cultural circumstance that has nurtured and sustained them. Two aspects of the Borgean journey merit comment at this point: the purpose that impels Borges' itinerants and the impoverishing, irreal quality with which Borges endows their travels.

The journey depicted in Borges' tales often takes the form of a search. Sometimes the object of this search is a person. The student of "The Approach to Al-Mu'tasim," crossing and recrossing India, seeks first for a woman of the thieving caste and then for the divinely good al-Mu'tasim; Lönnrot pursues Scharlach, a deadlier quarry, to the cardinal points on the map of a nightmarish city; and the British detective of "The Man on the Threshold," charged with finding a kidnapped imperial official, exhausts the byways of a Moslem capital in the Hindustan. Often, though, Borges' heroes hunt not for other characters but for bibliographic finds. The narrator of "Tlön, Uqbar, Orbis Tertius" consults encyclopedias and atlases for information about the mysterious country Uqbar. Babel's demoralized librarians scan pages of senseless characters, hoping to happen on a few coherent words. And Borges' luckless scholars—Averroes, for example—con learned treatises and try to extract from them enigmatic truths or, like the frustrated narrator of "Guayaquil," try to win access to the documents they are avid to read.

On occasion the search in Borges' stories becomes inverted and the Borgean hero, rather than striving to find something, tries to rid himself of a possession that threatens his sanity. The narrator of "The Zahir," for example, does his best to lose and then erase from his memory the uncanny coin that obsesses him. The Nilsen brothers, in "The Intruder," struggle to free themselves from the woman they both love. And the bibliophile who, in "The Book of Sand," covets and then acquires an infinite book ends by deliberately losing his bewitching treasure in a dank corner of Argentina's National Library. We should not be surprised that Borges at times represents a search as its opposite, the attempt to lose something. Freud, identifying the ways in which dreams may disguise latent thoughts, remarks that dreams sometimes reverse, or depict the opposite of, the ideas that the dream-thoughts truly express.[2]

While the searches, researches and antisearches of the Borgean hero very often entail travel from one place to another, they need not always involve physical movement. Sometimes Borges represents the journey, instead, as a purposive course of thinking and dreaming. Tzinacán, the Mayan priest of "The God's Script," never quits his prison cell but discovers, through reasoning and dreaming, the magic verbal formula that would confer omnipotence upon him if he uttered it. Frequently, too, Borges' characters accomplish their missions by combining travel with imaginative divagation. The priest of "The Circular Ruins" canoes downriver to a ruined temple and then abandons himself to creative dreaming. And Jaromir Hladík, of "The Secret Miracle," first dreams he is "running across the sands of a rainy desert" (*OC*, 508), is then conveyed by Nazi captors to a prison cell, and finally, as he awaits the morning of his execution, dreams that he is searching for God, with the help of a blind librarian, in the tomes of the Clementine Library.

Dreaming and imagining, then, must be counted legitimate representations of the Borgean pilgrimage. And, what is perhaps even more intriguing, the very act of narrating may be seen as a verbal journey. Just as Borges' travelers aim either to locate or to lose a marvelous person or thing, his fictional speakers advertise their narrations alternately as ways of retrieving a valued memory from oblivion or of exorcising an experience so unsettling that it undermines the narrator's mental integrity. Often it is the memory of a deceased friend that Borges' storytellers are eager to preserve. The insufferable men of letters who narrate "Pierre Menard" and "An Examination of the Work of Herbert Quain" propose to memorialize the dead writers whose work they assess and to correct, by their commentary, the distorting effect of unkinder eulogies. By contrast, the speakers of "Guayaquil" and "The Other," each shaken by an encounter with a double, aim to distance themselves from an unnerving experience by telling their stories. They set down their accounts in an effort to recover their psychic balance. These few examples suggest, in a tentative way at least, an analogy between narrating and other kinds of Borgean peripatetics.

Having inquired in a preliminary way into the purpose of Borges' expeditionaries, we can turn our attention to the peculiar and painful impoverishment that, in the course of their travels, attends them. "Impoverishment" may, at first, seem a stilted term to use in describing a broad gamut of unpleasant sensations that afflict Borges' protagonists during their journey. Yet Borges himself deploys it and, throughout his work, associates what is "impoverished" or "poor" with irreality. And I can think of no better term that, without itself implying an interpretation, refers alike to the physical degradation of Borges' fictive topography and to the attenuation of human connectedness itself. Together, these two kinds of impoverishment convey an irreality that subsumes and moves beyond simple solitude.

But how is this impoverishment figured? On rare occasions Borges' hero makes his way through magically pleasant surroundings, like the gently sloping English countryside traversed by Yu Tsun on his way to Dr. Stephen Albert's home. For the most part, though, the landscapes the Borgean traveler sees are eerily inhospitable. Dimly lit, low-ceilinged libraries whose patrons sleep propped standing in closets, sticky (or rainy) deserts, and gardens clogged with weeds and littered with broken statuary might be cited as typically devalued Borgean realms. Mud and dust, colors that have faded toward greyness, and an unnatural soundlessness combine to express the demeaned emptiness of worlds in which human consciousness subsides into a partial sentience. In these uneaseful surroundings the Borgean traveler, his own senses blunted by weariness or drunkenness or sleep, often encounters beings who seem less than fully human. Whether gauchos or immortals, Yahoos or Urnos, the primitivism of these strange tribes is of a special type, for the societies they comprise are not undeveloped but have long since fallen into degeneracy. Victims of what Ronald Christ calls "cultural senility,"[3] these overcivilized barbarians have nearly relinquished human relatedness. Their appetites are stunted, their linguistic faculties have lapsed into disuse, and, whether stupefied by old age or maimed by their fellows, they scarcely move about. Often they behave with a childlike callousness, the moral equivalent of their torpor. (Sometimes the creature Borges' wanderer happens upon is figured not as a human being at all but as a wolf or dog.)

Nothing in these perversely comfortless landscapes, where

human sensibilities are benumbed, responds with vivifying feeling to the passage of Borges' heroes. Danger itself recedes, unable to persist in realms unquickened by affect. And the depersonalized rarefication of the world portrayed in the text finds a reinforcing correlative in the emotional aloofness from the plight of his wanderers that Borges creates in his readers. Borges seldom equips his fictional creatures with motivating feelings; impelled by forces the reader neither questions nor altogether understands, Borges' protagonists most often simply act, and their actions, unanchored by any emotional freight, have a peculiar weightlessness. Moreover, when Borges does endow his impersonal heroes with hatred or fearfulness or shame, he does so by flatly informing his audience that these emotions have visited his automaton-like figures. The reader's empathy is never engaged.

The journey of the Borgean hero must be understood as an excursion into irreality. Now, irreality in Borges' writings takes two quite distinct forms, which I designate "the irreality of impoverishment" and "the irreality of annihilation." The first is the gradual detachment from his emotional world that the Borgean hero experiences as a tale proceeds. This affective impoverishment, which besets the Borgean traveler and progressively depletes his sense of being, is an important aspect of phase two of the paradigm. It complements—and finds expression in—the physical degradation of the Borgean terrain and the cultural degeneracy of its inhabitants. The second kind of irreality, the irreality of annihilation, entails the sudden collapse of the Borgean hero's self. It characterizes the fourth phase of the paradigm, and I shall return to it in my discussion of the conclusion of Borges' ur text.

Borgean impoverishment and the derealization it achieves appear in many ways in any given tale. Yet Borges almost never describes as such his hero's progressive attenuation of being. (To do so would counteract the irreal effect he aims to achieve.) Rather, and herein resides the genius of Borges' art, he reproduces in the reader the stilling of affectivity to which his protagonists gradually succumb. Thus, one way for a reader reliably to perceive impoverishment in Borges' tales is by consulting his own responses to a text.

Having accomplished a journey that abstracts them from ordinary human commerce—and from reality itself—Borges' adventurers come to rest in some sort of enclosing space. Basements, prisons, labyrinths, sickrooms, cities, walled gardens, houses, caves, palaces, factories, brothels, towers, circular temples, courtyards, and *almacenes* (small grocery stores), all do duty as the containing antrum that, in the third phase of the Borgean paradigm, immures his heroes. Sometimes the conveyances in which they travel—trains and tramways, wagons and automobiles—seem to function as ancillary representations of the enclosure Borges unfailingly depicts. So, too, can the hollow containers his travelers come upon, such as boxes, drawers, kilns and wells, serve as metonymic figurings of their eventual place of enclaustration.

However these enclosures are portrayed, they afford scant refuge to the Borgean traveler. Their physical features do not recommend them as havens; like the territories he has already traversed, they are by and large degraded, disorienting places. Misleading symmetries may confound and depress the new arrival. Or he may see that his new abode has been laid waste by fire or that it has in other ways fallen into ruin. Its furnishings, if furnishings there be, may be rough and rudimentary, or worse, they may be fashioned to accommodate some absent but monstrous inhabitant. Low ceilings, darkness, earthen floors, and reddish or rust-colored walls weeping with wetness are regular attributes of the Borgean protagonist's newfound quarters, whose access to the outside world is often limited to a single aperture, a window or a narrow passage or stairway.

In many of Borges' stories, it is true, the protagonist's journey not only ends in a place of enclaustration but begins from one as well. For example, before the fugitive student sets out, in "The Approach to Al-Mu'tasim," to find a woman of the thieving caste and then al-Mu'tasim, he spends a night in a tower ringed by a disordered garden. And Emma Zunz, hearing of her father's death, shuts herself in her room before embarking on her masochistic course of revenge. While the frequency with which Borges doubles the enclaustration phase in this way deserves notice, the repetition in a tale of any paradigmatic feature does not change the basic structure of the underlying ur text.[4]

Borges' heroes arrive at these interior spaces for a number of reasons. A few, like the priest in "The Circular Ruins" and Averroes, withdraw from the world in voluntary reclusion to engage in deliberate creative or scholarly pursuits. Several others—the narrators of "Tlön, Uqbar, Orbis Tertius" and "The Shape of the Sword" and Baltasar Espinosa, protagonist of "The Gospel According to Mark"—are forced by rising floodwaters to share quarters with back-country folk. For still others, physical ailments dictate an enforced quiescence. John Vincent Moon, for example, retreats to General Berkeley's Dublin house to convalesce from a wound; Juan Dahlmann, confined by blood poisoning to a hospital, imagines in his delirium that he travels through a series of other enclosing spaces—taxi, café, train, and *almacén*—that seem less ignominious than the sanatorium; and the paralyzed Funes and Recabarren resign themselves to an immobile, indoor existence. Frequently, though, the Borgean figure's enclaustration comes about because of his enmity with a ruthless adversary. He may, like the cringing narrator of "Tadeo Limardo's Victim" or like Villari in "The Waiting," go into hiding to conceal himself from the man he has wronged or, like Avelino Arredondo, in what seems like a latterday rewriting of "The Waiting," he may isolate himself in preparation for assassinating his foe. In still other tales, an encounter between enemies may result in the imprisonment of one of the antagonists. The priest who deciphers the God's script is shut in a pyramid by a conquistador, while the fictional Nazis of "The Secret Miracle" and *Deutsches Requiem* intern Jaromir Hladík and David Jerusalem.

In withdrawing to these imperfect sanctums Borges' protagonists relinquish, voluntarily or not, a measure of active control over their own movements. Once immured, reduced in these enclosed surroundings to a state of passive helplessness, they submit to a further experience that drastically abrogates the normal conditions of their lives. In the fourth and final phase of Borges' paradigm, his hero, simultaneously blighted and blessed, utterly gives up his claim to selfhood. His abruptly deepened experience of simultaneous omnipotence and self-loss constitutes what I have called the irreality of annihilation.

This fulminating experience may take any of several forms

in Borges' work. Often the protagonist comes face to face with another person in an encounter that annuls his identity. Sometimes he confronts his double. He may, like Yakub the Ailing or Lönnrot or Villari, be murdered without appeal by his remorseless other self. Or, like Droctulft, the Captive and Tadeo Isidoro Cruz, he may suddenly recognize his compenetration with his double and exchange his individuality for an alliance with his other self. (While hostile or perilous encounters are the rule in Borges' tales, on rare occasions, particularly in his later stories, the meeting Borges describes is a loving one. The elderly "Borges" who, in "The Other," happens upon his younger self feels affection for his arrogant alter ego. And in "Ulrike" the Borgean encounter is figured as the sexual union of the narrator and his ephemeral lover.)

Nearly always the encounter to be found at the climax of Borges' tales brings with it a revelation. Broadly understood, this epiphany entails a sudden divulging of the secret order of things—of the hero's true identity, say, or of the unexpected imminence of his death. Sometimes, however, epiphany becomes theophany, and Borges' hero encounters, instead of a human other, a god or some uncanny figuring of the infinite. In Borges' work as in many religious writings, to behold divinity straight on or to come into unmediated contact with the absolute, is to affront taboo. Those of Borges' heroes who are privileged to unmask the visage of God or to possess, in one of its manifestations, unbounded time and space incur the punishment traditionally visited on overreaching mortals. They may be killed outright, blinded or paralyzed, or their rationality may be hobbled; whatever impairment they suffer, it is tantamount to a relinquishment of selfhood.

Revelation has a visual character, and it is not surprising that many of the images Borges uses to represent the annihilating experience of self-loss have to do with seeing and, in particular, the seeing of a face. The countenance whose divulgation Borges describes may be sacred or profane. Similarly, what covers or shows forth that visage may have quasi-magical qualities, as do mirrors, disguises, and masks, or instead may appear as the mundane accoutrement of a character and his world. Dark glasses, *chambergos* (a kind of broad-brimmed felt hat), and beards obscure the faces of Borges' antagonists, while photographs serve to publish those faces abroad. The modest act of shaving takes on special meaning in Borges' tales, for it amounts to a symbolic rending of the veil behind which a wondrous face may be beheld.

The face is one of many figurings in Borges' work of the infinite. That subversive abstraction, as Borges delights to point out, undermines the comfortable conventions of time and space and, in doing so, topples the buttresses of self. Representations of the infinite serve, in Borges' tales, almost as emblems of the paradigm's fourth phase. And many experiences and objects represent the limitless absolute in Borges' work. The dilation of an instant into a year-long reprieve in "The Secret Miracle," the compressing of infinite space into a pullulating microcosmic point, and the ceaseless recording of Funes' absolute memory, all vividly stand for Borgean infinity. No less authentic figurings of the infinite, though, are the small, mysterious, often circular objects with which Borges' landscapes are strewn and which his protagonists appropriate, to their sorrow. Coins, rings, roses, compasses, historic medallions, terraqueous globes, and unnaturally heavy cones made from the metals of Tlön epitomize the infinite in his work. And so do mirrors, which replicate what they reflect and which, when they face each other, create unending chains of receding images. Fire, too, perhaps because a flame has ever-changing form, suggests infinity to Borges. And encyclopedias, uniquely suited as they are to representing the universe whose knowledge they condense, appear in Borges' writing as symbols of the infinite. In fact, texts of all kinds seem to stand for, or allude to, infinity in Borges' work, whether they are magical like the script of Tzinacán's god and the book of sand or, like the Bible or a simple piece of correspondence, appear to add docilely to the verisimilitude of a realistic tale.

These, then, are some of the ways in which Borges habitually represents each of the four phases of his narrative ur text. I shall now turn to specific stories and locate the paradigm in them. In some stories, the paradigm is relatively easy to find. In others, however, it is hidden, fractured, and reorganized.

We have already seen that reversal is one means by which Borges distorts his paradigmatic story as he gives it narrative form; he sometimes depicts his hero's search for a missing person or thing as the attempt to lose something—that is, as the opposite of a search. And other means of disguising the paradigm frequently exert their effect as well. Sometimes Borges represents the stages of his ur narrative out of their temporal sequence. The enclaustration phase, for instance, may precede the impoverishing journey, or it may both precede and follow it, appearing twice or even more often in a single tale. Indeed, the multiple representation in any single work of a paradigmatic feature is another effective means by which Borges masks the ur narrative while elaborating it. In literary terms, the vision of the god of fire that inspires and empowers the priest in "The Circular Ruins" foreshadows the revelation that fire brings at the end of the tale. In psychoanalytic terms, however, it states redundantly the act of revelation in the tale. Displacement, too, and other mechanisms that in dreams distort the representation of fantasy help to shape Borges' embodiments of the paradigm. To see how Borges manipulates these mechanisms in creative fictional art, we must turn our attention to individual tales.

It is easiest to discern the paradigm in those tales, written at nearly every stage of Borges' career as a writer of fiction, whose plots correspond in their broad outlines to the stages of the paradigm itself, that is, those that present the sequence of motivating mishap, impoverishing journey, enclaustration, and annihilation of selfhood primarily in regard to the actions of a single character, and without transposing significantly the order in which they occur. One such story is "The Garden of Forking Paths," first published in *Sur* in 1941. This tale, a particularly mysterious and beautiful one, unmistakably elaborates the paradigm, yet it does so in a complex and unmechanistic way.

In a manner of speaking, "The Garden of Forking Paths" has two beginnings, each containing a motivating mishap. The narrator of the story's first paragraph, which serves as a narrative frame for the account that follows, recalls Germany's bombardment of a British artillery park during World War I and promises that what we are about to read will shed light on events surrounding that surprise attack. Presented as a sort of corrective footnote to Liddell Hart's standard history, the tale claims our attention because it offers to account for this singular act of aggression in a new way. If the bombing of the munitions stored at Albert is the mishap that motivates the telling of the story as a whole—new insight into the causes for the attack prompts the tale's first-person narrator to speak—another act of violence, the murder of the German agent Viktor Runeberg, opens the first-person narration of Yu Tsun that comprises the rest of the tale. Yu Tsun's confession, or rather that part of it rescued for our scrutiny (the first two pages, Borges tells us, have been lost), takes up precisely at the moment when Dr. Yu, Runeberg's fellow spy, discovers that the implacable British agent Captain Richard Madden has murdered Yu's colleague. Yu Tsun's actions, including, perhaps, the act of relating his exploits, make up the remainder of the story. They constitute his response to what is, for him, a horrifying piece of intelligence.

From the outset the tale piles treason upon treason; Borges often links the motif of loyalty forsworn with the opening mishap that a tale describes. The story plunges the reader into a world where loyalty begets betrayal. Yu Tsun belongs to several Borgean confraternities, groups that constrain him to conflicting allegiances. Chinese by birth, he has turned, by his choice of profession, from his Oriental heritage to promulgate instead a Western culture: he teaches English in Tsingtao. Yet rather than ally himself with England in the European war, he secretly works for that nation's enemy. In turn, it is to confirm his loyalty to the sinister chief of Germany's espionage network that he murders a man who, under other circumstances, might have claimed his friendship as a fellow scholar and mentor. Dr. Stephen Albert, the sinologist who falls under Yu Tsun's attack, deserves better from his assailant, for he restores to Yu a veneration for his own ancestor Ts'ui Pên, whose lifework Yu has mistakenly misprized. Yu's misguided scorn for his great-grandfather represents still another disloyalty, a familial one, the more heinous because of the reverence for ancestors professed, at least as stereotype would have it, in Oriental cultures. Chinese, English scholar, German spy, colleague, descendant of an illustrious forebear, and disciple, Yu Tsun is caught in a web of loyalties that inevitably snarls. Nor is Yu Tsun the story's only traitor. Richard Madden, described as a "man accused of laxity and perhaps of treason" (*OC*, 472; *L*, 19), has betrayed his Irish fatherland by working for British masters.

"The Garden of Forking Paths" is one of Borges' tales in which the hero's derealizing journey takes as its point of departure an enclosed place, a chamber that both doubles and foreshadows the more completely irreal interior to which his travels lead. Yu Tsun's first response to the news of Runeberg's death is to lock himself in his London apartment, and details of what happens there make his quarters seem like an impoverished analogue of Stephen Albert's less modestly appointed home. Yu's "cama de hierro" ("iron cot") (*OC*, 472; *L*, 20), on which the spy throws himself, adumbrates the "portón herrumbrado" ("tall, rusty gate") (*OC*, 475; *L*, 23) at the entrance to Albert's Oriental garden. The silence of the boardinghouse room, a quiet Borges notes in three different ways, seems as unnatural as the syllabic Chinese music that fills the neighborhood of Albert's house. And several of the objects of everyday use that Yu Tsun finds in his pockets are recalled by less trivial items later found in the sinologist's library. The humble "red and blue pencil" (*OC*, 473; *L*, 21) parallels the valuable "*famille rose* vase and another, many centuries older, of that shade of blue which our craftsmen copied from the potters of Persia" (*OC*, 476; *L*, 24); the compromising letter Yu pulls from his pocket, a letter whose contents the reader never learns, has a double in the exquisitely penned fragment of a letter, key to interpreting Ts'ui Pên's chaotic novel, that Albert will later take from a lacquered drawer; and the inexpensive watch the spy turns up finds a more elegant analogue in the "tall circular clock" (*OC*, 476; *L*, 24) of Albert's study.

Through a graduated series of experiences that become progressively more irreal, Yu Tsun accomplishes a journey that not only takes him from the center of London to its outskirts but transports him as well from quotidian reality, with all its urgency and dread, to a charmed world whose events, rather irreal than unlikely, carry him forward with the soothing inevitability of a pleasant dream. At first Yu's circumstances are marked by impoverishment, not mystery. Alone in his London lodgings, he intuits that he is as good as dead, powerless to prevent Madden's hunting him down. Passively, lying prostrate on his bed, he gives himself over to a reverie in which his progress toward irreality begins. Daydreams that first recall to him his dead father and his childhood in a symmetrical garden of Hai Feng and finally conjure up before him "Madden's horse-like face" (*OC*, 473; *L*, 20) reproduce, as a sort of cameo, the larger action of the story and subtly afford a preliminary, mental analogue to the physical journey he will soon undertake. Yu Tsun emerges from these imaginings to take stock of his resources. They seem poor indeed. He possesses the secret—the name of the town where the British armaments are stored—but, he muses, "my human voice was very weak ['muy pobre']" (*OC*, 473; *L*, 20). Reviewing the contents of his pockets out of "the mere vain ostentation of proving my resources were nil" (*OC*, 473; *L*, 20), Yu only confirms his helplessness. Nor is the spy's almost willing acknowledgment of his straitened possibilities the only means by which Borges conveys the impoverishment of Yu's state. The sky that attracts Yu's absent stare is grey. The office of his hateful superior, whom he envisions scanning newspapers for ciphered news of his agents, is (improbably) "arid," the German nation itself a "barbarous country." And the entire scene in Yu's apartment takes place in a silence broken only by Yu's abject utterance "I must flee" (*OC*, 473; *L*, 20).

At length Yu Tsun conceives a plan that draws him away from his London flat, and he extends his mental wandering in an actual journey. Much later we are made privy to his scheme: he has resolved to murder a man named Stephen Albert, whose surname, coupled with his own in the newspaper accounts of the crime, will convey to Yu's chief the message he aims to transmit. But we do not know this yet. Borges withholds from his readers foreknowledge of Yu's plan, and our lack of information has two important effects. It heightens suspense, and so provides the tale, a spy thriller, with an element requisite to its genre. And, what is more important, the reader's ignorance derealizes the story, detaching Yu's actions from ascertainable causality. Events go forward with a logic of their own, a logic that the reader cannot plumb.

If the reader's ignorance of Yu's plan has a derealizing effect, it is because other aspects of the narrative also work to suggest

Yu's progressive estrangement from normal human connection. His trip from his flat to Ashgrove, the train station near Albert's home, is a solitary one. He emerges from his room into a "deserted street [where] I felt myself visible and vulnerable, infinitely so" (*OC*, 474; *L*, 21). Apart from the ruthless Madden, who, in hot pursuit, narrowly misses Yu's train, "there was hardly a soul on the platform" (*OC*, 474; *L*, 21). And when the train arrives at Ashgrove, "no one called out the name of the station" (*OC*, 474). His fellow passengers, to whom he does not speak, appear almost as aspects of his own self; one is in mourning, another reads with fervor a book in a foreign tongue, and still another is "wounded and happy." By the time the train reaches Yu's destination, his trip has become saturated in a facilitating irreality. "The train," he tells us, "ran gently along, amid ash trees" (*OC*, 474; *L*, 22). The magical part of the narrative has begun.

Yu Tsun is met at the station by a group of children who mysteriously know where he is going and direct him to Albert's house, the Borgean place of enclosure toward which he moves. These young guides, while they bear little superficial resemblance to the barbarians of Borges' other tales, occupy in this story the same position as Argos in "The Immortals" and Dahlmann's aged gaucho accomplice in "The South." If Borges here chooses children instead of, say, druids or other primitive folk, it is not merely in obeisance to verisimilitude, but because Yu's journey is one that will return him, in memory and in feeling, to his own childhood. As he approaches his victim's home, the landscape itself appears to welcome him with all the easefulness of recovered intimacy. Escorted by a circular moon, he follows paths whose gentle downward slope he finds restful. Chinese music fills the air, and the labyrinthine configuration of his route, which recalls the "symmetrical garden of Hai Feng" (*OC*, 474; *L*, 20) where he played as a boy, reminds him as well of his great grandfather Ts'ui Pên. He remembers that, years before, his powerful forebear renounced a provincial governorship in China and secluded himself, in an act of enclaustration that parallels Yu's own, to write a novel and build a labyrinth. Neither work, Yu muses, was ever realized; at Ts'ui Pên's death, the novel was shown to be a shameful confusion of mutually contradicting plots, and the labyrinth was never found. Lapsing into reverie for the second time, Yu loses himself in fantasies of that undiscovered maze, fantasies that make Madden's pursuit—and reality itself—recede from his consciousness until, he recalls, "I felt myself to be, for an unknown period of time, an abstract perceiver of the world" (*OC*, 475; *L*, 23). This is a sentence Borges has used before. It appears in his 1928 confession "Feeling in Death." There as here, it signals the dissolution of the limits of self that Borgean irreality entails.

Even before he reaches Stephen Albert's house, then, Yu achieves a numinous state that will permit him to accept—with wonder but wholly without surprise—the events that will soon befall him. Having reached his destination, he is admitted without fuss by the man he has marked for execution. He passes through a rusty gate, leaving behind the wall-less labyrinth of English countryside and entering a marvelous garden hung with Chinese lanterns. It is from this garden that the Oriental music has come. Ushered by his host along a "damp path [that] zigzagged like those of my childhood" (*OC*, 476; *L*, 24), Yu gains entrance to the sinologist's personal library of Western and Oriental books. It is in this Borgean enclosure that his journey ends.

The encounter that takes place in this charmed and private sanctum is an intimate one, charged with the reverence that deeply felt affection permits. Closeted together in that "intimate house" (*OC*, 475), the two discuss with pleasure a subject in which they, unique among men, share a passionate interest. From the man he is to kill, Yu Tsun, already the possessor of one secret, discovers another, one that holds great personal meaning for him. Albert reveals to him the key to his great grandfather's novel, an apparently indecipherable text. The scholar's researches (a more pacific version of the Borgean quest, as Madden's pursuit is an angrier one) have led him to a a fragment of a letter, copied on faded pink paper, from whose enigmatic message Albert has deduced the novel's principle of construction: Ts'ui Pên's masterpiece, for it is a masterpiece, not a failure, constitutes a literary labyrinth in which time, not space, forks and twists back upon itself.

The vindication of his disgraced forebear, one figuring of revelation in the tale and the beginning of phase four of the paradigm, leaves Yu Tsun reeling. As Albert concludes a reading of two parallel chapters of Ts'ui Pên's novel, Yu succumbs to a feeling of utter irreality. "From that moment on, I felt about me and within my dark body an invisible, intangible swarming. Not the swarming of the divergent, parallel and finally coalescent armies [of the novel] but a more inaccessible, more intimate agitation" (*OC*, 478; *L*, 27). He will have this same swarming feeling again in the seconds after he assassinates Albert. At these two nightmarish moments Yu's identity founders, merging with an infinite number of other souls that seem, outside ordinary temporality, to participate in Yu's being and annihilate it. "It seemed to me," he remembers, "that the humid garden that surrounded the house was infinitely saturated with invisible persons. Those persons were Albert and I, secret, busy and multiform in other dimensions of time" (*OC*, 479; *L*, 28). It is in this annihilated state that Yu confronts Madden and, almost simultaneously, murders Albert. Madden's pursuit, Albert's studies, and Yu's desperate plot converge in this fulminating instant, when all three, their beings fused, cease to exist. With Albert dead and the missions of Yu and Madden accomplished, the meaningful existence of all three is at an end; "the rest," Yu Tsun confides to us at the end of his confession, "is irreal, insignificant" (*OC*, 480).

To recapitulate, we have seen that the climactic final scene of "The Garden of Forking Paths" represents the disastrous foundering of individual selfhood in several ways. While Yu's double encounter with Albert and Madden functions in the tale as the primary figuring of the collapse of personal being, Borges relates to this event the motif of revelation. By killing Albert, Yu Tsun will reveal to his chief the location of the munitions park. And not only does Albert reveal to Yu Tsun the secret letter that unlocks his ancestor's novel to understanding, but the novel itself, a text that suggests the simultaneous playing out of infinite parallel histories, is a sort of literary aleph. The act of listening to a passage of that text, whose intricacies Yu miraculously comprehends, precipitates in Borges' hero a final release from selfhood.

At the end of his tale, then, Borges repeats in several ways the motif of revelation. Yet throughout the tale he has called attention to the seeing or not seeing of faces, an image he often links with the revelation motif. In his London flat, Yu's fantasies break off as he imagines "Madden's horselike face," a face he will see, to his horror, from his train window and which leaves him *aniquilado* ("annihilated") (*OC*, 474). (The word is significant, for etymologically it means "reduced to nothing," the Borgean hero's state as he gives up his selfhood in phase four of the paradigm.) Another moment when Yu connects the seeing of a face with the cessation of his being occurs early in the tale. Foreseeing his imminent death, he says goodbye to himself as he leaves for Ashgrove by looking at his face in a mirror. And other countenances figure in the tale, as well. At the Ashgrove station Yu cannot make out the faces of the children who direct him, nor can he see Albert's face when the sinologist admits him to his grounds. Later, though, as Albert reads to him, Yu does behold "his face, within the vivid circle of the lamplight" (*OC*, 478; *L*, 26). This circle of light is just one of several circles and round objects that Borges introduces in the course of his tale and which serve to extend even further, in still more attenuated visual echo, the motif of revelation. The sundry coins that Yu finds in his pockets (one, instead of being circular, is mysteriously four-sided), the "luna baja y circular" ("round, low moon") (*OC*, 474) that guides him through the countryside, and the gramophone record and "alto reloj circular" ("tall circular clock") that grace Albert's library all repeat this image, which Borges links elsewhere in his work to the infinite aleph experience.

The variousness of the imagery Borges associates in this tale with each phase of his paradigm disguises a good deal the underlying ur story he elaborates, but diverse imagery is not the only feature of the work that serves to mask Borges' underlying schema. Although in its broad outlines the plot of "The Garden of Forking Paths" adheres rather closely to the Borgean ur narrative, the story cannot readily be broken down—at least in any formulaic way—into four discrete and consecutive phases. Yu Tsun's enclaustration, we have already seen, both precedes and follows the derealizing journey he makes. And his experience of self-loss is repeated, in the course of the tale, as he hears Madden's voice on the telephone; takes leave of his mirrored self; feels "annihilated" at the train station by seeing the horse-faced Madden; loses himself (quite literally) in musings about Ts'ui Pên's dual endeavor; and listens to Albert read from his ancestor's book. What is even more intriguing, the story's principal motivating mishap—Runeberg's death and Yu's discovery of it—has enough of the revelation about it for us to perceive in that initial violent act a doubling of the story's final murder cum revelation.

Furthermore, each aspect of the paradigm is represented not once but many times. Two enactments of the motivating mishap begin the tale; Yu owes loyalty to no fewer than five ethnic and cultural groups; the spy's derealizing journey takes place partly in Yu's fantasied meanderings and partly in his physical removal to Ashgrove; the image of enclaustration recurs throughout the story, figured not only as Yu Tsun's sojourn in Albert's garden and library but also as the German agent's reclusion in his London flat and Ts'ui Pên's withdrawal to the Pavilion of Limpid Solitude; and Yu's loss of individual identity devolves not just from his simultaneous confrontation with Albert and Madden but also from his insight into the mechanisms of an aleph-like text. Just as in dreams a single person or event may be figured in more than one way, each element of the paradigm finds multiple representation in Borges' tale. This is so to such an extent that Yu Tsun, Richard Madden, Stephen Albert, and Ts'ui Pên—and perhaps even the sinister German chief—all seem to incarnate the prototypical Borgean hero. Their adventures coexist in the tale, not unlike the parallel and nonethelesss interlocking plots that unfold in Ts'ui Pên's novel. Traditionally, critics have seen, in the secondary characters of this tale, a series of Yu Tsun's doubles. (Borges himself doubtless thought of his fictional creatures in this way.) Yet the insight afforded by such an interpretation, while satisfying in itself, can be taken no further. It does not explain why Yu Tsun moves through a world peopled only by alternate selves. In the long run, I think it is more fruitful to see, in each one of the narrative's characters, an embodiment of Borges' ur protagonist. Each one enacts, completely or in part, the paradigmatic experience Borges repeatedly represents.

Still another way in which Borges' creating sensibility disguises, from itself and from the reader, the starkness of the informing paradigm is through displacement. To cite a single example, the walls of Albert's library—Yu Tsun's ultimate place of confinement—are lined with books and betray neither the spoiled quality nor the reddish coloration that Borges often associates with his enclosures. But the gate to Albert's garden is rusted (and therefore reddish in color), and the letter Albert shows Yu Tsun is copied on "a sheet of paper that had once been crimson, but was now pink and tenuous and criss-crossed" (*OC*, 477; *L*, 25). Dissociated, perhaps, from its original place in the paradigmatic fantasy material, the spoiled red cast of the Borgean antrum's walls may appear in this tale as the rusty corrosion of the gate and the faded pink of the letter's brittle paper.

In order to posit such connections—and, indeed, in order to be convinced that a Borgean paradigm exists—one must examine a much larger group of texts. At this point I shall extend my analysis to include a representative set of tales. Drawn from all five of Borges' collections of short stories as well as from his collaborative work with Adolfo Bioy Casares, these narratives all elaborate the paradigm in readily discernible ways. Leaving for last "The Twelve Figures of the World" (1942), a tale Borges wrote in conjunction with his friend Bioy, I shall examine the following works: "The Insulting Master of Etiquette Kotsuké no Suké" (1933), "The Approach to Al-Mu'tasim" (1935), "The Dead Man" (1946), "Emma Zunz" (1948), "The South" (1953), "The Gospel According to Mark" (1970), and "There Are More Things" (1975).[5] Table 1, which summarizes the discussion that follows, displays the principle figurings of the paradigm in each tale.

"The Insulting Master of Etiquette Kotsuké no Suké," which Borges adapted from Japanese folklore, tells the tale not of the story's titular villain but of an eighteenth century samurai warrior with the similar name of Kuranosuké no Suké. Borges sets the scene for the action of his tale by evoking a world in which elaborate rituals enact symbolic loyalty; he locates his narrative in eighteenth century Japan, and reminds his audience that the Japanese of that period believed their emperor to be divine and therefore due a special reverence. The story is about those who do their best to comply with the exquisite rites of Japan's court etiquette—and who, in so doing, affirm their loyalty to the emperor and fulfill their duty to other lords as well—and those who flout courtesy and betray the code of honor to which Japanese noblemen were traditionally bound.

The story's motivating mishap is the hara-kiri of the Lord of Ako, Takumi no Kami. This worthy noble disembowels himself to atone for having attacked a visitor at his court, the imperial envoy Kotsuké no Suké. Sent to prepare for the emperor's visit to Takumi's house by teaching the Lord of Ako the fine points of protocol, the master of etiquette has deliberately provoked his host. (Ironically, despite his expertise as teacher of decorum Kotsuké is himself insolent and discourteous.) Yet because Kotsuké is the emperor's representative, and thus officially his surrogate or "symbol," Takumi's justified assault is tantamount to an assault upon the emperor himself. The story, then, begins with an incident in which Takumi's loyalty to the emperor both falters and is proved. Intending to equip himself to entertain the emperor and thus to do him honor, Takumi has (symbolically) aggressed against his lord. His suicide, though, is an act that reaffirms his staunch devotion to the emperor.

The issue of loyalty apparently betrayed but actually confirmed is at the center of the tale. The story's protagonist, Kuranosuké no Suké, a samurai counselor in Takumi's court, responds to his master's death with conduct that seems to show him indifferent to Takumi's demise. His actions, however, eventually allow him to avenge his master's death and thus acquit his duty to his ill-used lord.

The impoverishing journey Kuranosuké undertakes leads him to forsake his family, remove to Kyoto, and lose himself in dissipation in that city's brothels and taverns. A Satsuma man, seeing him unconscious from drunkenness in the doorway of a bar, reviles the retainer for having forsaken Takumi's cause. But Kuranosuké's shameful conduct is a clever ruse, meant to allay the suspicions of his enemy Kotsuké, who is at first wary of reprisals from Takumi's men. Once Kotsuké is off his guard, the avenging

Kuranosuké rallies his master's warriors and mounts an assault on his enemy's palace. Assembling in a "barren garden" ("desmantelado jardín"), one Borgean enclosure, the warriors storm Kotsuké's house and trap him in a "gloomy little courtyard" (*OC*, 322). There they dispatch him and, because their own assault on him violates the emperor's law, they all atone with ritual suicide for their disobedience. The "annihilation of self" phase of Borges' paradigm thus figures in this story both as the

Table 1   Borges' Narrative Paradigm

	Motivating mishap	Journey (impoverishing factors)
"Kotsuké no Suké"	Takumi no Kami's death	Kuranosuké's degradation in Kyoto's brothels
"The Approach to Al-Mu'tasim"	presumed death of Hindu	1) student's flight to tower 2) student's search for woman, then al-Mu'tasim
"Emma Zunz"	1) Manuel Maier's suicide 2) embezzlement	1) Emma thinks about father 2) Emma goes to port, bars, hotel, then factory
"The Dead Man"	Otálora kills a man	1) Otálora flees to Montevideo; 2) goes to Bandeira's ranch
"The South"	Dahlmann's accident	1) trip to hospital 2) trip to *estancia*
"The Gospel According to Mark"	Espinosa scuffles with students	trip to cousin's ranch
"There Are More Things"	Arnett's death	1) speaker returns to Argentina, visits Muir; 2) visit to uncle's house
"The Twelve Figures of the World"	1) Molinari's presumed murder of Dr. Abenjaldún 2) robbery	1) bus trip to prison to see Parodi 2) train trip to Abenjaldún's house

murderous encounter between Kotsuké and Takumi's men and as the suicides that closely follow it.

One can immediately perceive parallels between this tale and "The Approach to Al-Mu'tasim," written some two years later. Again Borges locates his tale in a country that must have seemed to him exotic—"Al-Mu'tasim" is set in India—and again makes his hero someone who shows equivocal loyalty to a special cause. In this case the cause is a religious one. The Bombay law stu-

nclaustration	Annihilation of selfhood
) 47 captains meet in barren garden	1) Kotsuké's death
	2) captains' suicide
) Kotsuké's palace	
) tower	1) revelation of al-Mu'tasim
) al-Mu'tasim's gallery	2) revelation that al-Mu'tasim *is* student
) in hotel room	1) loss of virginity
) closeted with Loewenthal	2) murder of Loewenthal
) *almacén*	revelation of helplessness; death
) patio of house in Old City	
) Bandeira's sickroom	
) dining hall	
) operating room	Dahlmann's death
) *almacén* in Buenos Aires	
) *almacén* in country	
) the house	Espinosa's crucifixion
) the shed	
he Casa Colorada	confrontation with monster
) Parodi's cell	1) Abenjaldún's murder, fire
) Abenjaldún's house and library	2) unmasking of Molinari
	3) Parodi solves crime

dent who is the protagonist of the tale is an apostate Moslem who nevertheless is drawn to an Islamic procession, and who thinks he has killed a Hindu in sectarian strife. The motivating mishap of the tale, this Hindu's death, puts the student to flight, and his Borgean journey, which begins as his evasion of the police in the outskirts of Bombay, eventually exposes him to a squalid life among India's untouchables.

Mysteriously, his journey changes from flight to search; instructed, after a manner of speaking, by a ghoulish man whom he meets on the roof of a tower, the student resolves to seek out first a Palampur woman of the thieving caste and then a divinely good man named al-Mu'tasim. Crossing and recrossing the subcontinent, he falls in with "the lowest class of people . . . in a kind of contest of evildoing [infamies]" (*OC*, 416; *A*, 48). At the end of his degrading pilgrimage, he reaches at last a "corridor 'at whose end is a door . . .' " (*OC*, 416; *A*, 49), and in that Borgean enclosure draws aside a beaded curtain to reveal al-Mu'tasim's face. At that annihilating moment the seeker's story—and, we understand, his life—come to an end.[6]

"Emma Zunz," though a significantly later tale (it was first published in 1948), nevertheless restates the Borgean paradigmatic story. This time the characters are Jewish, and betrayals revolve around one Jew's dishonoring of another, as well as around the duties owed by child to parent and by a worker to fellow workers. The motivating mishap, Manuel Maier's suicide, impels his daughter Emma to forge a plan to kill the man who disgraced him and indirectly caused his death. The scheme she devises requires her to feign loyalty to her enemy, Aarón Loewenthal, and to seem to betray not only her father but her fellow workers as well. She gains access to Loewenthal by offering to inform on the strikers who work beside her in Loewenthal's textile mill.

Emma's plan is a masochistic one. It subjects her to awful sexual degradation—one kind of Borgean impoverishment. To muster in herself the feeling of outrage she will need to carry out the murder and to convince the police she has killed to defend her virtue, she engineers her own deflowering. Emma's journey takes her from her flat in Buenos Aires to the port district where she attracts a sailor in a bar and then to a tawdry hotel room, where she allows him to possess her. The impoverishment of Emma's experience appears in the tale not only as her sexual degradation. Her fatigue, the faded colors of the hotel room where she and the sailor retire, the failing light of dusk, and finally the blighted look of the "barren outskirts of the town" ("desmantelado arrabal") (*OC*, 566; *L*, 135) where she travels to seek out Loewenthal, all help to convey impoverishment at this stage in the narrative.

As for the third and fourth phases of the paradigm, they can be readily discerned. Emma makes her way, on a streetcar (one Borgean antrum), to the factory where Loewenthal waits. Closeted with him in his office, another enclosing place, she kills him with his own gun, then partially undresses him and takes his glasses off (a Borgean "uncovering") to make it seem as though he has tried to rape her.

I have examined "Emma Zunz" out of chronological sequence because so many points of commonality link it to "Kotsuké" and "Al-Mu'tasim." Like the first tale, it portrays a hero who wreaks revenge and in doing so subjects him/herself to infamy. And it is primarily infamy qua dissipation and sexual shame that figures Borgean impoverishment in all three tales. We recall that Kuranosuké's plan for avenging Takumi's death leads him to brothels and bars and that the student of "Al-Mu'tasim" "prays and fornicates in the pestilential stench of the Machua Bazaar in Calcutta" (*OC*, 416; *A*, 48). "The Dead Man," published in 1946, two years before "Emma Zunz," uses traces of these same elements. Although the revenge depicted in the tale is worked against the protagonist, not by him, revenge there is. And Otálora does make a brothel his first stop as he flees from the law at the beginning of the tale, and later covets the mistress of the man he seeks to supplant. Licentiousness, though, is not shameful in "The Dead Man." The sense of degradation, a key element in the three tales we have just seen, is starkly absent here. (The amoral objectivity of the narration does much to convey Otálora's sangfroid.)

Despite the change of tone, "The Dead Man," too, is informed by the Borgean paradigm. Benjamín Otálora, the Buenos Aires thug who is the story's protagonist, knifes a *compadre* at the beginning of the tale, and in consequence of this motivating mishap flees across the River Plate to seek protection from an Uruguayan political boss. That strongman, Azevedo Bandeira, deserves the murderer's loyalty; he gives refuge to the fugitive Otálora and finds him work as an apprentice cowhand on his back-country ranch. Bandeira's *estancia* is an impoverished place; lugubriously named "El Suspiro" ("The Sigh"), it is graced by no stream or tree, and the cattle that live there are lean and deprived.

Safe on the ranch, Otálora begins a campaign to usurp his benefactor's place. He appropriates to his own use the riding gear that is an emblem of Bandeira's power, and he seduces Bandeira's red-haired mistress. Yet, in the final scene, set in the dining hall at "El Suspiro" (a Borgean enclosure, as is Bandeira's sickroom earlier in the tale), Bandeira reveals his annihilating authority. He orders an underling to kill Otálora, who realizes as he dies that the man he has tried to replace has countenanced—and therefore ultimately controlled—his rivalry. Again, annihilation accompanies revelation at the end of one of Borges' tales.

Juan Dahlmann, in "The South," is a passive sort compared to the other Borgean heroes we have so far considered. Yet he, too, enacts Borges' four-part sequence of events. Like the protagonists of other tales, he acts out of loyalty, in this case loyalty to conspicuously Protestant forebears; a city-dweller himself, Dahlmann makes a sacrifice to keep up a family ranch he has never seen. That Borges makes his hero Protestant surely reflects the autobiographical nature of "The South"; Borges himself, whose near-fatal illness inspired this tale, came from Protestant stock on his father's side of the family. Yet one cannot help comparing this story to the others we have seen and noting that Borges very often assigns his protagonists unusual religious affiliations. Borges may, for more than one reason, have have endowed the hero of "The South" with Evangelical forebears.

The motivating mishap of "The South" is Dahlmann's striking his head on a freshly painted window frame. And his illness is one way in which the tale represents the ensuing impoverishment of his experience; Borges captures the humiliation and indignity that hospital patients feel at their own diminished powers. Dahlmann's Borgean journey figures in the tale either as the hallucination that visits him as he dies or as his literal removal to the Argentine South. Either way, Dahlmann's traveling, in the second half of the tale, to the hinterlands where his family's holdings lie constitutes another figuring of the paradigm's second phase. The emptiness of the pampa; the rusticity of the fare in the little store where Dahlmann stops to eat; the "poor architecture" (*OC*, 528; *BR*, 255) of that stopping place and the weather-worn reddish color of its walls; Dahlmann's drowsiness, induced by a glass of red wine, and his unnatural mood of estrangement from the people he is with; and the uncouth, anachronistic primitivism of the *compadritos* who molest him, all these aspects of the tale contribute to expressing the derealized impoverishment of Dahlmann's lot as he reaches the end of his journey.

Dahlmann's hospital room, which Borges describes as a "cell with something of a well about it" (*OC*, 526; *BR*, 253), is one Borgean antrum, the one that ultimately walls the sick man in according to one reading of the tale. But in the course of his journey, be it fantasied or real, Dahlmann passes from that hellish room through a series of other Borgean chambers—taxi, café, train and, finally, country store. The shabby wayside store, with its faded reddish walls and its iron-grilled window giving onto the plains and the night is another typical Borgean place of enclosure. Here Dahlmann, encouraged by a "timeless" aged man who wears the gaucho attire of a bygone day, answers the challenge of a group of ruffians who mock him. The story ends as he faces his new-found foes in a knife fight from which he cannot emerge alive.

The last two stories I shall examine here present elaborations of the Borgean paradigm that seem attenuated in several ways. The motif of loyalty and betrayal, already subdued in "The South," calls little attention to itself in these later tales. And in both stories the motivating mishap seems only incidentally linked with the protagonist's journey, not its direct cause. These changes, which surely signal a falling away of the emotions that quicken the paradigm and give it logical force, are an important feature of Borges' later works. Although in these stories the paradigm remains, some aspects of it seem only vestigial forms whose function no longer presses to be served.

For example, the only motivating mishap that appears in "The Gospel According to Mark" (1970) is the scuffle between the protagonist of the tale, Baltasar Espinosa, and some of his fellow university students. Borges includes this detail about his hero's life so as to portray his protagonist as a passive type; Baltasar fights in order not to take part in a student strike. Yet aspects of artistic works are overdetermined, and it may be that in addition to revealing Baltasar's character, Borges unconsciously supplies a paradigmatic detail.

Out of a spirit of acquiescence, Baltasar agrees to summer at his cousin's ranch, and his Borgean journey entails his abandoning Buenos Aires for more primitive surroundings. At the *estancia* he finds no folkloric glamour at all, but an abandoned hull of a house and its rustic caretakers. The Gutres, an unedifying lot who maintain the premises, are the scarcely verbal scions of a clan of Scotsmen better educated than they. After more than a century of intermarrying with Indians and living on the plain, the Guthrie family has reverted to a backward, childlike state. Impoverishment in this tale, then, is figured by the remoteness of Baltasar's cousin's ranch, its state of disrepair, and the backwardness of its keepers.

The Gutres occupy the same position in this tale as other characters who, in other tales, offer sustenance or instruction to Borges' protagonists. Referring only to the group of tales we have just seen, we can identify as homologous figures the ghoulish man who, in "Al-Mu'tasim," guides the fleeing student with his rant, the Norwegian-speaking sailor in "Emma Zunz" who initiates Emma in sexuality, and the timeless gaucho who throws Dahlmann a knife in "The South." If we take one common denominator among these figures to be their status as perverse mentors, we can associate with them the irreverent teacher of etiquette in "Kotsuké no Suké." And a teaching relationship links the Gutres to Baltasar Espinosa, although the roles of teacher and taught are here reversed; when flood waters strand Espinosa with the caretaker's family, he helps pass the time by reading them the Gospel according to Mark.

Confined in the dilapidated house until the water subsides— that is, enclosed in a Borgean antrum—Baltasar amuses himself with activities that serve as subtle figurings of the paradigm's fourth phase. He looks in a mirror at the growing beard that slowly has cropped out upon his face. He reads from the Bible (texts for Borges, we recall, often stand for the infinite and the Gutres understand the gospel as revealed truth). And he sleeps with the Gutre girl. These minor enactments of the final stage of the paradigm lead up to and prepare the reader for the drastic collapse of Espinosa's power; the ending of the tale doubly portrays the annihilation of Espinosa's self. As he opens the door to the toolshed and beholds, in that mean Borgean enclosure, a rude cross, a flash of enlightenment reveals to him the gruesome death the Gutres have devised for him. Moreover, we know that earlier in the tale Baltasar has mused, "the generations of men, throughout recorded time, have always told and retold two stories—that of a lost ship which searches the Mediterranean Sea for a dearly loved island, and that of a god who is crucified on Golgotha" (*OC*, 1070; *DBR*, 19). Not only is Baltasar fated to lose his life but, as his odyssey draws to a close, his identity merges with that of other men. "A-islado" in an Argentine Aegean, he reenacts the passion of Jesus. In almost a literal sense he has become both Ulysses and Christ, and his compenetration with these figures in effect dissolves his individual identity.

Borges wrote "There Are More Things," the last of our seven tales, much later in his career, publishing it in *The Book of Sand* in 1975. Its Argentine protagonist, who narrates the tale, is completing his doctoral exams in philosophy at the University of Texas when he receives the news that his uncle has died. This motivating mishap leads him to think nostalgically of his dead uncle, Edwin Arnett, and the reader learns that it was Arnett who first initiated the speaker in the metaphysical puzzles that were to become his métier. The two men, fellow enthusiasts in an abstruse field, have been collaborators in a privileged Borgean group.

The motif of loyalty and betrayal is attenuated in this tale; the narrator tells us that he feels a certain remorse at having let pass chances to be kind to his uncle, but his regret does not signal to the reader that he has betrayed Arnett. And, while Borges mentions that the English-born uncle has been a freethinker in religious matters, and that Arnett's friend Alexander Muir is a Scottish Calvinist, he adduces the characters' national and sectarian allegiances primarily in order to contrast with the Jewishness of the buyer of Arnett's house, and the blasphemous monstrosity of the house's new occupant.

So, too, is the Borgean journey present in the tale, but de-emphasized. In the other tales we have examined, Borges' heroes set out on a journey in what is clearly a direct response to the motivating mishap. Here, though, the narrator's return to Argentina takes place in due course, not apparently as a result of his uncle's death. Nevertheless, his journey home does take him from a cultural seat, the main campus of the University of Texas (Borges himself spent half a year there in 1961 and had a high regard for that institution of learning) to "the far end of the South American continent" (*LA*, 67; *BS*, 51). The town of Turdera, where Arnett has lived, is a place whose "almost coun-trylike solitude" (*LA*, 68; *BS*, 52) belies its proximity to the capital. When he returns to Argentina, the narrator inquires into his uncle's affairs, particularly when he finds that the new owner of Arnett's house has discarded his uncle's furnishings and ef-fects. The nephew gleans disturbing intelligence from his un-cle's friend Muir, from a neighbor, and from a carpenter in a nearby town who has made furniture for the new inhabitant of the house. He begins to suspect that the new occupant of his un-cle's home is a monstrous, inhuman creature.

Impoverishment, in this tale, is figured as the deformation of the house and the spoiling of its grounds. Passing by the front gate, whose bars are twisted out of shape, Arnett's nephew sees that the garden has grown all to weeds and that the edges of a shallow ditch have been trampled down. When he returns and trespasses on the premises during a storm, he notes that the flagstones have been pried up, and that the grass is unkempt. A sickening odor permeates the place. And, when he finds his way into the house itself, he sees, in the "single great bare room" ("sola gran pieza desmantelada") (*LA*, 75; *BS*, 57) that has been made by tearing down the partition between two rooms, weird furniture fashioned to accommodate some appalling crea-ture.

The house, of course, unambiguously represents the Borgean enclosure in "There Are More Things." Called "la Casa Colorada" ("The Red House"), it is associated by virtue of its name with the hue Borges assigns in many of his stories to the antrum where his heroes come to grief. Having admitted himself to the house and explored its contents, Borges' hero comes face to face with the hideous being whose dwelling Arnett's house has come to be. The tale concludes with the horrifying encounter between the nephew and his host. Is the intruding hero annihilated? Again we must remark an attenuation of the paradigmatic model. The fact that the story is narrated in the first person gives us to understand that the speaker has survived his meeting with the misshapen beast. Yet Borges is wise enough not to describe the encounter, and the reader who finishes the tale lays the book aside convinced that some awful fate befalls Arnett's nephew.

My own reader, having looked at eight of Borges' tales, ought by now to be able to locate the paradigm for himself in a very considerable number of Borges' works of fiction. What is more, he ought to regard in a different way many of the small details of Borges' narratives whose function may until now have seemed obscure. By relating stories to one another, he can identify homologous elements that function similarly in a number of tales. This technique of analysis sheds unexpected light on a tale like "The Waiting." One interprets the story differently if one understands that the protagonist's room is a Borgean enclosure, whose iron bed is homologous to Yu Tsun's iron cot or to the iron bars through which Juan Dahlmann peers. The room's scarlet wall paper, too, has parallels in other tales, such as the red walls of the remote country store in "The South" or the Casa Colorada in "There Are More Things." And the maté Villari drinks takes on a significance beyond that of a realistic detail, for it seems related to the glass of water Emma Zunz requests, the coffee Dahlmann and Baltasar Espinosa consume, and the tea Alexander Muir serves Arnett's nephew. Similarly, the dog Villari befriends, with which he speaks in a "rustic dialect of his childhood" (*OC*, 609; *L*, 167), reminds us of parallel figures in Borges' other tales: the ghoulish man in "Al-Mu'tasim," the sailor in "Emma Zunz," the timeless gaucho in "The South," and the Gutres in "The Gospel According to Mark." By recognizing in these small details of "The Waiting" signifiers of a particular kind of Borgean meaning, one revises somewhat the way one reads the tale.

Among the works that appear in quite a different light when read as vehicles for the Borgean paradigm are the tales Borges wrote in collaboration with Adolfo Bioy Casares. Many of the stories coauthored by the two friends, including all those included in the collections *Six Problems for Don Isidro Parodi* (1942) and *Two Memorable Fantasies* (1946), become recognizable as parodies, and not only parodies of the detective tale but of Borges' paradigm itself. As the two writers collude as H. Bustos Domecq to turn on its head, in the Parodi tales, the conventional detective story, they also spoof, probably unconsciously, the Borgean ur narrative. These collaborative works do elaborate the paradigm, portrayed with the same imagery that Borges employs, but with the crucial difference that irreality is utterly missing from the Parodi tales. Bereft of the disquieting intensity with which Borges endows them, the "impoverishment" and "self-loss" of Bustos Domecq's stories stand as a kind of private parody that Borges, knowingly or unknowingly, directs at himself.

Let us examine one of the Parodi narratives for signs of what is, in effect if not by intent, good-humored self-mockery. "The Twelve Figures of the World" begins with the confession of Aquiles Molinari that he has unintentionally killed a man. This inadvertent homicide, which motivates him to seek out the jailed detective Parodi and to recount his supposed crime, serves in the tale as the mishap out of which the rest of the story evolves. Molinari has killed, or so he thinks, the leader of a Druse sect, Dr. Abenjaldún, who has captured Molinari's slavish regard by initiating him in the rites of that heretical Moslem group. (Borges' heroes, we recall, regularly profess some exotic faith. Moreover, Borges often portrays the crucial theme of loyalty and betrayal, integral to the paradigm's first phase, as his heroes' devoutness or apostasy, or as the unorthodoxy of their sects.)

Eager to ingratiate himself with Abenjaldún, Molinari is punctilious in carrying out the process of spiritual cleansing the Druse leader prescribes, and the regimen to which the would-be convert commits himself parodies the second phase of Borges' paradigm. After subsisting for three days on weak tea (a Borgean beverage), he travels by train to a station near the villa of his spiritual guide. (We think of Yu Tsun's journey to Ashgrove or Dahlmann's train trip to the South or, in a tale we have not looked at here, Erik Lönnrot's journey on a train to Triste-le-Roi.) Panting with exhaustion, Molinari proceeds on foot to the *quinta* where Abenjaldún awaits. During the whole of this Borgean pilgrimage, the gull empties his mind, in a process reminiscent of the discipline of the priest in "The Circular Ruins," by repeating time and time again the signs of the zodiac, reeled off in proper sequence. By the time he reaches the home of Abenjaldún he has sunk into a state of idiocy. Borgean impoverishment, this, but with none of the seriousness that attends it in Borges' tales.

What follows seems, for a time, to parody "The Garden of Forking Paths," which Borges wrote just several months before this collaborative tale. Just as Stephen Albert meets Yu Tsun at the gate to his Oriental garden and conducts him to an intimate scholarly library, Abenjaldún greets his disciple at the *quinta's* gate, escorts him along a brick-laid walk, and ushers him finally into an office equipped with a scanty collection of books. Overawed by tomes like the *Illustrated Gardener* and *Criminal Woman,* Molinari takes little note of the bookkeeping in progress, whose intricacies Izedín, a member of the sect, is apparently engaged in revealing to his boss Abenjaldún.

Dr. Abenjaldún interrupts this financial epiphany to send his convert on a mock Borgean search. Enjoining him to recite again and again the signs of the zodiac, he ushers Molinari into the cult's assembly room where the faithful, draped in bedsheets, are ranged around the statue of a bull. There he requires the initiate to identify, through a process he says is mystical, four particular adherents from the many gathered there. By now Molinari is faint with fatigue, too lightheaded to notice that when he is sent to bring back Izedín he returns each time with a different man in tow: "I was absolutely exhausted," he reports to Parodi. "On the stairway my sight blurred. I figured my kidneys were acting up. Everything seemed different—even the man beside me" (*OCC,* 27; *SP,*

26). Now this blurring of the faculties, when we encounter it in a tale by Borges alone, signals the imminent falling away of selfhood and reality. The swarming sensation Yu Tsun has as he comprehends Ts'ui Pên's manuscript is a parallel moment. Hilariously, though, no vertiginous irreality is here involved; Molinari's kidneys are to blame! We are witnessing a joke or a con job, that is all.

To the amusement of his other followers, Abenjaldún sets Molinari a further test. Blindfolding him (is this a Borgean mask?), he tells the initiate to wait until the clock strikes twelve and then, using the incantation of astrological signs that has guided him before, to discover five Druses hidden throughout the house. The bogus divine then confers on Molinari what seems to the mystified dupe an awful power. As long as this second search lasts, Abenjaldún says, the continuity of the universe will depend on Molinari's accuracy in repeating the zodiacal signs. This sudden attainment of mastery, in this case a mastery we know does not exist, seems of a piece with the Borgean paradigm. Borges' heroes, in the moments that immediately precede their destruction, quite typically gain access to a marvelous power. But in Bustos Domecq's rendition of the paradigm, the reader knows in advance that the hero's supposed power is part of a practical joke. As Molinari stumbles from room to room searching for concealed Druses, lost in a house that, like any other Borgean labyrinth, seems "suddenly . . . interminable and unfamiliar" (*OCC*, 28), he hears a scream. He rips the blindfold from his eyes to find Abenjaldún dead before him and the villa afire. Of course murder, fire, and the uncovering of a face—here, absurdly, the face of the seeker and not the sought—are all associated elsewhere in Borges' tales with a final "revelation." And that term is used to comic effect at just this juncture in the tale, but in a context that deflates its seriousness: fleeing the scene of the crime he thinks he has committed, Molinari must scale the *quinta's* garden wall, and he confides to Parodi, "esa noche fui revelación en salto en alto"—"that night I turned into a champion high-jumper" (*OCC*, 29; *SP*, 29).

A fan of detective fiction who has not read a single one of Borges' tales will chuckle at "The Twelve Figures of the

World." To Borges, though, this story and the other Parodi tales must have afforded a special, secret delight. They undercut in a systematic way what functions in Borges' fiction to produce the irreal quality that is his personal stamp. To understand that the tales of Bustos Domecq contain and roundly spoof the paradigm, that they in effect parody Borges' other work, enlarges somewhat one's appreciation of the tales that Borges composed jointly with his friend.

But I must return to those of Borges' tales in which the paradigmatic sequence is obscure. What of a story that all but does away with character and plot, as do many of Borges' early fantastic tales? To locate the paradigm in stories that elaborate it in fractured, thoroughly disguised form, one must rely, to a greater degree than I have thus far, on evidence afforded by Borges' imagery. Borges regularly associates certain motifs and images with each phase of the paradigm. Let me return for a moment to the tales we have already seen, to point out the imagery linked with each stage of Borges' ur story. Table 2 records the motifs that, in these eight tales, surround the motivating mishap: heretical sects, master-apprentice pairs, and the issue of loyalty and betrayal. Table 3 registers some of the fictive elements with which Borges portrays the impoverishing journey: trips and searches, drinking, derealized states of mind, primitive beings who attend the protagonist, and the degradation of the hero's milieu. Details to which Borges returns as he depicts the enclaustration phase appear in table 4. They include stairways, enclosed spaces, and the color red or objects that are reddish in color—brick, rust (and, by extension, iron), and the remains of fire. Finally, table 5 displays in summary form the imagery with which Borges represents the annihilation of individual being. Although the motif of revelation encompasses all the details enumerated here, for clarity's sake I have listed separately mirrors, disguises and masks, faces, photographs, texts (such as letters, books and newspapers), precious objects, and things of circular shape.

With Borges' characteristic imagery in mind, let us turn to "The Babylon Lottery," a tale that dispenses with plot, to see whether Borges' narrative paradigm can be found. Although the Borgean ur story has been fractured, the tale nevertheless includes many details that Borges consistently associates with each phase of the paradigm. For example, we never learn what chance of fate made the narrator voyage from his native Babylon, and yet we infer that his journey has been prescribed by one—or many—drawings of the lottery. And the lottery has all the accoutrements of one of Borges' strange religious cults. Complete with sacred scriptures that confirm its "ecclesiastical power" (*OC*, 457; *L*, 31), it boasts devotees who spy upon their fellow men and betray them to the mysterious Company (we think of the Inquisition or the stern "Company" of Jesus). It boasts, too, masked heresiarchs and other veiled men who murmur "blasphemous conjectures" (*OC*, 456; *L*, 31) that impugn the Company's wisdom or its power. Present, then, are

Table 2   Motifs and Imagery Related to the Motivating Mishap

	Sects
"Kotsuké no Suké"	Japanese, with rites of courtesy
"The Approach to Al-Mu'tasim"	student is apostate Moslem
"Emma Zunz"	characters are Jewish
"The Dead Man"	smugglers' band; Bandeira's Jewish, Negro, and Indian blood
"The South"	Dahlmann's forebears are Evangelical; gauchos
"The Gospel According to Mark"	Gutres' primitive Christianity and Scottish ancestry
"There Are More Things"	speaker's consanguinity with Arnett shared interest in philosophy; Muir Calvinism vs. Preetorius' Jewishness
"The Twelve Figures of the World"	Dr. Abenjaldún's Druses

several of the key motifs linked with the paradigm's first phase: a subversive, pseudo-religious organization, heresy within that Borgean confraternity, and a shadowy event that has started the narrator on a long journey.

If no specific motivating mishap figures in the tale, neither are the circumstances of the voyager described. The impoverishment of the narrator's experience instead finds ciphered representation in the story. We are not surprised to learn that some of the destinies the speaker has fulfilled have subjected him to degradation and infamy. Slavery, imprisonment, even invisibility have fallen to his lot. Though he never tells us that his senses have dimmed, near the end of the story he reflects that he may, in telling his tale, have failed to note "some

Betrayal/loyalty/revenge	Master/student relationship
Takumi no Kami's loyalty to emperor; captains' avenging of Takumi no Kami's honor	Kotsuké no Suké is master of etiquette to Takumi no Kami; Kuranosuké is retainer of Takumi no Kami
student abjures Islam; flees reprisal of law	squalid man in tower instructs student
Loewenthal betrays Emma's father; Emma pretends to betray strikers; Emma turns on boss to be loyal to father	Norwegian sailor initiates Emma in sexuality
Otálora betrays Bandeira, and suffers Bandeira's revenge	Bandeira protects, instructs Otálora
Dahlmann keeps *estancia* out of family loyalty	the timeless gaucho tosses Dahlmann a knife
Gutres' perverted loyalty to, and betrayal of, Espinosa	Espinosa teaches Gutres from Gospel
	Arnett teaches philosophy to nephew; Muir advises speaker
Izedín's betrayal of Abenjaldún; Molinari's supposed killing of his spiritual guide	Abenjaldún initiates Molinari in Druse cult

mysterious monotony" (*OC*, 460; *L*, 35). The impoverishment that in other works attends the protagonist may here, perhaps, be displaced to aspects of the lottery itself. Its holiest spots include a cracked and dusty aqueduct and a sacred latrine, and part of its operations are revealed in the rubble of a factory that once manufactured masks. While the narrator himself neither drinks nor dreams, we learn that "drunkards" and "dreamers" may figure among the agents of the lottery. But the principal way the lottery degrades, or contaminates, to use Borges' own word, its patrons' lives is by infusing sheer randomness into their fates. The Company makes a mockery of free will by intervening infinitely in each life to alter its direc-

Table 3   Motifs and Imagery Related to the Impoverishing Journey

	Journeys, searches	Drinking
"Kotsuké no Suké"	entrapment of Kotsuké no Suké	Kuranosuké drunk in brothel door
"The Approach to Al-Mu'tasim"	student's search for woman, al-Mu'tasim	
"Emma Zunz"	trip to port, then factory	attracts sailor in bar; glass of water at Loewenthal's
"The Dead Man"	flight from Buenos Aires, later wandering	drinks at three points in tale
"The South"	trip to hospital, then to South	Dahlmann drinks coffee, then red wine
"The Gospel According to Mark"	trip to *estancia*	sweetened coffee
"There Are More Things"	return to Turdera; trespassing in uncle's house	drinks tea with Muir
"The Twelve Figures of the World"	trip to Dr. Abenjaldún's; "search" for members of cult; visit to Parodi	Molinari subsists on weak tea; beer also mentioned

tion in arbitrary ways, and this randomness is another form of impoverishment.

The narrator tells of having been in jail, as well as having wielded a sacrificial knife in a basement and eluded a strangler in a chamber of bronze. These places of enclosure, we recognize, are Borgean antrums. In addition, scattered throughout the tale we can find still other, free-floating allusions to enclaustration, as well as other details related to the third phase of the Borgean paradigm. A prison sentence, for example, may be meted out to the holder of a losing ticket, while the drawings themselves are held in the "labyrinths of the god" (*OC*, 458; *L*, 32). The unfortunate holder of a stolen ticket (the ticket,

Derealized states	Primitive beings	Degradation of milieu
Kuranosuké's drunkenness		Kuranosuké's removes to Kyoto's brothels, gaming houses, bars
	ghoulish man in tower; moon-colored hounds	student plunges into life of lowest castes
fatigue; *malestar*; coitus	non-Spanish-speaking sailor; barking dog	faded colors of hotel; failing light; ugliness of industrial district
Otálora drunk in final scene	gauchos and smugglers	desolateness and remoteness of El Suspiro
trip to *estancia* may be hallucination	the cat; the old gaucho	weather-beaten *almacén*, with "poor" architecture
	the illiterate Gutres	*estancia* in bad repair; bad weather
	Arnett's sheepdog	abominable remodeling of house
light-headedness		

rather than the prison walls, is red) has his tongue burnt out by a "white-hot iron" ("hierro candente") (*OC*, 457).

The inscrutable lottery chits are little aleph-like texts. Made out of bone or parchment and covered with symbols, they impose an infinite number of fates, which the drawings reveal. The number of drawings, too, is infinite, and the narrator, thanks to the lottery's vicissitudes, has been not one but an infinite number of men. Like the immortals of another of Borges' tales, he has relinquished individuality in the course of a life that subsumes all identities. Here is a kind of experience of self-loss, a figuring of the fourth phase of the paradigm.

"The Babylon Lottery" is an uncomfortable text. Composed early in 1939 at a time when Borges witnessed with dismay Argentina's slide toward fascism against the background of the

Table 4   Motifs and Imagery Related to Enclaustration

	Enclosed spaces	Stairways
"Kotsuké no Suké"	patio of Kotsuké's house; card factory	rope ladder
"The Approach to Al-Mu'tasim"	tower in garden; al-Mu'tasim's gallery	iron staircase of tower
"Emma Zunz"	Emma's room; hotel room; streetcar; Loewenthal's office	winding staircase of hotel
"The Dead Man"	brother's inner patio; sickroom; *estancia*'s dininghall	
"The South"	hospital room; taxi; coffee shop; train; country store	staircase is scene of accident
"The Gospel According to Mark"	house at *estancia*; toolshed	
"There Are More Things"	Arnett's house	vertical staircase
"The Twelve Figures of the World"	Abenjaldún's house; Parodi's cell	four mentions of stairs at Abenjaldún's house

Second World War and when his personal circumstances had suffered sharp reverses, its mood is dark; as well as any one of Borges' works, it conveys the subverting of human possibility. "The Elder Lady" is a work of a happier time. Borges wrote it during the 1960s, at the beginning of the quite prolonged old age that would bring him many pleasures and rewards. Even more than other tales he wrote during those years, "The Elder Lady" communicates an elegiac peace. Like "The Lottery," however, it elaborates Borges' paradigm in a somewhat atypical way, and so it may claim our attention now. Although the story does have a plot of sorts and a protagonist, the old woman of the title, the strong and disquieting feelings that seem to lie beneath the surface of most of Borges' tales—and actuate their narration—seem absent here. On its face the

Red	Rust and iron	Brick
red of Takumi's blood matches red of ritual cloth		
	iron staircase; "vías ferroviarias"	brick thrown by Hindu
Loewenthal's blood		
Bandeira's horse is "colorado," his mistress red-haired		
Dahlmann's house is "long pink house that once was painted crimson"	window of country store has iron bars	
Gutres have red hair	herramientas	
house is called "Casa Colorada"	struts of stair are iron	
Abenjaldún's blood	"el Tullido Ferrarotti"	brick paths at Abenjaldún's

story appears to be nothing more than a moving, very gently ironic portrait of an Argentine family that has come down in the world, a family in some respects like Borges' own. The highly charged issue of traduced loyalty, the shame in the sense that one's imposture has been unmasked, the fearful threat of nonbeing, all these fade, in what seems like a story unique among Borges' works. Nevertheless, the paradigm's

Table 5   Motifs and Imagery Related to Annihilation of Self

	Revelation	Mirrors	Scars, disguises masks, blindfolds
"Kotsuké no Suké"	Kotsuké realizes he's been tricked	mirror in box; bronze mirror	Kotsuké's scar
"The Approach to Al-Mu'tasim"	revelation of al-Mu'tasim's face	*A Game with Shifting Mirrors;* men mirror al-Mu'tasim	beaded curtain
"Emma Zunz"	news of suicide; Loewenthal's surprise	Paseo de Julio's mirrors	Loewenthal's beard and glasses
"The Dead Man"	revelation of being tricked	mirror in sickroom	Bandeira's scar
"The South"	Dalhmann realizes he's about to die		blood on Dahlmann's face; surgeon's mask; Dahlmann's beard
"The Gospel According to Mark"	Baltasar realizes he's about to be crucified	Baltasar looks at self in mirror	Baltasar's beard
"There Are More Things"	metaphysical revelations; seeing anfisbena	mirrors in Arnett's house	
"The Twelve Figures of The World"	"revelación en salto de alto"; solution of mystery		bedsheets; blindfold

traces are present in this tale. Committed to new uses, Borges' ur narrative can still be discerned.

The martial heroics of the old woman's father, Colonel Rubio de Jáuregui, are no real mishap, and yet they set in motion the events that culminate in the lady's death; Borges' speaker views the aged daughter as the last casualty of the war for independence. In this sense, at least, the battles of that war—

Faces	Photographs	Texts	Circular and precious objects
		story has inspired art	mirror in rectangular box
al-Mu'tasim's face	narrator's book has no illustrations	Mir Bahadur Alí's novel	
	photo of Milton Sills	letter	revolver in drawer
		letter of introduction	woman; trappings of horse
	daguerreotype of ancestor; X-ray	*1001 Nights*	box containing daguerreotype
		books at *estancia;* Bible	mailbox; cement lions
			prisms, pyramids, colored cubes, globe
		daily papers; Abenjaldún's books; letter of invitation	statue of bull

and in particular a wound Colonel Rubio once sustained—may be seen as the motivating mishap of the tale. As for disloyalty, Venezuelan chroniclers recording the conflict have been unfaithful to truth; they have bestowed on Bolívar the laurels Colonel Rubio deserved. Nationalism may serve as one analogue in this tale of the Borgean cults of other narratives. However, religious apostasy finds its way into the tale, as well; old Mrs. Jáuregui, it seems, makes no over-nice distinctions among sundry non-Catholic and thus irreverent groups. Protestants, Jews, Masons, heretics, and atheists are all the same to her.

Her mind is one that greatly simplifies. Although the speaker tells us of events that might pass for a Borgean journey—hard times have forced the colonel's family to remove from their original home in the center of Buenos Aires to a Palermo flat on the city's northside—Borgean impoverishment is chiefly rendered in this tale as the gradual extinction of the señora's mental lights. "Since 1932, she had been growing dimmer and dimmer" ("había ido apagándose poco a poco") (*OC*, 1049; *DBR*, 92), the narrator says of her, stopping a moment to defend a phrase he fears some readers may find trite. (The verbal poverty he makes excuses for is a further kind of impoverishment.) But the speaker's outworn locution exactly suits his purpose; he describes the lapsing of the old woman's mind into outworn habits of thought and speech that no longer correspond to experience. She prays the rosary without attending to the meaning of her words; persists in the use of certain archaisms, such as "orientales" for the more up-to-date "uruguayos"; and is incredulous when a relative asserts that the princess of Spain speaks like a common Galician girl. Moreover, impoverishment in the tale takes other forms. The señora is immobile, confined to her home. Her eyesight gradually fails and at a certain point she gives up talking. And the narrator assumes that little by little even her memories are stilled. He portrays her consciousness as subsiding at last into "entresueño," the state between waking and sleep, and describes her humble half-sentience as akin to the "modest, silent life" (*OC*, 1050) of the plants she tends.

Still another way in which Borges depicts impoverishment

in this tale, where irreality is rendered quietly as old age, is by depicting the family's decline. Bereft of their lands by Rosas, Colonel Rubio's heirs have sunk by degrees into penury, and the modest renown the colonel once achieved outshines by far the mundaneness of his grandchildren's petit bourgeois lives. One, an inspector of rents, lacks the energy to write the biography of his glorious forebear. Another marries a bureaucrat, and a third weds an Italian immigrant for whom a special apology must be made. History books and social registers drop their family name and even the street that commemorates the Jáureguis is lost in obscurity; it runs behind the Westside Cemetery, where workers, not heroes, are interred.

Borges is at his best when he describes the little pretensions the Jáureguis permit themselves. They drink tea instead of maté. And though they are poor, they proudly display the colonel's portrait, done in oil, and his sword, objects they plan to bequeath some day to the Historical Museum. Yet for all their snobbery, their values are those of the lower middle class; they have bought a dictionary in order to acquire its stand. Finally, their mother's sheer longevity seems to secure their claim to aristocracy. As the last surviving child of the patriots who wrested independence from Spain, Mrs. Jáuregui is to be honored on the occasion of her hundredth birthday. A government minister sends an official letter saying he intends to call to pay his respects, and the family put on airs as they show their friends the letterhead and signature of the important man. To prepare for the visit they polish and shine windows and floors, silver and furniture, and they open the piano so that their guests can see a velvet keyboard cover. An attentive neighbor lends them a potted geranium for the night.

These tender, slightly pathetic particulars work marvelously to evoke the household life of an "honorable family come down in the world" (*OC*, 1049). Yet when we look again at the details that endear the Jáureguis to us, we can identify in many of them paradigmatic details. In the maté which the family, like upper-class Anglophiles, replace with tea (and later in the port and sherry and champagne they serve) we see the beverage that is all but de rigueur in Borges' tales. And Rubio's portrait, like the photographs the journalists take, captures and shows forth a countenance. The letter, too—it inspires a kind of awe—reminds us of other letters we have seen in other stories, whose purpose is to reveal some new and surprising intelligence. The dictionary, although no one consults it, joins the unwritten "exhaustive biography" of Colonel Rubio (*OC*, 1049) as aleph manqué. And the old woman herself is another failed aleph; the newspapers, lying faithfully, call her an "eloquent archive" (*OC*, 1052) of one hundred years of Argentina's past. In reality, though, her memory is extinct. Oblivion has claimed the "tumult of passions" that was her life, experienced or recalled, and the narrator doubts that her consciousness supports even the "quiet chaos" (*OC*, 1050; *DBR*, 93) of senility. "Archive," "tumult," and "chaos" are all terms that connote Borges' image of ciphered infinity.

We have already seen that the señora never ventures out of doors, and her apartment is a Borgean enclosure of sorts. Located up a narrow flight of stairs, her flat consists of a darkened vestibule, a small parlor, and a dining room whose Venetian blinds—they are made of iron—admit a feeble light. In addition to this principal figuring of a closed-in place, the tale mentions "a series of hovels, not of galvanized-iron but of unplastered brick" (*OC*, 1049; *DBR*, 91), that the colonel's grandson recalls having seen from a streetcar. Both shacks and streetcar are Borgean antrums, as well.

The birthday festivities occupy, in the tale, the place of the paradigm's fourth and final phase; the excitement they bring hastens the death of the old woman who, even during the party, the narrator suggests, "perhaps . . . no longer knew who she was" (*OC*, 1052; *DBR*, 96). The commotion of the guests, which starts and ends with what Borges describes as unnatural abruptness, and the flashbulbs exploded in the señora's face make of the party a second version of the battle at Cerro Alto (also known as Cerro Bermejo—Vermilion Hill—presumably from the red of the blood spilled there). The conflation of two moments, separated by more than a hundred years, is exactly the kind of collapsing of time and space that Borges is fond of portraying at the end of his tales. Here the giving way of linear time is not cataclysmic, as it is in many of Borges' stories. The narrator merely reflects that "the last victim of that throng of lances high on a Peruvian tableland was, more than a century later, a very old lady" (*OC*, 1052; *DBR*, 96). In the work of another writer this flourish might pass for nothing more than a graceful figure of speech. But we are reading Borges, and we recognize, considerably softened but unmistakable nonetheless, one of Borges' favorite metaphysical tropes. We also recognize a figuring of the final phase of the paradigm.

We have now found evidence of the Borgean paradigm in two stories that for different reasons at first seemed to depend less on its structuring than do other of Borges' tales. In "The Babylon Lottery" the elements associated with his ur story are dispersed, not organized into a consecutive narrative. Yet the emotional tenor of the tale is one with that of the majority of Borges' greatest fictional works. "The Elder Lady," in contrast, does betray in its plot the progressive stages of the paradigm, but the story is affectively at variance with most of Borges' other narratives. Later in this study I shall return to the question of what causes Borges to distort the paradigm. I shall try to account on the one hand for the fragmenting of the paradigm and, on the other, for its emptying of mystery and infamy.

It would be impractical and tedious to analyze each of Borges' tales to prove that each rehearses the same underlying narrative. Yet one group of Borges' tales, if tales they be, deserves special notice in a discussion of the Borgean paradigm. With the exception of "Streetcorner Man," an original tale, the works that make up *A Universal History of Infamy*, Borges' first volume of fiction, stand as a halfway house between précis and independent invention. They adapt into pleasing vignettes material Borges claims to have unearthed in other books. As it happens, they, too, elaborate Borges' paradigm in recognizable ways. (We have already examined the story of Kotsuké no Suké.) But many of them differ markedly from Borges' mature tales, in tone as well as in the particular form that some aspects of Borges' paradigm assume in them. It is worth looking carefully at the *Infamy* texts, as I shall do in the next chapter, for by tracing their relationship to their sources one can do more than show that Borges was, in his reading and research, casting around for material of a rather specific kind. One can make good progress toward understanding why Borges obsessively restates the paradigm, by starting to understand what set of concerns so urgently pressed him to perform, again and again, a ritual narrative act. The Chinese emperor in "The Widow Ching, Lady Pirate" deployed multiple versions of a fable to subdue a disturbance in his realm. Borges' sending forth, in a like way, many versions of one story may have had, in psychic terms, a similar end. He may have aimed to allay, through writing short stories, a disturbance in his sensibility.

II

Origins of the Paradigm:
A Universal History of Infamy

What intrinsic interest can be accorded to a writer's technique? Who- ever savored in a writer's technique something that didn't reveal the psychology of a man?
—*Jorges Luis Borges*, The Language of the Argentines

The question of how to plumb the meaning of Borges' para- digm invites two kinds of critical approach which at first seem to have little bearing on one another. On the one hand, a reader may consult his own response to Borges' tales (and imagine that of others) and ask how the presence of the para- digm in Borges' works affects a reader. He may, that is, study this aspect of Borges' texts without taking into account the relationship of the writer to his work. Literary criticism as it is practiced nowadays favors just this sort of inquiry. On the other hand, however, a critic may try to shed light on what meaning the paradigm might have held for Borges. For mean- ing it surely had. To say that Borges rehearsed again and again the same ur story is to suggest that in his case the writing of a tale may have been, among other things, a compelling private ritual. And rituals, whether they are personal or social in nature, are designed to accomplish some function, whether or not their practitioners know what that function is. Borges, elaborating his paradigm time and again, must have acted to achieve some psychic end. A second way of understanding the paradigm, then, is to perceive what psychic issues Borges ad- dressed, what intimate problems he set out to resolve each time he recast his ur narrative.

I have chosen this second approach to interpreting Borges' paradigm. And I have done so, in part, because of the nature of the evidence at hand. It is almost impossible to document the responses of readers, whereas unusually promising textual data exist that enable one to explore Borges' relationship to his ur story. Borges did not, after all, begin his literary career by writing short stories, that is, by creating works that embody the paradigm. By the time he turned, in 1933, to experimenting with fiction,[1] he had published three books of verse, four collections of essays, and a curiously unbiographical biography.[2] These early writings, as well as his first narrative sketches, contain important antecedents of the paradigm, and by tracing how Borges' prototypical story evolved out of its beginnings, one can infer a good deal about the paradigm's role in Borges' inner life.

Although some elements of Borges' ur story first appear in his nonnarrative writings of the 1920s and 1930s, it makes sense to begin our look at the evolution of the paradigm by examining the first book of narrative that Borges saw into print. *A Universal History of Infamy,* published in 1935, affords a particularly good laboratory for studying what Borges was about as he shaped his first representations of the paradigm (or of something very like the paradigm). Because twelve of the thirteen sketches in the book draw on and reshape material Borges found in the course of his readings, one can go back to these sources and analyze rather precisely how Borges used them. Not only does such a study reveal a good deal about Borges' conscious aesthetic intentions, but it gives good evidence, as well, of some of the psychic conflicts that Borges, at least at that period of his life, was struggling to master.

What are these annals of infamy, and how did Borges come to write them? Borges almost surely conceived them as copy to help fill the Saturday Entertainment Supplement of Buenos Aires' sensationalist newspaper *Crítica,* a supplement he edited between 12 August 1933 and 6 October 1934. Borges' first narratives set down the fortunes of reprobates, either notorious real-life criminals or evildoers described in literature and lore. (In only one case does Borges invent a fictional antihero.) The *Infamy* texts are meant to entertain a mass readership, and in this they are very much of a piece with the rest of the supplement's contents. At the same time that the serious-minded Eduardo Mallea, editing the highbrow literary pages of *La Nación*, touted the books approved in Europe's salons, Borges assembled in *Crítica* week after week happy little celebrations of North and South American popular culture and Oriental lore. His columns, illustrated with cartoonlike color drawings done in the style of American funny papers, vaunted adventure stories like Jack London's "The Shadow and the Flash" and H. G. Wells' "The Cone"; detective fiction by G. K. Chesterton and Borges' Argentine friends Manuel Peyrou and Santiago Dabove; and assorted supernatural and science fiction tales. They hosted essays on the tango and the Negro spiritual and pieces by William Henry Hudson and Euclides da Cunha about life in the backlands of Argentina and Brazil. And they introduced to *Crítica*'s readers film directors like Ernst Lubitsch. Interspersed with fanciful excerpts from Marcel Schwob's *Imaginary Lives* and Rudyard Kipling's *Just So Stories*, Borges printed lurid feature articles on leprosy, the atrocities perpetrated even in those years by the Nazis, and the final hours of a United States convict condemned to execution in 1929. Borges did not entirely abjure in the supplement a more highminded literary aim; together with Ulises Petit de Murat he reviewed recently published works, among them Ezequiel Martínez Estrada's important treatise *Radiografía de la pampa*. And he used *Crítica*'s pages to publish a long piece of his own on the English translations of *1001 Nights* that eventually took its place among his "serious" essays, written at approximately the same period, in *A History of Eternity* (1936). Still, the chronicles of infamy that comprise most of his contributions to *Crítica* had much in common with the lighter contents of the supplement.

Borges must have regarded the composition of the *Infamy* texts as a sort of pseudoliterary play. In his "Autobiographical Essay" he recalls the "sheer pleasure" of writing them. And he describes his early narratives as being "in the nature of hoaxes." This is how he describes his method of composition:

In my *Universal History,* I did not want to repeat what Marcel Schwob had done in his *Imaginary Lives*. He had

> invented biographies of real men about whom little or nothing is recorded. I, instead, read up on the lives of known persons and then deliberately varied and distorted them according to my own whims. . . . I set down my free version . . . in flagrant contradiction of my chosen authority. . . . Since the general plots or circumstances were all given me, I had only to embroider sets of vivid variations. (*A*, 239)

This was the context in which Borges composed and published his first experiments with narrative. Together with his audience, he must have delighted in the glorious outlawry of the gangsters and pirates and impostors whose criminal lives he set down. And he must have delighted as well in secretly joining his villains in delinquency and fraud, for in writing these sketches he was acting the part of a literary marauder. To execute his first, covert attempts at story writing, he pirated, to a greater or lesser degree, other works. His own infamy, though, consisted not so much in pillaging his sources— he acknowledged them, if with less accuracy than show, in an index of sources at the end of *A Universal History*—but in betraying the works he consulted and in passing off as the work of others a great deal that he himself actually wrote.

The twelve fictional texts Borges published in *Crítica*, together with another he added to make up his 1935 book *A Universal History*,[3] afford a wonderful means of studying how the young writer worked as he made his first attempts at forging tales. Each of the thirteen texts points to and re-elaborates previously existing sources, although these sources are not always those a mischievous Borges cites. Many of the works Borges mines—Herbert Asbury's *The Gangs of New York*, Philip Gosse's *The History of Piracy*, and A. B. Mitford's *Tales of Old Japan*, to name a few—are English-language volumes, nonfiction accounts of treachery and violence, set in exotic regions of the globe. Burton's translation of the *1001 Nights* supplies Borges with material for two of his sketches, and two others adapt portions of Emanuel Swedenborg's eccentric theological writings. Still another piece is drawn from Don Juan Manuel's *Libro de Patronio*, a staple of the medieval Hispano-

Arabic tradition. And one of Borges' texts, "Streetcorner Man," relies on a "source" that Borges himself wrote, although "Hombres pelearon," the 1928 piece he subjects to reworking, itself retells a bit of Buenos Aires streetlore. But whatever the origin of Borges' literary raw material, these thirteen accounts do exist in "before" and "after" versions. Because each of the tales and sketches of *A Universal History* can be matched against the document Borges probably had at hand as he wrote, it is inviting to look for principles of selection and elaboration that may have governed Borges as he composed his first works of fiction.

Already some of the ablest critics of Borges' work have juxtaposed source and story. As early as 1958 Roger Caillois, in a "Postface du traducteur" appended to his French translation of *A Universal History of Infamy*, explored the nature of Borges' reliance on some of the volumes the Argentine writer claims to have plundered. Studying in particular detail the possible textual origins of "The Masked Dyer, Hakim of Merv," one of the last sketches Borges published and one that strays farther from its cited sources than do most of the *Infamy* texts, Caillois concludes that, at least in some instances, Borges owes little or nothing to any source but his own imagination.[4] Other critics have confirmed Caillois' view that Borges departs in radical and revealing ways from the works he drew on. Emir Rodríguez Monegal has pointed out the many changes—modifications characteristic of the mature Borges—that the young writer introduced in material he gleaned from an *Encyclopaedia Britannica* article, the source Borges cites for "Tom Castro, the Implausible Impostor."[5] Norman Thomas di Giovanni, who translated *A Universal History of Infamy* into English, has taken the trouble to locate and consult all of the sources Borges credits in the volume, plus a few he does not.[6] While noting that in some cases Borges' fictions coincide rather closely—both in content and in language—with the sources Borges used, di Giovanni affirms that often Borges' revisions are so thoroughgoing as to amount to independent creation. In particular, he traces Borges' freehand rewriting of history and of his sources in "The Disinterested Killer Bill Harrigan"[7] and shows how Borges' whimsy ignored what did not please it and grafted one source to another without apparent constraint. Finally, Ronald Christ's 1969 study *The Narrow Act: Borges' Art of Allusion* evaluates Borges' use of secondary material. Reviewing in detail the probable sources of three sketches, "The Dread Redeemer Lazarus Morell," "The Insulting Master of Etiquette Kotsuké no Suké," and "Tom Castro, the Implausible Impostor," Christ not only shows how Borges revised his original sources but speculates in a clear-sighted way as to why he did so. Christ points out that Borges, systematically if not always with perfect adroitness, undercuts the reader's sense that what the narrative recounts actually took place. That is, he adapts his source material by introducing into it touches of the irreal.

Much of the best commentary on *A Universal History* shows how Borges derealizes the stories he recounts in reshaping his source material. Christ, for example, points out how Borges, schooled in techniques of representation used by Robert Louis Stevenson, G. K. Chesterton, and Josef Von Sternberg, subverts the matter-of-factness of the adventure tales he retells. He shows how Borges undercuts the frank factualness of events that his sources anchor in a particular time and place, with "swift hints of a nightmarish reality which underlies all earthly appearances."[8] Christ identifies several of the techniques Borges uses to produce what is often a disquieting effect: Borges' refusal to enter the minds of his characters, his stripping away of explanatory background information, and his rapid cutting from one scene to another so as to deprive each action of relationship to any other. He concludes: "On the one hand Borges taints the reality which his sources describe; on the other he corrupts the authenticity of those sources themselves; in both cases the motive is to penetrate to the metaphysical world which lies beyond fact and substance, to pass through the covers of nonexistent books into literary landscapes which are equally phantasmal."[9]

David Gallagher, writing in 1973, tries, like Christ, to account for the unsettling quality of these fictive landscapes.[10] He reminds us that Borges himself, in his prologue to the 1954 edition of *A Universal History*, remarks of his violent early tales, "beneath the sound and fury there is nothing. The book is no more than appearance, than a surface of images" (*OC,*

291; *UHI*, 12). Gallagher contends that part of the irreality Borges achieves in *A Universal History*, as in the rest of his fiction, results from the value-free narrative stance he adopts. "All things," Gallagher points out, "from death to a packet of Hungarian cigarettes, tend to become equal components of a kind of aesthetic spectacle. . . . In this book a man's clothes, a corpse, a landscape, a violent crime, a country tavern or an oriental palace may each in turn be nonchalantly transformed— without moral discrimination—into pleasing spectacle."[11] Gallagher's insightful essay goes on to discuss many of the stylistic devices Borges uses in *A Universal History* to undo his reader's faith in history-making and ultimately in the solidity of the very events history claims to record.

Sylvia Molloy continues this same line of inquiry into the ways Borges, through narrative sleight of hand, conjures away the extratextual solidity of the stories he reports. Like Gallagher, she bases her analysis not on a study of Borges' sources but on a close scrutiny of the texts themselves. In her 1979 book *Las letras de Borges*, the chapter devoted to *A Universal History* strikingly demonstrates Borges' technique of derealizing his villains, paradoxically, by describing them. Molloy shows that by the very means most writers use to reveal their characters, Borges throws his "empty protagonists" into eclipse.[12]

Borges has been fortunate in his critics. The studies I have mentioned go far toward explaining the important ways in which Borges' first narrative experiments anticipate his fictional masterpieces. Moreover, they effectively rescue *A Universal History* from the relentless disparagement with which Borges himself treated his earliest tales. A severe critic of many of his own writings, Borges judged these sketches as "the irresponsible game of a shy young man who dared not write short stories" (*OC*, 291; *UHI*, 11–12). (Norman Thomas di Giovanni, the book's English-language translator, reports that Borges at first angrily refused to let him translate the work. Di Giovanni recalls that the usually courtly Borges at first "[balked] like a Missouri mule" at the thought of reviving in translation works that were, he claimed, "badly written to the point of embarrassment."[13] Implicit, then, in the body of commentary that now exists, is the intention of dignifying this apparently frivolous group of texts by showing it to be less derivative than Borges would have us think and a direct precursor of *Ficciones*. (Christ, alone among the critics I cite here, is outspoken in saying that parts of *A Universal History* strike him as "sophomoric frippery.")[14] Yet now that scholars have vindicated *A Universal History* as a crucial link in the evolution of Borges' authorial powers, it is important to recognize that in many important regards these texts, or at any rate the first of them to be published, do differ from Borges' fully realized work.

Despite the arguments of Christ, Gallagher, and Molloy, the *Infamy* texts seem to me far less irreal than the stories of *Ficciones*. Although, as Christ puts it, Borges "taints the reality of his sources," no *Crítica* reader had any reason to doubt that the real-life villains Borges described in his thumbnail biographies had actually lived and carried out heinous wrongdoing. In part, this is because Borges bills these accounts as nonfiction. In part, though, Borges' own choices in narrating his sketches create the impression that what he is recounting actually happened. To see how much more irreal Borges' later fiction appears than do his first experiments with narrative, it is useful to put side by side two descriptive passages, one excerpted from "Monk Eastman, Purveyor of Iniquities" (1933), the other taken from "The Approach to Al-Mu'tasim" and written two years later. In the "Monk Eastman" sketch Borges describes in the following way a battle between rival mobs:

> Uno de los pistoleros fue muerto, y el tiroteo consiguiente creció a batalla de incontados revólveres. Desde el amparo de los altos pilares hombres de rasurado mentón tiraban silenciosos, y eran el centro de un despavorido horizonte de coches de alquiler cargados de impacientes refuerzos, con artillería Colt en los puños. ¿Qué sintieron los protagonistas de esa batalla? Primero (creo) la brutal convicción de que el estrépito insensato de cien revólveres los iba a aniquilar en seguida; segundo (creo) la no menos errónea seguridad de que si la descarga inicial no los derribó, eran invulnerables. Lo cierto es que pelearon con fervor, parapetados por el hierro y la noche. Dos veces intervino la po-

licía y dos la rechazaron. A la primer vislumbre del ama-
necer el combate murió, como si fuera obsceno o espectral.
(*OC*, 314)

One of the gunmen was killed, and the ensuing flurry of
shots swelled into a battle of uncounted revolvers. Sheltered
behind the pillars of the elevated structure, smooth-shaven
men quietly blazed away at each other and became the focus of an awesome ring of rented automobiles loaded with
eager reinforcements, each bearing a fistful of artillery.
   What did the protagonists of this battle feel? First (I believe), the brutal conviction that the senseless din of a hundred revolvers was going to cut them down at any moment;
second (I believe), the no less mistaken certainty that if
the first shots did not hit them they were invulnerable.
What is without doubt, however, is that, under cover of the
iron pillars and the night, they fought with a vengeance.
Twice the police intervened, and twice they were driven
off. At the first glimmer of dawn, the battle petered out—as
if it were obscene or ghostly. (*UHI*, 56)

To this account, let us compare Borges' portrayal in the "Al-
Mu'tasim" text of a Moslem procession disrupted by a Hindu
mob:

Es noche de tambores e invocaciones: entre la muchedum-
bre adversa, los grandes palios de papel de la procesión
musulmana se abren camino. Un ladrillazo hindú vuela de
una azotea; alguien hunde un puñal en un vientre; alguien
¿musulmán, hindú? muere y es pisoteado. Tres mil hombres pelean: bastón contra revólver, obscenidad contra im-
precación, Dios el indivisible contra los Dioses. Atónito, el
estudiante librepensador entra en el motín. Con las deses-
peradas manos, mata (o piensa haber matado) a un hindú.
Atronadora, ecuestre, semidormida, la policía del Sirkar
interviene con rebencazos imparciales. (*OC*, 415)

It is a night of drums and prayers. Among the mob of the
heathen, the great paper canopies of the Muslim procession
force their way. A hail of Hindu bricks flies down from a roof
terrace. A knife is sunk into a belly. Someone—Muslim?

> Hindu?—dies and is trampled on. Three thousand men are fighting—stick against revolver, obscenity against curse, God the Indivisible against the many Gods. Instinctively, the student freethinker joins in the fighting. With his bare hands, he kills (or thinks he has killed) a Hindu. The Government police—mounted, thunderous, and barely awake—intervene, dealing impartial whiplashes. (*A*, 46–47)

Both passages convey the deafening chaos of streetfighting, and both to a degree derealize the violence they portray. Borges refers metonymically to the people in each scene, calling the mobsters "uncounted revolvers" and disembodied fists and describing the sectarians as "stick" and "revolver," "obscenity" and "curse." Yet in the first passage we visualize actual men— "hombres de rasurado mentón" ("smooth-shaven men")—while in the second Borges keeps us from imagining individuals. Instead of saying that a Hindu throws a brick from a rooftop, he writes that "*a hail of Hindu bricks* flies down from a roof terrace." To the same effect, Borges alternates, in both passages, between large abstractions and concrete images that derealize the people he describes. In the "Monk Eastman" text, for example, he writes that the gangsters formed "el centro de un desparorido horizonte de coches de alquiler." The phrase is one that figuratively expands the battle—it stretches from horizon to horizon— and, at the same time, focuses the reader's eye on the automobiles. And in the "Al-Mu'tasim" passage he juxtaposes in a similar way abstract terms and metonymic ciphers. "Three thousand men are fighting," he writes, "stick against revolver, obscenity against curse, God the Indivisible against the many Gods." The very concrete "stick against revolver" modulates into the more disembodied "obscenity against curse" and finally to the utterly abstract counterposing of two inimical religious faiths.

Another way in which Borges derealizes both passages is by using adjectives in unconventional ways.[15] For example, he assigns not to people but to things adjectives that denote emotion. Thus in the "Monk Eastman" passage the adjective "desparorido" ("terrified") modifies "horizonte," not the gunmen, while in the "Al-Mu'tasim" text the student's hands are desperate, not the student himself, and the "rebencazos" ("whiplashes"), not the police who deliver them, are impartial. Borges' use of adjectives to derealize what he depicts is visible in both texts, but is far more extreme in the second passage. His description of the Bombay police as "mounted, thunderous, and barely awake" is brilliant in this regard. The phrase combines two descriptive adjectives, "atronadora" ("thunderous") and "ecuestre" ("mounted") with a third that can only be understood figuratively. Moreover, while "ecuestre" frankly describes the noun it modifies, "atronadora" does not refer to the horsemen themselves but the noise that their mounts make. That the riders' corps is "semidormida" ("barely awake") marvelously conveys a hallucinatory feeling to the scene, much more so than does Borges' noting, in the previous excerpt, "the battle petered out—*as if it were obscene or ghostly.*"

Borges' use of metonymy and of adjectives deployed in unusual ways thus helps to create a more derealized effect in the second passage than in the first. In addition, his use of the past tenses in the "Monk Eastman" sketch serves powerfully to imply that the fighting described there actually took place. It is one thing to read, as we do in the "Al-Mu'tasim" passage, what purports to be the summary of a novel's plot. It is quite another to learn that "One of the gunmen was killed," or that "Twice the police intervened." The Borges of the *Infamy* texts has not yet adopted the trick of derealizing fictive events by presenting them in the present tense as a résumé of a nonexistent literary work.

Moreover, in the "Al-Mu'tasim" text Borges sows doubt about what takes place. He writes, "Someone—Muslim? Hindu?—dies and is trampled on," so that the reader is left in the dark as to precisely who died. And the student "kills (or thinks he has killed) a Hindu." The parenthetical uses of "creo" in the "Monk Eastman" text only feint at this effect. True, they call into question the narrator's authority, but only for a moment; the speaker's uncertainty prepares the way for a contrasting affirmation: "What is without doubt is that . . . they fought with a vengeance."

When Borges tells his reader that the Moslem student does not know whether he has killed someone, he does not venture much into the student's psychology. Quite a different impression is created in the "Monk Eastman" text, as Borges speculates about the gangsters' thoughts as they come under fire. Borges confirms the idea that the mobsters' battle actually took place by assigning to the participants human feelings. "What did the protagonists of this battle feel?" Borges asks, and goes on to divine their contradictory sense of imminent danger and invulnerability. Borges rarely, in his later and more irreal work, reports the inner life of his characters, and the reader's relative ignorance of what emotions actuate a Yu Tsun or an Emma Zunz is an important factor in the derealization of Borges' mature tales.

A comparison of any two excerpts does not, of course, prove that the whole of *Ficciones* is more irreal than the collection that precedes it. It is possible, though, to point out several important ways in which the narratives of *A Universal History* seem qualitatively unlike the stories Borges was later to write. Borges' use of narrative persona; the light in which he presents his reliance on previously existing texts; and the pleasure he derives from his heroes' outright badness are all important features of his texts that undergo change. Borges alters the way in which he exploits each one of these facets of his work, and as he does his fiction becomes increasingly irreal.

The Borges, for example, who, in "The Dread Redeemer Lazarus Morell," the first sketch to be published, reviews for his *porteño* readers the history of slavery in the New World, speaks unmistakably in his own ironic narrative persona. This is how he opens the piece: "In 1517, the Spanish missionary Bartolomé de las Casas, taking great pity on the Indians who were languishing in the hellish workpits of Antillean gold mines, suggested to Charles V, king of Spain, a scheme for importing blacks, so that they might languish in the hellish workpits of Antillean gold mines (*OC*, 295; *UHI*, 19). Later in the tale, painting a stereotypic portrait of pre-Civil War plantation life in the United States, he describes, with the same archness found in his opening jibe, Negro slaves whose "gentle falsetto voices intoned an English of drawled vowels":

> They worked in rows, bent under the overseer's lash. When they ran away, full-bearded men, springing onto beau-

> tiful horses, tracked them down with snarling packs of
> hounds. . . . The owners of this hard-worked land and of
> these black gangs were idle, greedy gentlemen with flow-
> ing locks, who lived in big mansions that overlooked the
> river—always with a white pine, Greek Revival portico. A
> good slave was worth a thousand dollars and did not last
> long. Some of them were thankless enough to fall ill and
> die. (*OC*, 296; *UHI*, 21)

The Borges who wrote these lines has not yet withdrawn behind an opaque narrative mask. He speaks with his own voice,
with the same irony one can perceive in his early essays and
in the hundreds of reviews he would later publish in *El Hogar*.
The crucial schism between Borges the man and the narrative
double who effaces him has not yet taken place.[16] Gradually,
in the texts of *A Universal History*, Borges can be seen distinguishing between his own voice, which he soon withdraws
completely from the tales, and that of an ambiguously fictional
self. The first-person speaker who narrates Borges' account of
the veiled prophet of Khurasan, one of the last of the *Infamy*
texts to be composed, is a creature of Borges' own invention.
"If I am not mistaken," a by now perfectly disingenuous Borges
has his narrator begin, "the chief sources of information concerning Mokanna, the Veiled (or, literally, Masked) Prophet
of Khurasan, are only four in number" (*OC*, 324; *UHI*, 79).
The four sources this fictional Borges, with hilarious scrupulous-
ness, proceeds to cite are of course apocryphal. They exist exactly in the measure that he does himself.

Concomitant with Borges' conjuring away of his own non-
fictional self is his deliberate exploiting, as narrative device,
of what was always a duplicitous reliance on his sources. At
no point does Borges merely transcribe the work of other writers. From the outset he selects and rearranges the material
he adapts. Even into the sketches—and there are several of
them—that correspond nearly verbatim to pre-existing texts,
Borges introduces significant changes of detail. Yet however
much these changes respond to aesthetic inclinations—principles of composition of which Borges may or may not have been
aware—the trick of deferring to nonexistent sources did not

initially form part of an integrated aesthetic. It probably evolved instead as a felicitous exaggeration of Borges' original timid but gleeful tampering with real texts.

The two formal transformations I have just described accompany a shift in the nature of the content of Borges' fiction, a shift that can be discerned within the series of texts that make up *A Universal History* and that becomes more pronounced in the tales that immediately follow them. As Borges sought out in the books that came his way exemplary acts of infamy, his notion of what infamy entails seems subtly to have changed. In a 1965 interview with Georges Charbonnier, Borges recalls the quality he set out to portray in his little sagas of infamy. "My characters," he says, speaking of the reprobates of *A Universal History,* "are, like most rogues, innocent people who don't realize the evil of what they are doing."[17] As Borges suggests, throughout his first book of narratives he depicts figures in whom "innocence hobnobs with infamy."[18] Yet Borges' delinquents are not all sociopathic naïfs; Kuranosuké no Suké, the protagonist of "The Insulting Master of Etiquette Kotsuké no Suké" although not its titular villain, suffers infamy precisely because of his acute moral sense. By the time Borges wrote this story, the ninth of the twelve *Infamy* texts to which original publication dates can be assigned,[19] he seemed less concerned with what Sylvia Molloy calls "pecado vistoso"[20]—flagrant wrongdoing—than with shameful degradation in its own right.

In the case of the repentant Kuranosuké no Suké this degradation attends the expiation of wrongdoing, not its initial commission. If, in his earlier sketches, Borges glories in the exploits of amoral simpletons who cudgel defenseless old men, pillage cities, fornicate with abandon, and coolly disembowel their victims, he eventually turns away from *infamia* as sheer egregious baseness toward an *infamia* that encompasses the shamefulness of ignominious deeds. The veiled prophet of Khurasan epitomizes infamy not just because he dupes the adherents to his cult but because he suffers from a hideous leprous affliction, infamous in itself, which leads to his downfall and disgrace. And the prideful Melancthon, protagonist of "A Theologian in Death," seems infamous not so much for his heretical preferring of faith over charity as for the nightmarish degradation that little by little afflicts his stubborn soul. As he persists, after death, in his erring theology, the furnishings about him fade into insubstantiality, spots of discoloration deface the walls and floor of his cell, his garments deteriorate mysteriously to a state of bestial primitivism, and the admirers who visit him, some of whom are faceless, seem to him an abhorrent lot. In short, it is the shameful conditions of Melancthon's punishment, not his initial sin, that strike us as infamous. That they strike us, as well, as irreal in one of the senses we have discussed is worth noting.

Having said this much about the ways in which the *Infamy* texts differ among themselves as Borges adjusts his narrative stance, I shall reverse my emphasis and concentrate, for the time being, on pointing out features that Borges' early narratives share with one another. The *Infamy* pieces evince so many structural and thematic parallels that one can identify, informing them generally, a sort of protoparadigm, a forerunner of Borges' ur narrative. This narrative formula is visible in all the *Infamy* texts, regardless of how Borges classifies them. When he collected them into book form, Borges saw fit to divide his early fiction into three separate categories. The first section of the book contains seven pseudo-biographical sketches of notorious villains, texts Borges originally intended to appear in *Crítica* under the lurid rubric that gives its title to the volume. Segregated from these sketches in the second part of the book is the short story "Streetcorner Man," which, despite its textual antecedents, Borges rightly thought of as a full-fledged original tale, not a thumbnail biography. The third section of *A Universal History*, subtitled "Etcetera," contains five shorter pieces, four of them drawing on Oriental lore, which aim at being magical, not gory. Two distinctions can be made between the "Universal History of Infamy" narratives and the "Etcetera" pieces; the former document the careers of real life villains, while the latter draw their subjects from literary works. And, while the "Infamy" pieces seem to dwell on criminal acts, the latter all culminate in and emphasize a moment—terrible or wondrous—of revelation. Yet all of the pieces in *A Universal*

History center around the portrayal of crime and retribution. One can think of these thirteen texts as embodying—with different emphases, to be sure—a single narrative model.

What, then, are the points of commonality that link the *Infamy* texts into a unified body of narrative that may have addressed, for Borges the apprentice writer of fiction, a single constellation of psychic concerns? At first glance the notion of infamy, as Borges uses it in these tales, seems to afford in only the laxest sense a common denominator. Examined from another perspective, however, the *Infamy* narratives do seem organized around a single basic story, one that accommodates within it infamies of more than one stripe. In each text Borges describes a famous reprobate who flouts the laws of society and is punished for his transgressions. What is more, the society whose mores the Borgean *infame* offends must be of a particular kind. It must be one that would have seemed "pointedly picturesque" (*A*, 239) (the phrase is Borges' own) to Borges and his *Crítica* readers: the marginal North American worlds of outlaw and sheriff, gangster and immigrant, runaway slave and poor white trash; Far Eastern realms—the Japan of the samurai warrior and the South China Seas during the nineteenth century Chinese dynasties—; Arabic lands, where necromancy seems a commonplace; and, in the case of "Streetcorner Man," districts that housed the quaint and mannered subculture of Buenos Aires' lowlife. When we recall that the Borges who here indulges in orgies of local color is the same Borges who, during the 1920s—indeed throughout his career—has consistently decried the use of local color as the last refuge of sentimental minds, we may well wonder at his reveling, in the texts of *A Universal History*, in the exoticism of these settings.

Whatever Borges' reasons for preferring these bizarre and foreign worlds, the scoundrels who plague them practice roguery of particular kinds. Some, like the confidence man Lazarus Morell, the Dean of Santiago, the pretender to the Tichborne title, or the corrupt master of ceremonies Kotsuké no Suké, defraud the trust of their intended victims. Others—Kotsuké no Suké might again be mentioned, together with the heretics Melancthon and Hákim of Merv and the usurper who, in "The Chamber of Statues," breaks into the tabooed tower—affront the decorum of religion or tradition. And, as often as not, the transgressions of Borges' villains reach such grand proportions as to threaten civil authority. Lazarus Morell captains an uprising of slaves, aiming to subjugate New Orleans, and Monk Eastman, with his gang warfare, vies for a time with Tammany Hall for control of New York's streets. The Widow Ching ravages coastal towns and threatens the power of an inept emperor. And the veiled prophet Hákim rivals the reigning Caliph, who sends an army to extirpate the infidel from Nishapur and Asterabad. Cities, it seems, are often the prizes of Borges' rebels. The three figures I have just mentioned take temporary possession of towns. And during the tenure of his illusory power Don Illán's pupil marches in triumph through the streets of Santiago, Tolosa and, finally, Rome.

Apart from similarities in the nature and venue of their crimes, Borges' ne'er-do-wells betray another common trait. Nearly all of them act in league with others, and if they traduce the doctrine and custom of their worlds, they promise fealty to their co-conspirators. Lazarus Morell heads a clandestine quasi-Masonic brotherhood whose members, ranked in strict hierarchy, take a loyalty oath. The Widow Ching exacts stern allegiance from her pirate crews and curbs their license with a written code. Similarly, Hákim constrains his heretical followers to the teachings of his Moslem splinter sect. Borges' antiheroes do not always take the lead in conspiracy. The Dean of Santiago, for example, apprentices himself to a sorcerer to whom he pledges gratitude; Arthur Orton has an evil genius in the black servant Bogle; and the *porteño* narrator of "Streetcorner Man" seems, at the story's beginning, obsequiously loyal to Rosendo Juárez. Even the lucky hero of "Tale of the Two Dreamers" acts at the instance of a man who appears to him in a dream. But whether or not Borges' *infame* is the leader, alliance in crime is certainly the rule in the *Infamy* texts.

By and large, the master-apprentice relationships and other shady alliances that Borges portrays go eventually awry. Virgil Stewart infiltrates Morell's fraternity, forswearing himself in order to bring Morell to justice; Hákim's devotees unmask him for a charlatan. The Dean of Santiago fails the test of character Don Illán sets for him and is turned out in disgrace by the aggrieved magician. And Bogle is killed before he can save Orton's beleaguered suit. Although in general the master-apprentice relationships Borges depicts originate in good faith, two of his sketches—"The Insulting Master of Etiquette Kotsuké no Suké" and "The Mirror of Ink"—describe teachers who willfully harm their pupils.

Vengeance is another recurring motif in these early works. The warriors who, led by their master's chief retainer, at last entrap the wicked Kotsuké no Suké, aim to avenge the betrayal of their unfortunate lord. And Virgil Stewart, in Borges' version of Morell's story, acts on behalf of his uncle, whose slaves Morell has set free. The sorcerer who does away with Yakub the Ailing not only frees himself but avenges at the same time the murder of his brother and coconspirator, who has died at Yakub's hands. And the narrator of "Streetcorner Man," in knifing his tarnished hero's rival, carries out a sort of revenge, as well. Borges, fascinated as he is with issues of loyalty and betrayal, sees in acts of revenge deeds that combine loyalty to one master with the betrayal of another.

Borges' antiheroes are virulently wicked, but pathos, in these texts, colors their actions and attaches, too, to other characters. As he told Charbonnier, Borges intends in these sketches to portray naive scoundrels, not remorse-ridden sinners who answer to the proddings of conscience. In this spirit he exaggerates a detail from Herbert Asbury, making much of Monk Eastman's fondness for cats and birds so that the gangster will seem childlike. And, by endowing Ebeneezer Bogle with cleverness, Borges clears the way for making Tom Castro a near-imbecile bent only on conciliating everyone he meets. Billy the Kid, too—Borges supplements the epithet by calling him "el casi niño" ("the almost child")—kills wantonly but with a guiltlessness that seems boyish; to Pat Garrett's boast that he has practiced his marksmanship on buffalo, Billy coolly answers back that he has practiced his on men. By making these heroes seem childlike Borges surrounds their demise with pathos. Eastman's bullet-riddled body, found, as Borges would have it, on Christmas Day, is watched over by a perplexed cat. Billy the Kid's corpse, in Borges' version of the tale, is placed on public display, a prey to ridicule and to rot. As for the fate of the Tichborne Claimant, it

is, to my mind, one of the most painful details in all of Borges'
work. Borges ends Castro's story by inventing for the ruined
fraud a vaudevillian speaking career. Released from prison, the
impostor makes a speaking tour of England, ingratiating himself with audiences by adapting the story of his misdeeds—and
changing his claim to either innocence or guilt—to suit his
hearers' liking. Borges' characterization of the pretender to the
Tichborne estate is entirely of his own devising. He invents an
infame whose whole life is taken up with trying to impersonate
a creature worthy of celebration or love. In each of these instances, and in others as well, Borges modifies his sources to in-
ject pathos into the stories he retells.

To recapitulate, the thirteen works of *A Universal History*
portray heroes who, generally in league with others, transgress
the laws of their markedly quaint—and thus, for the reader,
nonserious—social worlds. Each narrative develops in multiple
ways the motif of betrayal, or the abuse of trust. Not only does
the delinquent hero traduce law or social decorum but he may,
as well, renege on a loyalty he has pledged. Alternatively, an
erstwhile ally may double-cross him and become the agent of his
pathetic demise. At length, in each work an avenging justicer
puts a stop to the hero's wickedness.

In this narrative formula, displayed in table 6, it is easy to
see much that resembles the Borgean paradigm. The pattern of
wrongdoing redressed will be recast, in Borges' later tales, in a
schema that moves from a motivating mishap toward a moment
at the end of the tale when the hero's impotence is suddenly revealed. And the motif of loyalty and betrayal that appears in
Borges' later tales is pronounced in his early texts. What is
more, the criminal gangs that Borges' villains head are early
avatars of the secret societies and heretical religions of his mature work. The scholars who covertly invent Tlön and prepare
for the Congress of the World, the practitioners of the Cult of
the Phoenix or the Sect of the Thirty, even the degenerate immortals, the Gutres and Yahoos and Utopians evolve out of these
feisty bands of pirates and gangsters and religious zealots. And
the paired antagonists of *A Universal History*—Lazarus Morell
and Virgil Stewart, Billy the Kid and Pat Garrett, Monk Eastman and Paul Kelly, to name a few—are forerunners of the

doubles of his later tales. (That they are not yet, at least in most of the *Infamy* texts, portrayed as doubles is worth noting.) Moreover, the cities on which Borges' *infames* have designs prefigure the labyrinths of *Ficciones*. Beyond this, however, it is difficult to locate aspects of Borges' ur story in the *Infamy* texts as a group, or to guess why Borges' narrative paradigm evolved in the direction it did. It is hard, too, to find further meaning

Table 6   The *Infamy* Schema

Protagonist	In league with	Transgresses
Lazarus Morell	quasi-Masonic sect	frees and resells slaves
Monk Eastman	1) Jewish father 2) gangsters	1) cudgels old man 2) Battle of Rivington
Widow Ching	pirates	sacks coastal towns
Dean of Santiago	Don Illán	1) practices magic 2) betrays Don Illán
1) narrator 2) Francisco Real	Rosendo Juárez Northside toughs	*compadres'* swagger humiliates Juárez
Tom Castro	Ebeneezer Bogle	impersonates Roger Tichborne
Yakub the Sick	sorcerer	practices magic
King in "The Chamber of Statues"		opens forbidden tower
1) Kotsuké no Suké		provokes Takumi no Kami
2) Kuranosuké no Suké	47 captains	fails to prevent master's demise
Hákim of Merv	heretical followers	rebels against Islam and the Caliph
Melancthon	wizard	rejects doctrine of charity over faith
Mohamed El Magrebí	father seen in dream	does not himself break law, but thieves rob Cairo house
Billy the Kid	Swamp Angels	kills Villagrán and others

either in the *Infamy* schema or in the paradigm itself without taking a further interpretive step.

This step is to see that, in portraying his reprobates, Borges was in one sense portraying himself. A betrayer of sources, a marauder of texts, Borges may well have styled himself a kind of literary *infame*. Conversely, at many points in the *Infamy* narratives he hints that his villains remind him of artists. Castro

punished by	Betrayal or revenge motif
irgil Stewart	1) defrauding of slaves;
	2) Stewart avenges uncle
aul Kelly	
hinese Emperor	Mr. Ching defrauds stockholders
on Illán	ingratitude toward Don Illán
rancisco Real	Juárez betrays speaker's trust;
arrator	—
) British courts	
) carriage that kills Bogle	
irror image of Yakub	sorcerer avenges brother
árik	affronts taboo
uranosuké no Suké	betrays courtesy
mperor's law	avenges Takumi no Kami
aliph Mehdi	misleads followers
izard	deceives visitors
ersian captain	
at Garrett	Garrett betrays Billy

and the inspired Bogle, engaged as they are in creating and foisting on Lady Tichborne a facsimile of her son, resemble in no small degree artists confronting the problem of how to represent life. Emir Rodríguez Monegal has pointed this out[21] and has seen, as well, that the pool of ink that, in another of the *Infamy* texts, mirrors marvelous visions is a metaphor for a work of art.[22] Yakub's imprisoned sorcerer works, therefore, a magic that is tantamount to artistic creation. Indeed, to extend the conceit only a little, all magic in these tales may well allude to creative processes. The temporal and spatial illusions that Don Illán unfolds for his pupil seem akin to the expanse of fictional worlds that a novelist, say, opens up before his reader. And magical feats are not reserved, in these texts, to Arabic divines. Borges associates even Billy the Kid with mysterious deeds. He calls him the source of "invisible bullets which (like magic) kill at a distance" (*OC*, 316; *UHI*, 61). Frederick Watson, in one of the works Borges cites as a source, refers to Billy the Kid as "the super gunman of the West, inhuman, nerveless, implacable," and goes on to say, "it is just that perfection of balanced technique which Americans [and, we might add, Borges] adore. . . . He was without question both a supreme expert and *an artist in homicide*."[23] A biography of the Kid that Borges also credits as a source concurs in painting Billy both as artist and as sorcerer. Distinguishing him from the run-of-the-mill desperado "who loved melodrama and felt called upon, as an artist, to shed a few drops of blood," Walter Noble Burns says that such common types "lacked the afflatus that made him [Billy] the finished master. They were journeymen mechanics laboriously carving notches on the handles of their guns," says Burns. "He was a genius painting his name in flaming colours with a six-shooter across the sky of the Southwest."[24] Elsewhere, wondering at the Kid's agility in eluding death, Burns marvels, "He escaped by apparent miracles; he was saved as if by necromancy."[25]

While Borges does not always imply that his indecorous heroes are themselves artists of sorts, he often relates them and their violent deeds to things artistic. His account of Lazarus Morell, for example, begins by placing Morell alongside, and by implication on a par with, other "consequences" of Fray Bartolomé's skewed philanthropy. That sixteenth-century humanitarian, determined to protect the Indians in America, helped bring about the importation of African slaves into the New World. He was thus indirectly responsible, Borges suggests, for Morell and for the following list of things:

> W. C. Handy's blues; the Parisian success of the Uruguayan lawyer and painter of Negro genre, don Pedro Figari; the solid native prose of another Uruguayan, don Vicente Rossi, who traced the origin of the tango to Negroes; the mythological dimensions of Abraham Lincoln; the five hundred thousand dead of the Civil War and its three thousand three hundred millions spent in military pensions; the entrance of the verb "to lynch" into the thirteenth edition of the dictionary of the Spanish Academy; King Vidor's impetuous film *Hallelujah*; the lusty bayonet charge led by the Argentine captain Miguel Soler, at the head of his famous regiment of "Mulattoes and Blacks," in the Uruguayan battle of Cerrito; the Negro killed by Martín Fierro; the deplorable Cuban rumba "The Peanut Vender"; the arrested, dungeon-ridden Napoleonism of Toussaint L'Ouverture; the cross and the snake of Haitian voodoo rites and the blood of goats whose throats were slit by the *papaloi's* machete; the *habanera*, mother of the tango; another old Negro dance, of Buenos Aires and Montevideo, the *candombe*. (*OC*, 295; *UHI*, 19–20)

Many of the entries in this enumeration have to do with the arts. Music and painting, statue and film, novel, poem and dance— and Lazarus Morell—all have a common stimulus in Fray Bartolomé's act. In a similar way Borges connects the Widow Ching to the lady pirates of a musical comedy that had recently played in Buenos Aires. And, in his account of Monk Eastman, he likens to ballet the wary footwork of *compadres* wielding knives.

Why was Borges so taken with the likeness of wrongdoers to artists? And why did he, in constructing thirteen separate texts using source material of various kinds, consistently create variations on a single basic plot? In comparing his criminals to artists, Borges aligned himself with a literary tradition; Oscar Wilde had touted lying as creativity par excellence, and De Quincey, Chesterton, and Poe had treated murder as a fine art.[26] But

Borges' own circumstances may have drawn him to this conceit. He may have been wrestling, as a journeyman writer of tales, not just with the technical problems of composing narrative art but with psychological conflicts that writing fiction may have aroused or made more acute. Borges returns time and again in the *Infamy* texts to the issue of how one can be at the same time a devoted son and a successful artist. His *infames* are in several ways analogous to upstart sons who defy paternal sway. Initially in league with mentors or companions in crime, figures who may represent one aspect of a father's role, they flout laws until an avenging type, acting in the name of paternal interests, punishes them—punishes them, that is, for the very enterprise that, we have seen, Borges associates with artistic creation.

Borges' mention of fathers in two of the *Infamy* sketches, when none appears in his sources for those texts, suggests how taken up he may have been with the issue of father-son relations. He invents Monk Eastman's father and makes him the proprietor of a Kosher restaurant "where men wearing rabbinical beards could safely partake of the bloodless and thrice-cleansed flesh of ritually slaughtered calves" (*OC*, 312; *UHI*, 53). And, in the story of Lazarus Morell, he refers to the cleric Bartolomé de las Casas not as "Fray," as history remembers him, but as "Padre." In addition, in what is admittedly a less eye-catching phrase, he accords the Mississippi River its traditional epithet "The Father of Waters." He does so in a paragraph that recounts how the explorer of that river, Hernando de Soto, betrayed the Incan Prince Atahualpa, whom De Soto had befriended and taught to play chess. This detail, which anticipates Lazarus Morell's betrayal of the Negro slaves he promises to free, restates a motif that is common both in this sketch and others, the motif of the master-apprentice relationship gone sour.

The master-apprentice pairs portrayed in the *Infamy* texts— Bogle and Orton, Kotsuké and Takumi no Kami, Don Illán and the Dean of Santiago, to name the clearest examples—present problematic relationships between symbolic fathers and sons. While in no case is the mentor portrayed in Borges' tales the actual father of the *infame*, we may plausibly see in these paired characters paternal and filial figures. Certainly Borges' own father was in many ways his mentor. In his "Autobiographical Essay" and in his public dialogues Borges makes clear that his father, Jorge Guillermo Borges, was a valued teacher. It was the elder Borges who initiated his son into the metaphysical puzzles of Berkeleyan idealism, and who put at his son's disposal a "library of limitless English books" (*OC*, 101). It was Borges' father who counseled him not to rush into print. Himself a writer manqué, the author of a play, a historical novel, and a number of poems, Borges' father did all he could over the course of several decades to foster his son's literary career. It seems inviting, then, to guess that the master-apprentice pairs that Borges depicts in his first volume of tales draw on his own experience as apprentice.

As portraits of Borges' own relationship with a parent he consciously revered, the *Infamy* vignettes may startle us, for they describe awful disruptions in the teacher-student bond. Bogle is unable to rescue his creature Tom Castro from the law; Don Illán's pupil betrays him and is punished for his ingratitude; and Kotsuké no Suké provokes his student to attack him. In a variant whose implications are even more sinister, the prisoner of Yakub the Sick instructs him in sorcery until Yakub has acquired the power to destroy himself. The talent the mentor imparts is often, in these tales, the means by which the student, aggressing against his teacher, brings harm upon himself. The ubiquitousness in Borges' early narratives of soured relationships between mentor and pupil deserves notice, for it may reflect Borges' own unconscious dilemma as he undertook an activity—fiction-writing—that his father had essayed. Did Borges unconsciously regard the writing of tales as a competitive activity hostile to his father and thus deserving of punishment? We can never be sure. But it is tempting to speculate that he did.

It is possible to hypothesize that in writing the *Infamy* texts Borges expressed and tried symbolically to resolve a psychic problem: how to reconcile his duty as a son with his literary ambition, an ambition fostered by his father. Yet to be convinced that questions of oedipal rivalry lie at the center of these narratives, one must analyze in greater depth Borges' use of his sources. By studying Borges' methods of selecting, excluding, and elaborating his textual raw material, one can test this hypothesis, in some degree at least.

"The Disinterested Killer Bill Harrigan" recommends itself for this purpose. In many respects it exemplifies the ways Borges adapted source material. Its overall degree of adherence to the accounts Borges drew on is neither extremely great nor slight; it stands a middle ground between texts like "Tale of the Two Dreamers," which departs only in small details from its source, and "The Masked Dyer, Hákim of Merv," which alludes in only the most abstract way to antecedent historical and poetic accounts. What is more important, the manner in which Borges treats the raw material about Billy the Kid's life as he reworks it into his own tale is typical of his methods of revision in *A Universal History*.

What are the sources to which Borges owes a debt for his information about Billy the Kid? In the Index of Sources that ends *A Universal History* Borges cites two books, *A Century of Gunmen* by Frederick Watson and *The Saga of Billy the Kid* by Walter Noble Burns. To these sources Norman Thomas di Giovanni, in a 1973 article, adds Herbert Asbury's *The Gangs of New York*, pointing out some details that Borges must have gleaned from that work.[27] (In the same essay di Giovanni discounts *A Century of Gunmen* as a likely source for Borges' tale.)

Let us briefly review the saga—Borges', not Burns's—of the disinterested gunman Billy Bonney, or, as Borges calls him, Bill Harrigan. Borges' text has five sections, each with its own subheading. The first section, like a scene from a Western movie, paints a desert panorama of flat-topped buttes and buzzard-stripped, calcined bones, and superimposes on this stock landscape the image of Billy the Kid. The second etches quickly Billy's "apprentice years" in the tenements and sewers of New York City. There, raised among blacks, the Irish Billy is schooled in gang thuggery until finally, lured by the frontier glamour of Wild West theatricals and in flight from the law, he joins the migration westward. The story's third section provides an eclectic array of quaint facts about the North American West. At this point, having devoted fully half of his tale to placing his hero in a picturesque context, Borges locates Billy in the foreground of a bit of narrative and recounts, in the story's fourth section, an episode that shows Billy's famous sang-froid. The incident Borges picks is the account of Billy's first killing. The tale's final segment steps back from this dramatic act and surveys in a few sentences the remainder of Billy's career. The section ends with a second dramatic moment, a brief one, which relates Pat Garrett's shooting of Billy in Fort Sumner. Borges rounds his story off with an account, gruesome but full of humorous pathos, of the Kid's blasphemous death throes, and of the townspeople's equally blasphemous mistreatment of his corpse.

In composing his fictional remake of Billy the Kid's life story Borges deliberately plays on a theme that will intrigue him throughout his life, the pathos-ridden disparity between things as they are and the symbols by means of which we grant them meaning. Selecting a legendary figure as his subject, he exploits to the hilt Billy's famed cold-bloodedness, only to say that Billy "never completely matched his legend, but he kept getting closer and closer to it" (*OC*, 318; *UHI*, 65), as if Billy's whole concern had been to live up to the heroic dimensions of his own notoriety. Borges mines his tale with reminders of the distance between artifice and what is real. Adding a detail to his sources, he imagines his hero a Bowery street urchin, enthralled by wild west shows, "perhaps without an inkling that they were signs and symbols of his destiny" (*OC*, 317; *UHI*, 62). These symbols of a glamorous West that Borges, too, describes stereotypically for his readers, will not in the end coincide even with so brilliant a destiny as Billy the Kid's. The image of the Wild West as Borges paints it is grand indeed; among its attributes are "the redwoods, going down before the ax; the buffalo's huge Babylonian face; Brigham Young's beaver hat and plural bed; the red man's ceremonies and his rampages; the clear air of the deserts; endless-stretching range land; and the earth itself, whose nearness quickens the heart like the nearness of the sea" (*OC*, 317; *UHI*, 62–63). Yet this land of extravagance and promise holds out to Billy, even to Billy the Kid, a destiny we feel is, in the end, a paltry one. If Billy can murder in his twenty-one years an exorbitant number of Anglos and Mexicans, he ends up a pitiful parody of his myth. Borges, diverging from his sources, ends Billy's career in shame, and it is the particular shame of not quite having managed to be himself. We see the Kid at last demeaned, lifeless, and unburied, his face masked with make-up. Borges' hero becomes, in the end, quite literally a false image of himself.

We are now in a better position to understand why Borges not only tolerates but goes out of his way to include in the *Infamy* tales the banalities of picturesqueness. If, in "The Disinterested Killer," he revels in the clichés of local color—from redwoods to redmen—and translates into Spanish, catch-phrases like "trigger finger" ("dedo del gatillo") and "cattle rustler" ("ladrón de hacienda"), it is so that he can cast a suddenly human and human-sized protagonist against a background so stereotypic as to strike us as patently fake. The contrast between a flat, unlifelike setting, a setting Borges paints with happy glibness, and the unexpected and painful vulnerability of his outlaw, supports the pathos of the story's central theme.

We can also gain insight into Borges' private joke, one he practices in all of the *Infamy* texts, of misleading his readers as to how he has relied on previously existing books. To cite an example from his story of Billy the Kid, Borges implants, at precisely the dramatic climax of his tale, a bit of false erudition that hilariously distracts the reader's attention from the act of violence at hand. In the fourth section of the tale Billy meets up with a bullying Mexican, the first man he will kill. Learning that his antagonist is none other than the dread Belisario Villagrán, from Chihuahua, Billy shoots the Mexican without ceremony. Borges writes: "Sin dignarse mirar el muerto lujoso, Bill reanuda la plática. '¿De veras?', dice.* 'Pues yo soy Billy Harrigan, de New York'" (*OC*, 318). ("Without deigning to glance at the showy dead man, Bill picks up his end of the conversation. 'Is that so?' he drawled. 'Well, I'm Billy the Kid, from New York.'" (*UHI*, 64).) In the footnote he so punctiliously supplies, Borges (or, rather, his narrator) purports to provide the original English—"'Is that so?' he drawled"—from which he has supposedly made a direct but inadequate translation. He has interrupted the dramatic movement of his tale to salvage the "authentic" tonalities of a perfectly colorless phrase. Yet the sentence that Borges takes such pains to document appears in Spanish, not in English, in the Burns biography and in quite a different context. He has not only subverted to humorous effect the impetus of his story, but presented in a false light its relationship to textual sources. We can now see that this maneuver, one Borges will use again in *Ficciones,* has a hidden function in this tale, although the readers of *Crítica,* unused as they must have been to Borges' trickery, could hardly have suspected it. Just as Billy the Kid fails to correspond to his legend, Borges' story itself, like a narrative false image, cannot faithfully map the sources on which it draws. By playing on the question of his own text's authenticity, Borges expresses on a formal plane the central concern of his tale, the disjunction between an account of a thing and the thing itself.

In organizing his sketch around this unifying theme, one that can scarcely be discerned in his sources, Borges almost certainly molded his tale in a conscious way. Nor are the narrative gambits I have already pointed out the only ones through which he exerts on his material a well-considered control. It seems likely, though, that some of the changes Borges works on his sources respond to impulses, equally creative ones, of which Borges may not have been fully aware. In appropriating to his own uses Billy the Kid's story, he may have exercised, unconsciously but in a systematic way, other habits of composition that also bear understanding.

Why was Borges attracted in the first place to the saga of this famous desperado, and how did he tailor his source material to please himself and his Argentine readers? Of necessity, he selected for his twelve-hundred-word précis of the Kid's career a small percentage of the information in his sources. But when one juxtaposes Borges' sketch with the books on which he drew, one is struck with the large quantity of material that his sources, particularly Walter Noble Burns's biography, contain that must have piqued Borges' interest. Some of this material Borges places unchanged into his own narrative. Further details, though, find their way into the *Infamy* sketch in greatly altered form. These details are telling, for they serve as evidence that facets of the sources that do not figure in Borges' text nevertheless did catch his eye.

One of these elements is Billy's loyalty to his friends. Given what we know of Borges' predilections, we can easily guess that Billy's carelessness of danger, his *coraje,* must have appealed greatly to Borges. Burns, too, makes much of the Kid's unflinching nerve. He apostrophizes:

> His courage was beyond question. It was a static courage that remained the same under all circumstances, at noon or at three o'clock in the morning. There are yellow spots in the stories of many of the West's most famous desperadoes. . . . but no tale has come down that Billy the Kid ever showed the "yellow streak." Every hour in his desperate life was the zero hour, and he was never afraid to die. "One chance in a million" was one of his favorite phrases, and more than once he took that chance with the debonair courage of a cavalier.[28]

This "nerveless imperturbability" is the trait Borges chooses to set off in his portrait of the child turned outlaw. Yet Burns describes, as well, a more genial side of Billy's nature, a side that must have impressed Borges almost as much as his murderous insouciance but that Borges rigorously excludes from his own portrait of the Kid. Billy Bonney, it seems, was proverbially loyal to his friends and quick to avenge any wrongs they chanced to suffer. Burns's account of him is rich in anecdotes that prove the steadfastness of the Kid's affections, and one of these, which details the Murphy-McSween vendetta that for years made a battleground of New Mexico's Lincoln County, describes exactly the sort of clan warfare that Borges includes in several of the *Infamy* tales. The Lincoln County War, as it was called, deserves a place in our discussion. Although it does not figure directly in Borges' sketch, the conflict must have caught Borges' eye. We can deduce this because a few details from Burns's account of it do survive, although in much-changed form, in Borges' own text.

To document Billy's unswerving loyalty to his friends, Burns gives special note to one incident in that war, the murder of a British rancher named Tunstall. Tunstall is brutally killed by Murphy's strongmen, and the murderers, as Billy watches helpless from a nearby ridge, indulge in a little sadistic fun with Tunstall's corpse:

Half-drunk with whisky and mad with the taste of blood, the savages turned the murder of the defenseless man into an orgy. Pantilon Gallegos, a Bonito Cañon Mexican, hammered in his head with a jagged rock. . . . They killed Tunstall's horse, stretched Tunstall's body beside the dead animal, face to the sky, arms folded across his breast, feet together. Under the man's head they placed his hat and under the horse's head his coat carefully folded by way of pillows. So murdered man and dead horse suggested they had crawled into bed and gone to sleep together.[29]

Later, when McSween's men retrieve the dead man's body, they sling his long-suffering corpse across the back of a pack mule, and on the homeward trip Tunstall's face is torn by nettles and briars growing beside the trail.

Two traces from this vivid episode can be found in Borges' narrative, although Borges makes free to insert them in his own tale in wholly different contexts. The image of Tunstall's body, composed as if for sleep next to his horse's cadaver, may have suggested to Borges his own *infame*'s bravura in stretching out for a night's rest by the side of the corpse of a man he has killed. And the cruel, mocking treatment Tunstall's body receives, combined with the later mutilation of his face, may have influenced Borges' imagination as well. Billy's own cadaver, in Borges' version of events, is exposed to indignities at the hands of a vindictive populace, and Borges dwells with particular relish on the incipient decay of the Kid's face, to which the townsfolk at last apply make-up, a sort of Borgean mask.

The burden of Burns's account of the Tunstall murder is to underscore Billy's loyalty to his friends, a loyalty not sullied by mercenary self-interest. While the godly McSween is able to dissuade from vengeance those of his men who are actuated by greed, he cannot shake Billy's resolve to hunt down the murderers of his ambushed employer and friend. Burns waxes proud as he reports Billy's stark view: " 'Tunstall was my friend,' declared the Kid, and that seemed to him to cover the situation."[30] Burns goes on to describe the nature of Billy's fellowship with the dead man:

> Tunstall and Billy the Kid had been worlds apart in every-
> thing. Tunstall had had a background of breeding and
> culture; the Kid's background was the frontier. They dif-
> fered as night from day in character, thought, outlook on
> life. White for Tunstall was black for the Kid. But
> strangely enough, a strong friendship had developed be-
> tween them. Their friendship was their only common
> ground. Friendship was one of the few things the Kid
> held sacred.[31]

This friendship, securing as it did the loyalty of an untamed
prodigy in murder to his cultivated employer, may well have
impressed a Borges for whom the vicissitudes of filial love
were of lively concern. And if Billy's relations with Tunstall
betray hints of feelings Borges may have likened to a son's
affection for a father, Billy's biography describes the Kid's
encounter with another man of learning, Governor Lew Wallace, in terms that make explicit the Kid's filial stance.

Late in Billy's career Governor Wallace offers amnesty to
the Kid if he will hang up his guns and forswear further lawlessness. Again, as he does in portraying Tunstall, Burns lays
stress on the governor's civilized demeanor. Describing Wallace's interview with the Kid, he writes, "One was a product
of culture and refinement; the other of a rough frontier; one
finished, the other primitive; one constructive, the other ob-
structive. . . . The governor was an intellect; the Kid a trigger
finger."[32] As Burns envisions their meeting, Billy confronts a
kindly gentleman who offers him a pardon and some advice.
" 'I am,' " Burns imagines the governor saying to Billy, " 'let
me see—just thirty-two years older than you. Old enough to
be your father. So, Billy, I am going to talk to you like a
father.' "[33] Eventually, the issue of loyalty and betrayal asserts itself in Billy's dealings with the fatherly Wallace. Having
once refused a truce with the law, Billy later falls into a sheriff's
hands and faces trial and the gallows. By this time, though,
the governor has rescinded his offer of a pardon, and Burns
makes a point of noting that Billy felt betrayed by what looked
to him like the reneging on a promise.

Burns touts Billy's loyalty so much, and so little of his portrayal survives in Borges' text, that one is forced to wonder that Borges avoided this trait, which must have made Billy a uniquely eligible *infame*. It is not hard to guess that Borges deliberately excised from his source material all evidence of humane emotion on his hero's part, so as to make the Kid's infamy more stark. His task, after all, was to paint archvillainy and make it amusing to his *Crítica* readers. But before we conclude that, in leaving out of his sketch this part of Burns's account, Borges was simply trimming away unuseful facts, we should continue our look at the revisions he works on his sources. Consistently, the passages Borges selects for reworking are ones that ring with oedipal overtones. Borges is quick to mute the harmonics of conflicts and strivings with which he may have been much taken up himself. But he proceeds not so much by deleting this highly charged matter from the narrative he composes as by subjecting it to a kind of creative distortion. This distortion may accomplish the same end that dream-work has in screening from a dreamer's consciousness the latent fantasies that stand behind a dream.

To see how Borges used material that may have been particularly interesting to him—and particularly troubling—one can compare the dramatic centerpiece of his Billy the Kid sketch with the rather different account Burns gives of the same event. The fourth section of Borges' tale depicts Billy's first homicide, his barroom confrontation with a Mexican named Belisario Villagrán. Borges places a fourteen-year-old Billy, newly arrived in the West, in a frontier saloon, cowed and diminished by the rough men around him and too poor to pay his bill. In Borges' version of events, the Mexican bully swaggers into the bar, intimidates the patrons, and loudly abuses their mothers. Billy repays the affront with an insolence born of fearlessness. "¿Quién es?" he coolly asks, and when the frightened cowhands whisper Villagrán's name, he shoots the bandido, appropriates the knife of a would-be admirer, and, to prove his utter intrepidness, beds down for the night beside his victim's body.

The original text Borges recasts is a much more elaborate account, and should interest us as much for what Borges leaves out as for what he reworks and includes. Burns, taken though he is with Billy's nerveless courage, is at pains to explain why Billy, at the tender age of twelve (not fourteen, as Borges would have it), felt compelled to kill for the first time. He makes clear that the Kid killed only to defend an ally, a man who had previously stood up for Billy in a fight. Burns's biography claims our attention here, for a more patently oedipal little fable can scarcely be conceived than the account Burns gives of Billy's first murder. As the biographer tells it, Billy left New York at the age of three in the company of both parents, bound for Coffeyville, Kansas. Upon her husband's death there shortly afterward, Mrs. Bonney remarried and moved her family west to Silver City, New Mexico, where her second husband worked in the mines. It is there, not in Llano Estacado as Borges says, that Billy is provoked to kill for the first time.

The story is one that enlists our sympathy. Walking past a saloon one day in his mother's company, Billy heard a bullying blacksmith drop "some light remark, directed, possibly with flirtatious intent," at his mother.[34] Inflamed by the insult, Billy hurled a stone at the offending smith, knocking off his hat but not hurting him enough to prevent his giving chase. A passerby named Moulton defended Billy by knocking the enraged blacksmith down. A few weeks later, Burns says, Moulton was quietly drinking beer in Dyer's Saloon and Billy was standing idly by when two drunkards stumbled through the swinging doors and knocked Moulton's hat from his head. Moulton, much provoked, had engaged the two offending drunks in unequal battle when the blacksmith, seeing a chance to settle his own score, joined the fight and aimed a heavy chair at Moulton's head. Seeing his erstwhile defender outmatched, Billy rushed the blacksmith and killed him deftly with his pocketknife (Borges gives the youngster a pistol). Having proved his loyalty to Moulton, Billy, knowing he must flee, exhibits no bravado, nor does he stay to claim the plaudits of the assembled company. Instead, he pays a furtive visit to his mother before slipping out of town. Here is Burns's sentimental description of Billy's farewell:

> He went to his mother's room, told her he had killed the man who had insulted her; not boastfully, nor yet re-

gretfully, dealing coldly with a fact. Heretofore we have had dim pictures of this mother in the humdrum of prosaic existence. Here was her crisis, and in the revealing light of it she stands out a Spartan. She shed no tears; it was no time for tears. She thought only of the safety of her first-born. She agreed with his plan to dodge arrest; gave him the few dollars she had on hand; drew him to her bosom for the last time and kissed him good-bye. The boy slipped out into the night, his mother's eyes straining after the slight, furtive figure hurrying away, growing dimmer and dimmer, fading out at last in the darkness. It was the final parting on earth; mother and son never saw each other again.[35]

Burns's account has much in it that casts Billy as the son in an oedipal triangle. Burns dwells on Billy's love for his mother—a love that pitted him against one flirtatious older man—as well as on his loyalty to another, more friendly male figure. Billy's fight with the blacksmith thus enacts an assault on one paternal adult, the rival for his mother's love, while his barroom defense of Moulton confirms his loyalty to a second father figure, a more benevolent one. How does Borges, having selected this episode as the event that will stand at the center of his own tale, rework his source material? Clearly, he does a good deal more than strip Billy's crime of extenuating detail. He replaces the blacksmith with the Mexican, a comic caricature; conflates into one fight the two encounters of Burns's original account; and almost entirely omits any mention of Billy's mother.

In making his Irish-American hero scornful of Mexicans, Borges directly contradicts a passage from Burns's account. Although Burns gives us, in Billy, no model of racial ecumenism (his subject is biased against Indians and Jews), he absolves the Kid from anti-Mexican prejudice. In what strikes the modern ear as a patronizing passage, Burns imagines the rapt reminiscence of a Mexican housewife from the region through which Billy ranged: " 'Billee the Keed? Ah, you have hear of heem? He was one gran' boy, señor. All Mexican pepul his friend. You nevair hear a Mexican say one word against Billee the Keed.

Everybody love that boy. . . . Ah, many a pretty *muchacha* cry her eyes out when he is keel.' "[36] Why did Borges replace the anonymous blacksmith of Burns's account with the pistol-packing, big-sombreroed Belisario Villagrán? Perhaps he was playing to his own Spanish-speaking but utterly un-Mexican audience. Borges might well have expected his stereotypic Mexican bandit to bring a condescending smile to his Argentine readers' lips. Perhaps, though, Borges perceived, either consciously or not, the same oedipal undercurrents that I have pointed out in Burns's tale. If he did think of Billy's victim as embodying paternal traits, his merciless caricature may secretly ridicule paternal prowess.

Yet no reader could guess this. Borges obscures from the reader (and, very probably, from himself) almost every hint that he is retelling an oedipally charged tale. He almost—but not quite—suppresses from the surface of his text the motif of a son's affection for his mother. Billy's mother does not figure in part four of Borges' sketch. While one might argue that Borges omits from the barroom scene Billy's tenderer emotions so as to create an unregenerate type, Borges does not, after all, entirely dispense with this sensitive theme. He very obliquely alludes to it. By placing in the Mexican's mouth a rude salutation that impugns the drinkers' mothers—Villagrán calls the company "gringos hijos de perra" ("son of a bitch gringos")— Borges includes in his tale but almost entirely obscures the highly charged question of threatened oedipal love.

Another example of Borges' including in his own text a detail that seems to allude to Burns's story may be his invention of Villagrán's hat. The Mexican, worthy forebear of Pancho Villa that he is, is equipped with an "immense sombrero" (*OC*, 318; *UHI*, 64). Now while Burns does not say whether Billy's victim was wearing a hat when he set upon Moulton in the bar, he does mention headgear at two other points in his story, and in each case the knocking off of a hat is a serious act of aggression. The rock Billy shies at the blacksmith's head to chastise his discourtesy is a dangerous missile indeed; Burns remarks that "an inch or two lower and it would have caught him full in the forehead and probably killed him.[37] And the two drunks who later pick a fight with Moulton do so by knocking his hat to the ground. Borges may, in giving Villagrán his exaggerated Mexican sombrero, incorporate in his narrative but render comic and unoffending the aggression against two father figures that he found in his source. Just as, according to Freud, the details of a dream's manifest content are significant not necessarily in themselves but as signposts to the associations of the dreamer, this sombrero may stand, for Borges (not, of course, for his readers) for two aggressively charged anecdotes that he found in Burns's account.

In other ways, too, Borges alludes to the conflicts contained in Burns's original story, and disguises and denatures them. In conflating into one fight Billy's original attack on the blacksmith and his defense of Moulton, Borges merges into a single act encounters that express both sides of a son's ambivalence toward his father. Of course, what appears on the surface of Borges' text is itself a story of filial triumph over a father who is held up for ridicule. Yet not only does this sketch unveil to its public one face of a set of conflicts to which Borges may well have been prey, but it also encodes and expresses—covertly but in a way that is far more complete—other aspects of these same troubling concerns.

A further detail from the barroom scene is worth noticing, one Borges removes from its original context in Burns's account and places in his own narrative to strikingly different effect. As Borges tells the story, Billy answers Villagrán's challenge with a mildly spoken "¿Quién es?" before shooting him. Burns's biography documents no verbal exchange in the description of the incident. But Billy utters the words "Quién es?"—set down in Spanish in the English source—at another fatal juncture. They are, in fact, Billy's own last words, addressed to members of Garrett's posse just moments before the sheriff guns him down. Borges, who instead has the dying outlaw pour forth defiant obscenities, inserts the phrase in the barroom encounter. What are we to make of this transposition? By changing the context of the remark, Borges has excised a phrase that, in Burns's original, signals the Kid's uncertainty and defenselessness, and located it in a scene in which Billy triumphs. It may be that the revision expresses Borges' wish that his filial champion succeed over paternal antagonists.

In examining Borges' adaptation of the barroom scene I have argued that Borges chose from his source an episode with strong oedipal themes and, in reshaping it, disguised and made more tolerable these painful but compelling motifs. The final event of the story, Billy's death and burial, stands in a like relationship to Burns's biography and bears analyzing in a similar way. Burns's version of events surrounding Billy's death occupies fully ten pages and differs sharply from Borges' account. In addition to abbreviating the original story and changing its details, Borges empties it of the human passions that, according to Burns's report, engage its principals. Here is Borges' version:

> The night of the twenty-fifth of July, 1880, Billy the Kid came galloping on his piebald down the main, or only, street of Fort Sumner. The heat was oppressive and the lamps had not been lighted; Sheriff Garrett, seated on a porch in a rocking chair, drew his revolver and sent a bullet through the Kid's belly. The horse kept on; the rider tumbled into the dust of the road. Garrett got off a second shot. The townspeople (knowing the wounded man was Billy the Kid) locked their window shutters tight. The agony was long and blasphemous. In the morning, the sun by then high overhead, they began drawing near, and they disarmed him. The man was gone. They could see in his face that used-up look of the dead.
>
> He was shaved, sheathed in ready-made clothes, and displayed to awe and ridicule in the window of Fort Sumner's biggest store. Men on horseback and in buckboards gathered for miles and miles around. On the third day, they had to use make-up on him. On the fourth day, he was buried with rejoicing. (*OC*, 319; *UHI*, 65–66)

The most striking thing about Borges' comic but unpleasant account is its detachment from the emotions that Burns both describes in his characters and evokes in his reader. Burns portrays Billy as the sympathetic victim of a man whose enmity the Kid had done nothing to deserve. Burns, who throughout his book extols Billy's loyalty to friends, implicitly censures Pat Garrett, once Billy's ally, for drawing back from that friendship. Garrett, it seems, had accepted the post of sheriff and formed a posse to gun his former buddy down. And when he does kill the Kid it is in an unequal fight.

Here is the story as Burns tells it. Pat Garrett had tracked the Kid to Fort Sumner but had lost the trail and, on arriving at the garrison, went at once to enlist the help of the Mexican Pete Maxwell, a mutual friend of his and the Kid's. As Garrett, late at night, was making his way to Maxwell's house and admitting himself to the darkened bedroom where the Mexican lay asleep, Billy the Kid, not knowing his pursuers were in town, had entered Fort Sumner as well, to pay an amorous call on a female member of Garrett's own family. By chance he, too, had gone to Pete Maxwell's house to cut a steak from a just-killed carcass hung from Maxwell's porch. Garrett's two deputies, seated on the porch, miraculously failed to recognize the Kid from the voice with which he asked them in alarm "¿Quién es?" But Garrett, by that time at Maxwell's bedside, did recognize his quarry and, with the advantage that forewarning gave him, shot Billy through the heart as the Kid entered the bedroom to rouse his friend. The news of Billy's death rallied Fort Sumner's inhabitants in defense of their flamboyant favorite. The women of the town, grief-stricken by the Kid's murder, gathered to sorrow at his wake, and the menfolk muttered vengeance against Garrett and his men.

Again Borges reshapes an account in which he may have perceived oedipal motifs, and again he all but removes—one is tempted to say "represses"—these aspects of the story from the *Infamy* text. Burns's version presents the fugitive Billy as the friend and gallant of a female relative of Garrett's. Both this and Garrett's lapsed friendship make Burns's story suggest oedipal relationships. Moreover, as in the other episode Borges chose to adapt, this one has, in addition to a punitive father figure, another man who might have seemed to represent a father's more benign aspect; Pete Maxwell, to whom Billy applies for food, is connected with Garrett (during the shootout Garrett is in Maxwell's bedroom) but is more favorably disposed than Garrett to the Kid.

Whether oedipal tensions actually came into play in Billy's relationship to Pat Garrett, we can never know. But in adapting

Billy the Kid's story Borges responded not to lived events but to a written text, and it is easy to see how Burns's account affords him grist for an oedipally colored fantasy. Yet when Borges retells the tale, he de-emphasizes this oedipal material. He alludes only glancingly to Garrett or his betrayal of the Kid, describing Garrett only as Billy's "friend, the sheriff who later killed him" (*OC* 318; *UHI*, 65). Nor does he mention the women who figure so prominently in Burns's account. Neither Billy's ladyfriend nor the women who mourn him appear in Borges' text. Instead, Borges replaces Billy's touching romantic tryst with "populous orgies that often lasted four days and four nights" (*OC*, 318; *UHI*, 65). And he makes a grim burlesque of a scene that, in his source, is a respectful wake. Instead of sadness, the townsfolk of Borges' account show self-righteous, gloating voyeurism when they display Billy's corpse.

Why did Borges change this episode in the way he did? Was he so intent on ending his sketch with a Borgean mask that he was willing to reverse the affective valence of the scene? Was he determined to avoid sentimentality? Probably. But it may be that Borges' transformation of the episode disguises aspects of the original story that were too disturbing for him to contemplate openly.

Once one perceives that Borges' changes, or some of them at least, have the effect of repudiating facets of his sources, it is tempting to ask whether the scores of small details Borges alters in adapting the *Infamy* sources may represent a symbolic effort on his part to deny troubling aspects of the stories he reworked. It matters not at all to the effect of the barroom scene whether Billy is twelve or fourteen years old, or wields a knife or a gun. And whether the confrontation itself takes place in Llano Estacado or Silver City is likewise a matter of indifference. Nearly every sketch is riddled with similar details that Borges alters to no apparent effect. Most of the details Borges tinkers with are trivial, not themselves charged with psychic import, and Borges must have taken conscious delight in betraying his sources in tiny, invisible ways. His many changes of detail, though, may symbolically have warded off larger, troubling concerns that his sources led him to contemplate.

A look at some of the ways in which Borges recasts his

sources in forging his version of Billy the Kid's life powerfully suggests that oedipal themes preoccupied him as he reworked this material. A more extensive look at Borges' *modus operandi* as he composed other of the *Infamy* texts would confirm the central importance of oedipal concerns to the Borges of the early 1930s. By identifying this oedipal latent content in this early volume of tales, one gains insight into the *Infamy* sketches themselves. At the same time, one illuminates in important ways several aspects of the Borgean paradigm. The motivating mishap, colored as it is by the motif of loyalty betrayed, probably represents a filial assault on a paternal rival who is both confederate and foe. The pursuit of the *Infamy* by an agent of paternal justice is one aspect of the journey Borges' later heroes undertake. And the final annihilation of the Borgean hero enacts the vengeance of that aggrieved symbolic father. But what of the other aspects of the paradigm? Is it possible, by analyzing Borges' use of sources, to assess the psychic freight of other paradigmatic features? In particular, can one shed light on the two kinds of irreality that are present in Borges' mature tales? Although the many of the principal antecedents of irreality in Borges' work appear in his early nonnarrative writings, the *Infamy* texts do clearly contain forerunners of irreal Borgean impoverishment and the Borgean aleph.

To find a precursor of Borgean impoverishment one need only turn to the second section of the Billy the Kid sketch. Subtitled "The Larval Stage," it ascribes to Billy an almost wholly fictional childhood, and one far more depraved than the upbringing Burns documents. The real Billy Bonney was born in New York City, the legitimate son of Irish immigrants and the elder of only two children. Borges, piecing together tidbits from another (and rather unlikely) source, Herbert Asbury's *The Gangs of New York*, writes the following account:

> Along about 1859, the man who would become known to terror and glory as Billy the Kid was born in a cellar room of a New York tenement. It is said that he was spawned by a tired-out Irish womb but was brought up among Negroes. In this tumult of lowly smells and woolly heads, he enjoyed a superiority that stemmed from having freckles and

a mop of red hair. He took pride in being white; he was also scrawny, wild, and coarse. At the age of twelve, he fought in the gang of the Swamp Angels, that branch of divinities who operated among the neighborhood sewers. On nights redolent of burnt fog, they would clamber out of that foul-smelling labyrinth, trail some German sailor, do him in with a knock on the head, strip him to his underwear, and afterward sneak back to the filth of their starting place. (*OC*, 316; *UHI*, 61–62)

To this description I shall add another, similar one drawn from another sketch. In "The Dread Redeemer Lazarus Morell," Borges sets the scene for Morell's exploits by painting a picture of the Mississippi River:

It is a river of muddy waters; each year, disgorged by it, over four hundred million tons of silt profane the Gulf of Mexico. From time immemorial, so much ancient and venerable muck has built up a delta, where gigantic swamp cypresses grow out of the debris of a continent in perpetual dissolution, and where labyrinths of mud and rushes and dead fish extend the bounds and the peace of this foul-smelling alluvial domain. Upstream, between the Arkansas and the Ohio, is another stretch of lowlands. Living there is a sallow race of squalid men, prone to fever, who avidly gape at stone and iron, for in their environs there is little but sand, timber, and muddy water. (*OC*, 296; *UHI*, 20)

Both the cloacal New York of Bill Harrigan and the mud-clogged estuary of the Mississippi prefigure the impoverishment found in Borges' later tales. Although no hint of irreality marks these passages, the degradation of physical circumstances they depict anticipates the demeaned quality of Borgean landscapes in the second stage of the Borgean paradigm. Moreover, the avid, unclean boys who dart from sewer and basements to rob decent folk, and the squalid yellowish race who, in their backwardness, hoard stones and bits of iron stand very close indeed to the subhuman tribes Borges' later heroes meet in the course of their journeys. Yet what most calls our attention in these early Borgean degenerates is not the atrophy of their sensibilities or the affective barrenness of their worlds. It is the sheer filth in which they live and their fierce acquisitiveness. Both of the passages, too, stress the mazelike, chaotic quality of the polluted worlds they describe. Harrigan's New York is a "foul-smelling labyrinth" ("laberinto fétido"), a "tumult [caos] of lowly and woolly heads," and Morell's "foul-smelling domain" ("fétido imperio") is a "labyrinth of mud."

Can one detect, by studying the way Borges employed his sources as he forged these two excerpts, any underlying psychic concerns? In both instances it is Borges, not his source, who stresses the fetor of the scenes he portrays. The New York Asbury describes is not a filthy place. Yet the city where Borges' hero, like a subhuman grub, lives out his "larval stage" is an evil-smelling place, whose gangs "operated among the neighborhood sewers." Swamp Angels, Borges calls them, assigning Billy and his friends to the only one of several streetgangs Asbury describes whose name connotes dirtiness. In a similar way, Borges departs from his source when he portrays the Lower Mississippi as the resting place of vegetable and human detritus. Mark Twain, in the two passages from *Life on the Mississippi* on which Borges bases his text, betrays not the slightest disgust either at the river's silty effluvium—he cites a statistic that puts its quantity at 406 million tons annually[38]—or at the victims of a yellow fever epidemic that ravaged Memphis, Tennessee.[39] Commenting only that the outbreak of the fever has decimated the population of the town, he dwells on the city's graces, not the least of which is a newly installed sewerage system designed to prevent the spread of future sickness. Borges, in a startling revision of his source, makes of the yellow fever victims a primitive race, a "sallow race [estirpe amarillenta] of squalid men, prone to fever." Both the slime and decay of the delta and the backwardness of its people are inventions of Borges' own.

What are we to make of Borges' changes? Freud, in his 1908 essay "Character and Anal Eroticism," perceives in the attitudes adults hold toward cleanliness, order, and money the vestiges of feelings, most keenly felt during a stage of early childhood, toward feces and bowel control. He points out that "cleanliness [and] . . . orderliness give exactly the impression of a reaction-formation against an interest in things that are unclean and intrusive and ought not to be on the body."[40] As for the symbolic equation of money with feces, Freud finds precedent for it in the myth, fairy tale, superstition, and linguistic usage of many cultures. Our geese, for example, lay golden eggs, and our lucre is filthy. He speculates, too, that "the contrast between the most precious substance known to man and the most worthless . . . has contributed to this identification of gold with faeces."[41] It is telling, then, that Borges introduces into each of these passages details having to do with dirtiness, chaos, and rapacity. The triple presence of these motifs in passages that foreshadow his portrayal of impoverishment may signal that Borges sometimes struggled unconsciously with anal-sadistic wishes, hostility whose roots lay in pre-oedipal experience. (If one makes an analogy between the evolution of the race and the development of the individual, it is possible to see in the primitivism of Borges' cultural degenerates the archaic quality of this sort of regressed state.)

But why should the passages in Borges' later tales that express these conflicts be marked by impoverishment, a generalized depreciation of the hero's experience? The muting of affectivity that supervenes during the second phase of the Borgean paradigm may well express self-punishment for anal-sadistic impulses. These impulses, directed toward the father who comes to grief in the paradigm's first phase, might well engender guilt in Borges' fictional other selves.

I must confess that the two passages I have just singled out are not typical. Both in the overtness of their imagery and in the pleasure their tone conveys, they deviate from Borges' normal reticence, in the *Infamy* texts, in treating the motifs of greed, filth, and disorder. One should not suppose, though, that these motifs are absent either from *A Universal History* or from those portions of Borges' sources to which his sketches specifically allude. Displayed in the *Infamy* texts themselves, disorder may appear, in decorous inversion, as ritual or ceremony or etiquette. Witness the Kosher observances of Monk Eastman's father, an orthodoxy Borges himself invents, or the niceties of imperial protocol that Kotsuké no Suké must teach his host.

When a thing of value figures in his sketches, Borges deploys all his authorial skill to distract his readers from its monetary worth. Borges adds to Walter Noble Burns's biography of Billy the Kid the "large silver coins" that the men in the barroom scene cavalierly spend. But the coins attract our notice not so much for their value as specie as for the Mexican eagle and serpent emblazoned upon them. Neither are the "faceless coins" that a whimsical Borges invents in "The Masked Dyer, Hákim of Merv" valuable as money; they are a kind of abbreviated codex, an apocryphal source of information about the veiled prophet Mokanna. And in "The Chamber of Statues" Borges modifies Burton's *1001 Nights* to keep the reader from thinking of the contents of the forbidden tower as mere riches. The renegade king of the original Burton breaks into the tower and finds there nothing but "figures of Arabs on their horses and camels"—the harbingers of Tárik's invasion—and a scroll predicting the ruin of the kingdom. Burton then records the sacking of the realm and enumerates the "great loot" Tárik plunders from the vanquished, stressing not its pricelessness but its price. Borges, emphasizing instead the fabulous nature of the objects Burton lists, incorporates some of them into his tale, but rather than treating them as booty, includes them among the marvels contained in the king's forbidden tower. In his version the intruding king, not Tárik, discovers them. And he changes the description of these treasures so as to deemphasize their character as wealth. To cite just one example, Burton describes an emerald table in the following way: "He [Tárik] found there the table of food for the Prophet of Allah, Solomon son of David (peace be with both of them!), which is extant even now in a city of the Greeks; it is told that it was grass-green emerald with vessels of gold and platters of jasper."[42] Borges strips the table of its vessels of gold and platters of jasper but endows it with supernatural powers. He writes instead:

> In the second [chamber], they found the table set for Solomon, son of David—peace be on them both! It was carved from a single emerald, whose color, as everyone knows, is green, and whose hidden virtues are real and indescribable, for they quiet tempests, protect the chastity of the owner, dispel dysentery and evil spirits, assure a favorable out-

> come in litigations, and bring great relief in childbearing.
> (*OC*, 337; *UHI*, 110)

In the context of the present discussion, we are not surprised that one of the table's marvelous properties is to banish dysentery.

In this passage as elsewhere in *A Universal History of Infamy* Borges de-emphasizes the costliness of the treasure an *infame* comes by, and instead calls attention to the object qua marvelous thing. One of the most striking impressions to be gained from a comprehensive review of Borges' use of source material is this, that Borges systematically expurgates from the lives of his archvillains almost every hint of venality. He omits from his tables any mention of the stuss games and extortion Monk Eastman oversaw, the bribe Kotsuké no Suké was hoping to invite, or the ample inheritance Arthur Orton stood to gain if he successfully foisted himself on the Tichborne clan. Nor does he mention that the mirror of ink, as Edward William Lane describes it in *The Manners and Customs of the Modern Egyptians*, was used to call up the image of a common house thief[43] or that John A. Murrell, real-life precursor of Lazarus Morell, was a name that was "attached to legends of lost or buried treasure."[44] It would be no exaggeration to say that swindles and robberies, in short, the illicit acquiring of wealth, constitute in the original sources the principal crime of most of Borges' *infames*. Borges' suppression of this material must have been quite intentional; nothing could have been more inimical to his aim of presenting pure, disinterested wickedness than to impute mercenary motives to his innocent-seeming heroes. But what amounts to a wholesale omission of this sort of material may also bespeak Borges' uneasiness with acquisitive impulses, his own or those of others.

Borges' distaste for financial dealings was notorious. Alicia Jurado, one of Borges' close friends, attests: "His lack of interest in money matters is extraordinary. . . . Once he was offered a rather large sum for a lecture and he asked that the amount be reduced, because it seemed excessive to him. He is wholly unconcerned with money; he leaves it between the pages of a book that he then forgets in his library; he gives it away;

he looks upon it with indifference; he never makes a calculation."[45] One of the constants in Borges' writings and interviews is his scorn for those who act out of avarice. Speaking with María Esther Vázquez, for example, he disparages "people who 'pursue a career' as a writer merely to garner fortune or fame."[46] And he quite often ascribed self-interest to those he did not admire, accusing Peronists of "[trying] to cadge all the money they could"[47] and even blaming Argentina's political violence of the 1970s on the terrorists' greed: "[The violence] is criminal, not heroic; the disappearances are carried out for pay."[48] We can only guess at the reasons why Borges refused to concern himself with money, and why he valued so much a gentlemanly disinterestedness in pecuniary affairs. It is interesting, though, to see that one of the forerunners of the mystical aleph in Borges' writings is surely simple lucre. Even more interesting is the hint that the marvelous—and eventually irreal—quality with which Borges invests his aleph may constitute a distraction from or defense against a psychic issue that may have troubled him.

Money, though, is not the only antecedent of the aleph to be found in the *infamy* texts. Borges mines his early narratives with objects hindsight reveals as early figurings of the Borgean symbol of the infinite. A number of his characters wear rings that signal special prowess. Adding to the accounts of Twain and DeVoto, Borges pictures Lazarus Morell's liegemen flashing their "momentary wealth of rings" ("momentary" because they do not own the rings) in order to awaken respect among the slaves they deceive. And he culls a detail from Asbury in the Monk Eastman sketch to mention Johnny Dolan, a mobster famed for his eye-gouging ring, which Borges describes with relish as a "fine copper device that he could wear on his thumb to scoop out an adversary's eyes" (*OC*, 311). So, too, does Francisco Real's ring in "Streetcorner Man" betoken special status; no sooner has Real died than rapacious *compadres* cut off his finger to despoil him of it. Yet none of these rings has any magic attached to it. The only thing they have in common is the prestige they represent and the sadism they further or provoke.

Sometimes the rings Borges describes are too big to be worn. He adds to Burton's account of the breaching of the proscribed tower an "iron key ring" (*OC*, 336) that holds the keys to the sanctum. Similarly, to El Conde Lucanor's exemplum, which he alters scarcely at all in drafting "The Wizard Postponed," Borges adds a trapdoor that leads to Don Illán's underground cell and graces it with "a great iron ring" (*OC*, 339). We recall that iron appears consistently in Borges' paradigmatic story.)

And sometimes it is the image of a circle in a square (or a square in a circle) that Borges inserts into his texts. Consistently, he uses this slightly mysterious figure in contexts that hint at altered states of consciousness. While Philip Gosse reports that Mrs. Ching's pirate crews "are much addicted to gambling and spend all their leisure hours at cards and smoking opium,"[49] Borges envisions "cards and loaded dice, fan-tan's rectangle and cup, opium's visionary pipe and little lamp" (*OC*, 308). To Gosse's portrait of the drugged pirates' repose, he thus adds fan-tan's four-sided counter and bowl. The opium dreams of the pirates seem somewhat akin to Ebeneezer Bogle's visionary state in the Tom Castro sketch. In describing the moment when Bogle is inspired, Borges again uses the image of a circle in a rectangle. Bogle, as he would have it, "wandered about until a honey-colored moon repeated itself in the rectangular basins of the public fountains. The god visited him" (*OC*, 304). The circular moon mirrored in the rectangular London fountains brings the illumination Bogle seeks. The same configuration of circle in square appears in "The Mirror of Ink," again connected with magical revelation. The circular pool of ink, to have its effect, must be cupped in a palm onto which a rectangular grid has been drawn. In adapting his source, Borges exploits the phrase "magic square" to enhance the mystical properties of the design. Lane, who provides a drawing of such a square in his account, makes clear in a footnote that the square, subdivided tick-tack-toe fashion, is magic in the mathematical sense, since the numbers inscribed in each of the nine compartments of the grid add up, along horizontal, vertical, and diagonal axes, to the same sum.[50] Borges, however, adopts the phrase "cuadro mágico" without mentioning the numbers, and leaves his readers to impute to the square a frankly mystical significance.

Two of the three representations of circles in squares have

to do with mirrors, and mirrors recur in several other *Infamy* narratives, as well. The samurai warriors of the Kotsuké no Suké sketch gather in a chapel whose only adornment is a "rectangular box containing a mirror" (*OC*, 321; *UHI*, 71). Later in the same tale the warriors wrest aside a bronze mirror that disguises the access to Kotsuké's hiding place. Borges invents both of these mirrors and creates as well the bronze mirror that Hákim destroys, presumably by using it after he has beheld God and been blessed with special power. Several mirrors, though, do figure in Borges' sources, and it is revealing to see how Borges uses them. Burton, for example, detailing the luxuries Tárik plunders, describes in the source for "The Chamber of Statues" "a marvelous mirror, great and round, of mixed metals, which had been made for Solomon, son of David (on the twain be peace!) wherein whoso looked might see the counterfeit presentment of the seven climates of the world."[51] Borges, adapting this passage, perhaps taking his cue from the mention of Solomon, son of David, alters the nature of the image that the magic mirror displays. He writes: "They came upon a circular mirror, the work of Solomon, David's son—forgiveness for them both!—whose price was great, for it was made of mixed metals and whoever looked into it could see the faces of his fathers and his sons, from the first Adam to those who will hear the Trumpet" (*OC*, 337). Not only does Borges change the specular scene so that it reveals, instead of the world's seven climates, the faces of the viewer's male progeny and ancestors; he subtly alters the wording in other ways, to make of Solomon an artificer and to hint at a tension between David and his son. The mirror *"made for* Solomon, son of David" becomes, in Borges' text, *"obra de* Solimán" while the pious aside "on the twain be peace!" becomes the more ominous "¡sea para los dos *el perdón!"*, as if both David and Solomon had transgressed.

We are back in the realm of dissension between father and son. Unmistakably, some of the *Infamy* texts—"The Mirror of Ink" for example—relate the seeing of a mirror image with punishment visited by symbolic father on symbolic son. Yet anxieties other than those produced by oedipal strife surely underlie Borges' use of the mirror, in these texts and elsewhere in his work. Borges' use of the mirror as symbol is quite complex and many able critics have explored it.[52] This study will add to their wisdom one further comment, one arising from an examination of Borges' manipulation of sources. In addition to "The Chamber of Statues," two other of the *Infamy* sketches rely on works that mention mirrors and that do so in a way that links mirrors to the idea of forebears and their infirmity. Lane, recounting the wonders of the mirror of ink, tells how a skeptical Englishman required the magician to conjure up, in the ink, the image of his own father, whom the necromancer had never seen. Lane writes:

> An Englishman present ridiculed the performance [of the magician] and said that nothing would satisfy him but a correct description of the appearance of his own father. . . . The boy, accordingly, having called by name for the person alluded to, described a man in a Frank dress, with his hand placed to his head, wearing spectacles, and with one foot on the ground, and the other raised behind him, as if he were stepping down from a seat. The description was exactly true in every respect: the peculiar position of the hand was occasioned by an almost constant headache; and that of the foot or leg, by a stiff knee, caused by a fall from a horse, in hunting.[53]

While Borges, inventing both characters and plot of "The Mirror of Ink," does not portray this scene, he certainly had read it. In the epithet he assigns Yakub—"Doliente"—we may perceive a hint of the ailments of the father in Lane's account. Moreover, to this possible allusion we can add another which, in a similar way, links a mirror image to the idea of impaired forebears.

Roger Caillois has guessed that Marcel Schwob's 1920 parable *Le roi au masque d'or* served Borges as one source for "The Masked Dyer, Hákim of Merv."[54] Schwob tells of a king who wears a mask of gold and lives in a sumptuous palace attended by masked retainers. Oracles have warned that the king should not behold a human face, but he admits to his court a beggar who, blind but unmasked, divines that the king's servants are false to him. The king expels the beggar but that night looks for a mirror (they are forbidden in his court) and, finding none, ventures out of the palace. In a wood he sees a beautiful maid spinning but, when he asks that they look at each others' faces and lifts his mask, the girl cries out in horror and runs away. In the water of a stream the king beholds his own face. He is a leper. Stung by pain and anger, he replaces his mask and steals back to his court. That night he goes to the chamber where the portraits of his ancestors hang. He rips the masks that, in the paintings, hide his forebears' faces, exposing the bare wall behind each portrait. Bitterly, he blames his ancestors for having transmitted the curse of leprosy along with the royal title; it is by using the royal cup, bed, and clothes that he has been infected.

Schwob's story does not end here. But even a partial précis shows the connection Schwob makes between inherited privilege and a grimmer legacy. And Borges may have had reason to identify with the unmasked king. Endowed with special intellectual gifts, he had been weak-sighted from childhood. His own family's curse, blindness, had afflicted the Borges men of five generations before him, and he had every reason to fear that he himself would one day go blind. Behind his deployment of mirrors in three of the *Infamy* texts lies the fantasy of seeing one's forefathers, and in two of the three cases the ancestors to be seen in the mirror are sadly impaired. Whatever other meanings the image of the mirror has in Borges' work, it may also contain and express Borges' fear of blindness and his blame of those from whom he had inherited a congenital ill.

In addition to the mirrors, rings and coins to be found in the *Infamy* texts, other early figurings of the aleph appear in these early narratives. (The Chinese emperor's kites that give their name to this study are a notable example.) Borges often connects these marvelous objects with the idea of special privilege and sometimes with revelation that incurs punishment. But it is not the rule in the *Infamy* sketches for Borges' protagonists to meet their final doom in a moment of revelation. Although the Widow Ching, the dean of Santiago, and Yakub the Ailing are brought low in a moment of sudden insight as they gaze at a wonderful thing, for the most part Borges' early protagonists, unlike the heroes of his later tales, do not end their careers with an experience of epiphany. What is more, the proto-alephs of Borges' early narratives impart little sense of mystery, nor are they connected with access to the infinite. It is in other writings Borges produced during the 1920s and early 1930s that he explores the theme of temporal and spatial infinity, an important motif that he will later compound with the other meanings of these early alephs.

If Borges' alephs take on meanings in the *Ficciones* tales that they do not have in the texts of *A Universal History,* so do other aspects of Borges' protoparadigm assume new forms as he moves toward his ur story. Table 7 shows some of the important shifts that take place as Borges modifies the *Infamy* schema and makes of it the paradigm of his mature tales. The criminal bands he paints so gleefully in his first narratives become less

Table 7   Shifts in Borges' Narrative Schema

Infamia Schema	Paradigm
Criminal bands	Less openly harmful alliances, e.g., utopian societies or intellectual elites
Protagonist is wrongdoer	Motivating mishap not portrayed as protagonist's crime
Pursuit of protagonist by agent of right	Pursuit of protagonist is coterminous with protagonist's search for something or someone
Filth and primitivism	Derealizing impoverishment
Various enclosures, including prisons, hideouts, and squalid places of origin	Labyrinth or enclosure that immures protagonist
Protagonist may capture city	Enclosure sometimes portrayed as city
Protagonist brought to justice (not by a double)	Annihilation of hero often entails encounter with double
Treasure, marvelous things	Aleph, epitome of infinite
Little suggestion of irreality	Heightened irreality

openly violent confederacies in the *Ficciones* texts. The Tlönists are a utopian secret society whose sinister aim is covert, and the writers who memorialize Funes and Pierre Menard are a more decorous lot by far than the mobsters and pirates and outlaws of Borges' earlier book.

So, too, is the pursuit of the criminal by the law transformed in most of the later tales into something apparently less ominous. The motif of the search is scarcely to be seen in the *Infamy* texts; "The Chamber of Statues" and "Tale of the Two Dreamers" are the only sketches in which the hero undertakes a journey in the hope of finding something. The most important precursor of the Borgean journey in these early works is not travel on the hero's part but his pursuit by an agent of law and order. As for the impoverishment that attends the Borgean traveler in the later tales, when Borges portrays it at all in these early texts he usually depicts it as filth.

One can identify in the *Infamy* texts antecedents of the enclosures where Borges' heros are immured in phase three of the paradigm. The forbidden tower the renegade king unlocks, the "gloomy little courtyard" (*OC*, 322; *UHI*, 73) where Kotsuké no Suké hides, the sorry quarters where Melancthon's soul is confined, and the "old house whose patios were filled with statues and vines" (*OC*, 299) where Lazarus Morell stalks from room to darkened room anticipate the enclaustration phase of the paradigm. So do the "labyrinth of sewers" (*OC*, 311; *UHI*, 52) of Monk Eastman's New York and the muddy mazes of the Mississippi delta. But Borges does not appear to use in a systematic way these early figurings of his labyrinth. They do not fit into the plots of his narratives in a prescribed way.

As for the annihilation phase of the paradigm, its most important precursor in *A Universal History of Infamy* is the bringing to justice of each of Borges' *infames*. In three important ways the representation of the protagonist's nemesis in the *Infamy* texts differs sharply from the paradigm's fourth phase. The person who avenges the antihero's wrongs is not his symbolic double. The motif of revelation in the early sketches may have to do with the *infame*'s downfall but need not be related to it. And the notion of infinity—and the vertiginous irreality

that Borges links with it—is all but absent from his early narratives. The profusion of kites that end the story of the Widow
Ching is the only hint of infinity in these texts.

To pursue an understanding of how Borges' paradigm
evolved, we must examine its other antecedents in Borges' nonnarrative work. Then we shall be in a better position to understand the full range of material that Borges had at his command
in 1935 when he wrote his first mature tale, "The Approach to
Al-Mu'tasim." Only at that point will we be able to speculate
about what stimulated Borges to fuse in his narrative paradigm
aspects of his writing that he had long kept separate from one
another.

III

Origins of the Paradigm: Irreality

To respond to Jorge Luis Borges' work, and in particular to his narrative art, is to be subtly disquieted by it. His writings explore ingenious ideas, but it is not the novelty of Borges' tales that engages the reader's mind; if Borges' stories were merely clever we would by now have ceased to value them so highly. We would rank a tale like "Tlön, Uqbar, Orbis Tertius" alongside C. S. Lewis' very intelligent science fiction, and "Pierre Menard, Author of the Quixote" with Frederick Crews' spoof of literary criticism *The Pooh Perplex*. It is because Borges' work transcends ingeniousness that we find it so compelling. We read it because it evokes in us a haunting feeling of irreality.

Just as we mean, when we call something "Kafkaesque," something more specific than "nightmarish," we think of Borges' fictive universe as irreal, and mean by that term something slightly different from "unreal"—nonexistent—or "fantastic" or "uncanny" or "dreamlike." Our intuition embraces at once the Spanish expression *irreal,* for it refers alike to the mysterious, unsettling quality of much of Borges' work and to the idealist notions of contingent being that many of his writings explore. Ana María Barrenechea, the first to devote a book-length study to Borges' work, was quick to identify irreality as the fundamental impression that Borges' art conveys. Her pioneering book *La expresión de la irrealidad en la obra de Jorge Luis Borges* (1957) attempts, in her words, "to analyze how Borges has constructed his sharply etched world of shadows."[1] In her classic study, she identifies Borges' favorite themes and goes on to show how specific aspects of Borges' style work to "undermine our belief in a concrete existence."[2] Barrenechea was the first—she remains one of the ablest—of many perceptive critics of Borges' work whose aim has been to point out the remarkable economy of Borges' texts, that is to say, the effectiveness with which Borges expresses, in the structure, themes, and language of his works, a sense of the irreal. Yet few have asked precisely what we take Borgean irreality to be, and even fewer have asked why Borgean irreality is so affecting.

Borges himself, though, never tires of posing these very questions. His nonfiction prose, in particular, is, among other things, a lifelong set of musings as to the nature and value of irreal experience and the possibilities for expressing irreality in literature. Whether he turns his attention to a particular writer's work, the history of an idea, or the efficacy of a rhetorical device, Borges nearly always addresses, directly or indirectly, issues that arise from his fascination with the irreal. And it is in Borges' early essays and short confessional prose texts that we must look if we wish to trace the origins of—and thereby interpret—those aspects of Borges' narrative paradigm that have to do with irreality.

Both the impoverishment of the Borgean hero's lot in phase two of the paradigm and the sudden collapse of his selfhood at the end of the ur narrative have antecedents in Borges' early work. In chapter 2 we found early representations of both kinds of irreality in *A Universal History of Infamy*. Descriptions of dirtiness, for example, constitute early (and by no means irreal) figurings of Borgean impoverishment. And the lucre that Borges' villains illegally acquire, in most of the *Infamy* sources, is one forerunner of the magical objects that empower and blight Borges' later protagonists. But *A Universal History of Infamy* fails as fiction exactly to the degree that it does not completely capture Borges' intuition of the irreal. It is chiefly in his nonnarrative writings that Borges explores irreality during the 1920s and early 1930s. We must now turn to other of Borges' early texts, as well as to the writings of several of Borges' contemporaries, to gain insight into the complex and emotionally charged meaning that irreality held for Borges.

One must begin by understanding that Buenos Aires during the 1920s was a city whose cultural life was in ferment. When he returned to Argentina in 1921, Borges joined an ardent fellowship—some scores or even hundreds strong—of cultural evangelists who were coming to regard Buenos Aires as the artistic hub of South America, and perhaps even of the Spanish-speaking world. During the 1920s Borges the young man of letters was prodigiously active. The bibliographic work *Las revistas literarias argentinas (1893–1960)*, compiled by Lafleur, Provenzano, and Alonso, documents Borges' collaboration, as contributor or director, in ten of the more or less ephemeral literary magazines that flourished and died in Buenos Aires during that decade.[3] The poems and literary essays Borges wrote, when collected and republished in book form, make up three volumes of essays and three collections of poems. Arriving from Spain bearing the gospel of ultraism, an avant-garde poetic movement, Borges achieved almost at once some small renown in *porteño* literary circles. Emir Rodríguez Monegal points out that during these years Borges participated full tilt in Buenos Aires' literary life.[4] It was in this atmosphere of enthusiasm and camaraderie that Borges began to formulate and articulate for the first time a set of aesthetic principles. He also pursued his fascination— one shared by a number of his fellow intellectuals—with idealist metaphysics. In addition, he began to turn both of these rational preoccupations to the task of forging an effective mode of literary self-expression. His essays and poems of the 1920s show him feeling his way toward a single internally consistent program of principle and praxis, a vision that would integrate his aesthetics, his metaphysics, and his intimate psychic experience. What emerged was seldom a very successful amalgam. The Borges of the essays of *Inquisitions* (1925), *The Extent of My Hope* (1926), and *The Language of the Argentines* (1928) is a different Borges from the poet of *Fervor of Buenos Aires* (1923), *Moon Across the Way* (1925), and *San Martín Copybook* (1929). As a poet Borges was doing one kind of task, as a critic another. Both as poet and as critic, though, Borges was beginning to conceptualize using a vocabulary that would later coalesce into a set of notions about irreality, notions that for a time simply coexisted, sometimes confirming each other and sometimes conflicting or having little bearing upon one another.

The degree to which Borges' formulations about irreality

derived from the ideas of others, or at least formed part of the common currency of ideas that circulated among those of Borges' set, is important to recognize. In his "Autobiographical Essay" Borges credits his father, a man knowledgeable in philosophy and psychology of the school of William James, with initiating him, during his childhood, into the mysteries of Berkeleyan idealism. He recalls, as well, his father's illustrating for him, with the aid of a chessboard, the paradoxes of Zeno. Borges must have experienced as a boy the intellectual vertigo of imagining the precariousness of being. The idea that *esse rerum est percipi,* that is, that the existence of things resides in their being perceived, was certainly available to him, together with its corollary that we may vanish at any moment if the creature who is dreaming us awakes. Similarly, Borges must have played with the notion that time and space, because they are infinitely divisible, defeat movement through temporal and spatial dimensions, since before one can travel from *a* to *b* one must first arrive at the midpoint between them, *c*, and then at the midpoint between *c* and *b*, and so on. These concepts will form the basis, throughout Borges' life, of his speculations about metaphysical concerns. What is surprising, though, is the extent to which the cluster of ideas that are related to these basic propositions formed part of a shared store of already minted formulations.

El Caudillo, the novel Borges' father wrote during the family's stay in Majorca in 1919 and published two years later, is one of the texts written by people known to Borges in which motifs having to do with irreality after the Borgean mode appear. As a whole, *El Caudillo,* a historical novel laced with ironic social comment, creates no sensation of irreality in the reader; set in Entre Ríos during the civil wars of the 1870s, it follows the adventures of a sallow, citified youth, Carlos Dubois, as he encounters the family of a rural power broker. Yet the narrative contains several images that the author's son will later elaborate and exploit in his own writings. (Although, in his "Autobiographical Essay," Borges writes that he himself suggested to his father several of the novel's images, it is doubtful that all of the passages I shall here point out originate with the younger Borges. Some of them—one describes a romantic encounter, another reflects on the way a mother's face looks to her child—seem utterly foreign to Jorge Luis Borges' work. It seems improbable that Borges helped his father with passages so unlikely to have aroused his own interest.)

The image of a divine countenance unveiled, which Borges will later incorporate in his paradigm's fourth phase, appears in several contexts in his father's *El Caudillo*. "The night's face is veiled," one not very effective descriptive passage runs.[5] And when the protagonist finds himself in peril, death is figured as "the face hidden beneath the awful mask."[6] Elsewhere, the elder Borges writes that, to her child, "A mother's face never changes, it is always the same, sacred like the face of the gods."[7]

Borges' father also explicitly deploys in his book the idea of the eternal return. When Carlos Dubois, a phlegmatic young man with little taste for passion, is set upon by the strongman's amorous daughter Marisabel, he fends off the girl's advances by musing about his and Marisabel's counterparts in other possible times: " 'What would be curious,' " he observes, distracting Marisabel from her flirtation, " 'is to know if we have ever walked this same road together, thought what we are thinking today and spoken the same words.' " And minutes later, when the couple are joined by another girl, Dubois continues his metaphysical fantasy. " 'Perhaps we shall meet on the infinite path of time and, perhaps, millions of years from now, I shall talk with you both as I am doing now.' " Not only does Jorge Guillermo Borges invoke the concept of cyclic time but he associates with it the same enfeebling, exhausting effect that his son will attach to it. Dubois remarks that to contemplate the idea of the eternal return makes him feel worn and spent, "gastado" to use the elder Borges' word.[8]

What is more, the sense of being detached or withdrawn from one's own life is admirably caught in several passages of the novel. Thinking back on his "grey, blurry childhood" ("infancia gris y borrosa")—the same conjunction of adjectives later appears in the younger Borges' writing—the narcissistic Dubois perceives his own childhood as something not quite his, "a past so remote that it seemed to him like a long snatch of a story he had learned by heart. The story of a beloved and intimate friend, rather than his own personal history." And a little later Jorge G. Borges goes on, "Carlos Dubois did not know himself, but he knew intimately the history of his memories." Further, the ghostliness and utter solitude of feeling cut off both from others and from self finds expression in another image that may adumbrate the younger Borges' work. Summoning back his earliest memory, Dubois envisions in his thoughts "a stairway where many people were going up and down. He could see himself sitting on the first steps, playing. The steps climbed to inaccessible, mysterious regions."[9]

In its tone this passage surely anticipates texts to be written later by Borges' son. And another passage, also one that describes unrealized people who only halfway live, likewise deserves comment. It is an aside, which interrupts the presentation to the reader of Marisabel's sisters, unexceptional girls endowed with no special grace or redeeming faculty. The narrator, having described them, stops to reflect:

> The world is full of half souls, of ill-defined characters infinitely multiplied who are nothing but a copy and repetition of their age's salient features and concerns, who in no way stand out, have no anomalies nor any atrophied faculty or super-sensitivity, who are duplicates of vulgar, inferior models, like works of artists who worked out of necessity and routine without a love of their art. Not even moral ugliness or beauty saves these souls; they pass through the world like dreams and shadows.[10]

The passage equivocates (*"like* dreams and shadows"); the reader feels it would be off the mark to view as irreal in a literal sense these imperfectly turned out creatures. Nevertheless, these ill-defined half souls, the botched handiwork of bored divinities, presage the golems and dreamed protagonists that Borges will later portray. And, as we shall see, the notion that life, not to be completely fulfilled but to be wholly real, must be lived intensely, is one that Borges shared both with his father and with others in his own circle.

Another text that enunciates the view that to have true value life must be intense is an essay by Borges' fellow editor of *Proa* Brandán Caraffa. Published in the August 1924 number of *Proa* under the title "Palabras de Aprendizaje" ("Words of

Apprenticeship"), the essay is a metaphysical polemic on the theme of carpe diem. It contends that, since a man's life consists of a succession of discrete states that embody, well or ill, a certain quantum of impersonal creative energy, one should strive to make his life "so intense that one's whole personality can be manifest in it."[11] The goal of every human being should be to concentrate the energy allotted to him and expend it fervently in action. Brandán argues: "Surely an individuality lasting just thirty years but who in that short lapse of time *develops himself intensely in various kinds of action,* is worth more than an ascete in Tibet who dies at the age of a hundred but who lives isolated from everything, without having bound his soul to the universe through the creation of innumerable concrete states."[12]

Exhorting his readers to regard their lives as a sequence of present moments, each one of which should be prized for itself, not for its relationship to past or future, Brandán Caraffa goes on to conjure up a vision of immortality. He surmises that if there is immortality, it consists in living forever to perform into eternity the same pursuits, whether transcendent or trivial, that one has performed in life. Thus a man who wastes his life in banalities risks being condemned to have "his ridiculousness or his uselessness preserved for all time";[13] he forges his own hell.

One further passage in this essay cannot fail to catch the eye of a reader of Borges' work. It extends a little the notion that to contemplate through infinite time the barrenness of one's life would constitute hell. "Papini," writes Brandán, "in one of his fantastic tales, depicts the anguish of a man obliged to pass in review and contemplate every single one of his thoughts, even those that are most secret. I think the most awesome punishment for us would not be flames or liquid fire, but the eternal vision of our whole life projected eternally before our eyes."[14] For a moment Brandán Caraffa leaves aside the choice between filling one's life with passion worthy to be immortalized or with stale drudgery. He conceives of man's worst punishment as having to survey forever the sum of his own actions and thoughts. We are close indeed to the conception of Funes' total lucidity, or to Borges' notion of the aleph in any of its forms. Brought together in this passage is the idea of eternal punishment and the act of watching an infinite unfolding of self.

The double habit of regarding consciousness both as vivified by an impersonal force and as being made up of a series of discrete moments, each one of which is absolute and self-contained, found defenders besides Brandán. Another who subscribed to these idealist fancies and whose influence Borges often has avowed was the *porteño* Socrates, Macedonio Fernández.[15] Practiced in locating his perceiving eye outside himself, Macedonio records again and again the results of a radical detachment from self. He writes, for example, that it is bliss "to happen upon a seat filled with oneself on a streetcar filled with others."[16] And, having been struck by an adversary, he sighs, "if only I had been able to find an instant replacement for myself a second before the punch landed."[17] One consequence of Macedonio's bent for looking at himself from the outside in is that objects seem to take on a peculiar life of their own. Invested with the intrinsic attributes that we normally ascribe to people, not to things, the inanimate, as he conceives it, acts upon man instead of the reverse. Thus it is that he writes, conveying his own passivity, not that he steps off curbs but that "sidewalks have always left me in the street."[18] Or the following:

> It suits a new walking stick to have been lost once: it's a kind of youthful fling that one should make sure it does not miss. Although it would be more convenient if one could buy them already lost and found. And bookstores, too, would save us a good deal of trouble if they dispensed some books in already-read form. Better still, in the case of a good book, if they sold it to us already returned by borrowing friends.[19]

This is a charming fantasy. Yet to regard the losing of a walking stick or the reading and lending of a favorite book not as one's own experience but as that of the cane or volume in question, in effect deprives the self of complex, emotionally dense, perduring being. Causality falls away. Each action drains the self, with the result that it is rendered more and more irreal. In turn, the objective world, which, Macedonio believes, exists only by virtue of being perceived by the self, grows ever more ghostly as the self becomes more and more attenuated.

Macedonio's views were decidedly whimsical, designed much more to startle than to convince. Yet some of the radical notions he advanced deserve our attention, for Borges seems to have adapted to his own use certain ideas he shared with Macedonio. For example, Macedonio championed intensity of feeling, so adamantly that, in an essay in *Proa* in which he vindicates mysticism as metaphysics' emotional counterpart, he affirmed, "Intensity is the mystical category."[20] And not only did Macedonio embrace the idealist view that reality exists only in that it is perceived, but he went one step further to assert that spirit itself, the perceiving faculty, is likewise a dream. In a passage that defies exegesis, he declares:

> The world, being, reality, everything, is a dream without a dreamer; an only dream and the dream of only one, therefore the dream of no one, all the more real the more it is utterly a dream. What is irreal, nonexistence, is Matter, which supposedly activates that dream; matter, that which could never be, is thus not dreamable.

> El mundo, el ser, la realidad, todo, es un sueño sin soñador; un sólo sueño y el sueño de uno solo, por tanto el sueño de nadie, tanto más real cuanto más es enteramente un sueño. Lo irreal, la inexistencia es la Materia, supuesto excitante de aquél sueño; la materia, lo que nunca pudo ser, pues, no es soñable.[21]

Contained in this elliptical set of propositions is a reversal of terms, a reversal Borges sometimes adopts, according to which the tangible, material world to which we often assign the epithet "real" is, quite the contrary, irreal. Conversely, what is most real is what is dreamed. And for Macedonio the subjectivity that dreams is as evanescent as the Cheshire cat. It is interesting to compare the passage quoted above with one of Borges' own, published a year earlier in the essay "Berkeley's Crossroads." Borges writes:

> Berkeley claims: Things exist only insofar as one fixes one's mind on them. It is licit to answer: Yes, but the mind

exists only in that it perceives and meditates on things. In this way not just the unity of the world collapses, but the unity of spirit itself. The object lapses into nothingness, and with it the subject. Both enormous substantives, spirit and matter, vanish simultaneously and life becomes a jumbled rush of states of mind, a dream without a dreamer. (*I*, 115)

The few metaphysical essays Borges wrote during the first several years of his literary career bear the idealist stamp that marked the philosophizing of Borges' intellectual group. Yet even in his earliest writings Borges is concerned to explain what relationship metaphysical concepts might bear to lived experience. "The Nothingness of Personality," his first essay on a metaphysical theme, examines the proposition that the self does not exist, if by self we understand that aggregate of experience that a consciousness retains as it persists through successive time. The topic may be theoretical but Borges' occasion for taking it up, he insists, is not merely his delight at a "piece of intellectual mischief." Rather, "una certidumbre firmísima," a deeply felt certainty, has left him wholly convinced of the spuriousness of the self. The core of the essay is Borges' account of the experience out of which this certainty grows.

It is his taking leave of a close friend, Borges says, that has made him suddenly understand that no self redeems man's life from meaninglessness. He recalls that on the night of their farewell he and his friend, probably his Spanish mentor Rafael Cansinos-Asséns, walked and conversed self-consciously, aware that in retrospect their final talk would acquire special meaning. Here is his emotional account of their last moments together:

> There clamored in my chest the wish to show my soul completely to my friend. I would have liked to strip myself bare of my soul and leave it there throbbing. We went on talking and debating, on the verge of saying goodbye, until suddenly, with an unsuspected firmness of certainty, I understood that the personality we are used to tout so exorbitantly does not exist. It struck me that no full, absolute moment would justify my life, no moment that contained

all others, that all moments would be provisional stages that obliterated the past and confronted the future, and that apart from the episodic, the present, the circumstantial, we were no one. And I cursed all mystery-mongering. (*I*, 90)

Just what is the experience Borges describes, and what conceivable connection does it have to the existence or nonexistence of the self? Borges tells us that on his final evening with his friend he strains to create a moment worthy of the occasion, worthy, that is, to express his affection for his friend and to sum up the momentousness of their parting. But, disappointingly, no privileged moment ensues to epitomize Borges' intensity of feeling. It is at this point, if we take Borges at his word, that he falls to reflecting on metaphysical themes and intuits, suddenly, the nonexistence of the self. Quick work, this. It may well be that Borges accurately reports this touching episode and that, faced with the double task of expressing friendship and enduring the prospect of loss, he took refuge in abstract thinking. But to assert that this experience demonstrates the nonexistence of self requires of the reader no small leap of faith. In later texts Borges reconciles with better success his personal experience and the metaphysical terms in which he chooses to frame it.

I have stopped to show that during the decade between 1919 and 1929 other Argentines besides Borges couched their thoughts in terms Borges associates with two kinds of irreality in his later work. I have done so not in order to imply that Borges' own writing is less original than critics have deemed it to be. Nor do I claim that the three men of letters whose works I have discussed are the only writers whose work evinces habits of mind that Borges must have shared with other friends than these. Nonetheless, it is worthwhile to see that Borges did not devise out of whole cloth all of the ideas and images that he will come to link with a unique and personal evocation of irreality.

Another important way in which Borges' intellectual world may have influenced his notions about irreality is by shaping his ideas of aesthetics. It is no accident that the metaphysical ideas extant among Borges' confreres during the 1920s are compatible with, and even in some measure complement, the avant-garde theories of poetic art that Borges and others were eagerly propounding. In particular, ultraism, as adapted by *porteños* from its Spanish beginnings, reflects in its precepts several of the ideas I have just discussed. Borges, who, returning to Buenos Aires from Spain and his tutelage by the Spanish *ultraísta* Rafael Cansinos-Asséns, was chief spokesman for the movement in Argentina, drafted in 1921 the following program of ultraist principles. He prescribes:

1. Reduction of lyric poetry to its basic element: the metaphor.
2. Elimination of connecting phrases, links, and useless adjectives.
3. Abolition of ornamental devices, confessionalism, the circumstantial, preaching, and deliberate vagueness.
4. Synthesis of two or more images in one, which thus enlarges its capacity for suggestion. The ultraist poems consist, then, of a series of metaphors, each one of which has its own meaning and holds an unedited vision of some fragment of life.[22]

By saying what an ultraist poem ought *not* to include, Borges delineates his *ars poetica*. The poem, purged alike of verbal excess and ornamental language and of sentimentalism and the psychological, should present the reader with, as Borges writes elsewhere, "a limpid art that might be as atemporal as the eternal stars" (*I*, 96–97). The idea of capturing and rescuing from time a moment of intense experience coincides with, and is vindicated by, the notion that life ought really to be viewed as a series of discrete moments, each one lived with as much intensity as possible. And the notion that impersonal energy, not a fiercely individual soul, animates men, is consonant with the ultraists' avowed goal of abstracting from concrete, temporal circumstance essential experience.

It is useful to examine the premises and the aims that Borges and other artists of his day espoused, for by doing so one is better able to see how Borges' conception of irreality evolved. In particular, one can see that the concept of impoverishment, crucial to one mode of the Borgean irreal, emerges not from a single point of origin in Borges' early thinking, but from several contexts and diverse usages.

The Borges who wrote *Fervor of Buenos Aires* conceived of himself as an anti-*modernista* poet. In his preface to *Fervor*, Borges contrasts his own purpose and his own poetics with those of what he takes to be the prevailing literary school of his day. Declaring that his aim has been to write feelingly—even with reverence—about a humble subject, he warns the reader not to expect a portrait of Buenos Aires qua cosmopolitan emporium. He will write instead about the "friendly neighborhoods" where he grew up, neighborhoods that have witnessed and perhaps nurtured his "love . . . pain and . . . doubts." This modest Buenos Aires of the outlying districts, or *arrabales*, deserves Borges' poetic celebration because, Borges says, "Here a divinity lies concealed." Comparing himself to "the Latins, who, when they walked through a grove, would murmur '*Numen inest*,'" he justifies writing about an unexalted part of the city by noting that it is bound up with his own intimate life, and with a feeling of transcendence that he tries to convey in many of the poems in the book.

Borges says he understands that his purpose will seem strange to those who embrace the *modernista* aesthetic. With "justified rancor" he inveighs against more traditional poets "whose lyric is so often watered down with quasi-music that it has the cut-rate rhythm of a heap of gaudy trinkets." He will not dupe the reader with musicality for its own sake or trot out the baubles that ornament *modernista* Beauty. "How," he scoffs, "can one help disliking a writer who recites words willy nilly, without savoring the hidden wonder they contain, or a writer who, like some lapidary of inanities, overloads his writing with gold and jewels, humbling with so much splendor *our poor, opaque verses*, lit only by the *indigent* glow of suburban sunsets" (*FBA*, unnumbered p. 2, my emphasis). "Poor," in this context, is the opposite of the infatuation of *modernista* writers with artifice and with beautiful (and costly) things. If Darío and Lugones linked beauty with gems and porcelain and mother-of-pearl, Borges connects it with the authentic portrayal of human emotion. And the particular emotion that Borges strives to express, he experiences only in humble surroundings.

In requiring that art flow from and express the emotions and personality of its creator, Borges is in accord with a great many young *porteño* literati who, like him, debunked established aesthetic norms. Nearly every page of the important periodical *Martín Fierro*, whose second and more important period of publication spans the years 1924–27, irreverently clamors for art that will reveal and convey true intimacy, not prettify it with "rhetorical petticoats."[23] Pablo Rojas Paz, in an enthusiastic review of César Fernández Moreno's *El hogar en el campo*, praises the "coloring of feeling," the "contained emotion" and the "intimate emotion of the landscape." Fernández Moreno, he says approvingly, "prizes emotion more than expressiveness. . . . When he sings his intimate happiness, he does it with discreet lovingness, so intimately that it seems like the confession of a friend."[24] Leopoldo Marechal, claiming that "to be a poet means to reap one's whole self, one's whole personality," damns Leopoldo Lugones as "a cold architect of the word . . . [who] erects structures where emotion cannot abide."[25] Alberto Prebisch, reviewing an exhibition by the sculptor Irurtia, complains that "Mr. Irurtia oscillates indiscriminately between one of those influences [Michelangelo, Donatello, Neoclassical sculptors and Rodin] and another, without ever giving us clear evidence of his own personality."[26] And Santiago Ganduglia, in an article blasting the naturalism of the left-wing Boedo group, rails against an aesthetic that "has insisted on aesthetic professionalism, and in the process stifled personality." He goes on to demand that literary descriptions not serve merely to paint a backdrop for action but that they "[define] a state of mind."[27]

Authentic expressions of intense, intimate personal feeling were, then, the order of the day. But not just any feelings might appropriately become the subject of this new kind of poetry. At least among the so-called ultraist writers, a strict decorum prevailed that not only banished mawkishness and pretension but abstracted feeling from actual experience. If the *Martinfierristas* call for the artist to portray his most intimate sensibility, the writers of the *Proa* group, with whom Borges himself was even more closely allied, go further and actually specify the way intense personal feeling should be distilled in timeless art. The statement of principles with which the editors of *Proa*—Jorge

Luis Borges, Brandán Caraffa, Ricardo Güiraldes and Pablo Rojas Paz—inaugurate, in August 1924, that magazine's second era declares:

> The only credential we demand is *disinterested fervor* for the life of the spirit. We have imposed on ourselves a stern discipline so as to lay to rest every petty passion that might make us put a personal situation before an effective value of art. . . . The only way to free our spirit from those simplistic, false positions in which only intuition—or only intelligence—reigns, is by ruling life with *spontaneous convictions*.[28]

The writer, according to this manifesto, must renounce the "petty passions" of his particular "personal situation" to the end of communicating to the reader, in its pure form, intensely felt and intimate experience. This "disinterested fervor"—emotion unencumbered by the ballast of circumstances that ordinarily weighs it down—is to be the stuff of art. And this stripping away of the circumstantial constitutes another kind of impoverishment.

It is only when one recognizes this precept—it is the keystone of ultraist poetics—that one can fully make sense of the essays Borges wrote in 1924 and 1925, many of which appeared in *Proa*.[29] *Inquisitions*, the volume in which these essays were eventually collected, should be read as Borges' musings on the proper stance a poet should assume toward his subject. Again and again, in reviews, portraits of men of letters, and metaphysical reflections, Borges identifies what he believes are two opposing attitudes. The first, held by the ultraists and by Borges himself, requires the writer to abstract from his life essential feelings and lay them before the reader. The second, which Borges identifies in writers as different from one another as James Joyce, Ramón Gómez de la Serna, and the Uruguayan poet Pedro Leandro Ipuche, impels the writer to enumerate zestfully the small particularities of everyday living. Commenting on Joyce's "novel of cathedral-like grandeur," Borges writes: "On the pages of *Ulysses* all of reality teems. . . . *Not the mediocre reality of those who only perceive in the world the abstract operations of the soul* and its ambitious fear of not overcoming death, nor that other half reality that filters in through the senses and in which our flesh coexists with the sidewalk, and cisterns with the moon" (*I*, 23–24, my emphasis). Borges marvels approvingly at Joyce's verbal richness, which he describes, curiously enough, in pecuniary terms. Joyce, he writes, "is a millionaire where words and styles are concerned. In the commerce of his art, Castilian doubloons and shekels of Judah and Latin dinars and ancient coins where the Irish shamrock grows flow together with the prodigious treasury of words that make up the English language" (*I*, 24–25). At the same time, Borges professes, whether with disingenuousness I cannot tell, his own linguistic penury; he claims not to have read all of Joyce's masterpiece.

That the Borges of 1925 links Joyce's "innumerable pen" with coins, an image he will later associate with the overpowering aleph (or zahir) experience, is worth noting, for elsewhere in *Inquisitions* he reiterates the view that writers of the non-ultraist camp, writers, that is, who do not winnow from exemplary experience the chaff of circumstantial detail, confront the reader with a kind of literary aleph. Indeed, it is in this very context that Borges uses in his writings for the first time the term "aleph." In a review of Ramón Gómez de la Serna's *La Sagrada Cripta del Pombo*, a suprisingly favorable review considering Borges' often-expressed preference for Don Ramón's literary rival Rafael Cansinos-Asséns, Borges admires precisely that quality in Don Ramón's work that is absent from his own; he rejoices in Gómez de la Serna's hearty, all-encompassing enthusiasm for detailing every facet of life. Likening the Spaniard's passionate enumerations to those of Walt Whitman, Borges alleges that he prefers those of Don Ramón, which focus the reader's mind not on a "welter" of things that taken together make up the world but on individual things seen sharply, one by one. "What sign," writes Borges,

> can capture in abbreviated form the sense of Ramón's work? I would put over it the sign Alef, which in the new mathematics stands for the infinite cipher that contains all the rest, or the bristling weathervane that untiringly urges its darts in every direction. . . . Ramón has inventoried the world, including in his pages not just the

exemplary events of the human adventure, as poetry is wont to do, but the anxious description of each one of the things which, assembled, make up the world. (*I*, 124)

Borges seems in this passage implicitly to disparage poets who, like himself, write only of "the exemplary events of the human adventure." In a similar way, he pejoratively compares his own writing—and by extension his own sensibility—with that of Pedro Leandro Ipuche. In "Ipuche's Americanism," he admires the Uruguayan poet's "awed feeling for the forest," his gift of "feeling deeply rooted in and bound up with the living earth" (*I*, 58). This telluric richness, Borges laments, is lacking in his own poetic evocations of city life. Comparing his own use of the word "honda" ("deep") to Ipuche's use of it in *Tierra Honda*, he reflects: "I once applied the adjective 'deep' to 'city,' thinking of those long streets that reach beyond the horizon, down which the suburbs gradually fade and fall away on the outskirts of evening; but the word in Ipuche's mouth means something very different, and speaks of an almost physical feeling for the earth, the earth solemn beneath wandering footsteps and in which a primordial, busy life is seething up" (*I*, 58–59). Borges' self-criticism, of course, is mitigated by the pleasure he clearly betrays in this highly poetic description of Buenos Aires' receding streets. Nevertheless, he ends his essay with what seems to repeat a confession of his own scrawniness of spirit: "One last confession. I have already remarked the joy that swelled my chest as I read over some stanzas of *Tierra Honda*. I would also like to confess a cause of shame. Reciting its words, I have been shaken with longing for the countryside, where what is truly American is reflected in each little weed, and I have suffered the shame of my ill-defined urbanity" (*I*, 60). Borges yearns, here, to experience the raw, untutored exuberance he associates with the Argentine (and Uruguayan) frontier; he longs to shed his urbanity—however one understands the latinism. Both his erudition and his destiny as a singer of the city deprive him, he implies, of a deeply gratifying, elemental aspect of the experience of being *criollo*. But the passage is revealing in another way, as well. It shows Borges connecting his urban(e) intellectualism, and indirectly his poetic stance itself, with a kind of irreality. His urbanity is "ill-defined" ("borrosa") and therefore shameful. Irreality, in this context, connotes an attenuation of vital experience in intellectualism.

Having examined the Zeitgeist in which Borges worked during the 1920s and identified some of the aesthetic ideas he then espoused, one can draw some inferences about the formulations he made, at this early stage in his career, about irreality and its relationship to impoverishment. Coexisting in the essays of *Inquisitions* are several ways of conceiving of *pobreza*. To abstain from using the "prestigious words" (*I*, 149) and ornamental tropes with which the *modernista* poets studded their verse was to prefer language that was "poor" but, for all its plainness, wholesome and authentic. Used in this sense, impoverishment was, for Borges, a desirable attribute. To a second way that Borges understood the notion of impoverishment he attached no small ambivalence. The stripping away of circumstantial detail that an ultraist writer strove for, in order to present to the reader an impersonal, distilled feeling, purified of quotidian residues, effects a kind of impoverishment; the very minutiae of daily life that an ultraist would rigorously exclude from his verse strike Borges as filled with human vitality and thus worthy of enumeration. And yet a third use of impoverishment asserts itself in these passages, an indigence of spirit that causes shame to Borges the intellectual. Whether constrained by straitening aesthetic norms or deprived by his nature and training of the capacity for certain kinds of intense experience, Borges regards himself as less endowed—poorer in being—than some others who go in for pleasures less mediated by reason. He contrasts the intellectual, who lives intimately, as he does, with "concepts that are pure abstraction" and "the man of the senses, carnal man, [who lives] in contact with the external world" (*I*, 148), and he seems to envy the latter. After all, a writer who sets great store by intense affective life must necessarily regret any attenuation of his power to feel.

Integral to Borges' thinking about impoverishment are his ideas concerning the function of language, metaphor, and art. In "Examination of Metaphors" Borges points out that language is far poorer than the experience whose cipher it is. "Seeking out absences in language," he argues, "is like looking for space in the sky" (*I*, 67). Confronted with the aleph that each moment offers him, man copes with a superabundance of perceptions by reducing his experience to language. "The world of appearances," writes Borges,

> is a welter of jumbled perceptions. A glimpse of country sky, that smell, like the smell of resignation, that the fields give off, the pleasant pungency of tobacco burning one's throat, the slackening wind lashing the road before us and a walking stick's submissive uprightness as it offers itself to our hand, all fit together in any consciousness, almost all at once. Language is a functional ordering of this enigmatic abundance of the world . . . its aim is wholly practical: it is a meticulous map that orients us by appearances, a useful password that our fantasy may at times deserve to forget. (*I*, 65–66)

The language we use to encode experience, Borges argues, inevitably impoverishes it. And, in turn, the language with which we eventually express our thoughts and feelings filters from them some of their immediacy and renders them less intense. The task of the poet, Borges would persuade us, is to reinvest life with its original vividness and emotion. The metaphor, born of language's indigence, compensates for the inexpressiveness of language itself. Thus, commenting on Quevedo's elaborate conceits, Borges sees in them "the zeal to restore to every idea the brusque, daring quality that made it startling when first it presented itself to the spirit" (*I*, 45). Like Quevedo's arresting metaphors, the bizarre comparisons of the ultraists were to startle the reader and awake in him fresh imaginative powers that would mirror or respond to the poet's experience. In accomplishing such a revitalizing effect, the artist achieved true magic. "The image," Borges asserts, "is witchcraft." And images were not to be frivolously used. "There is someone," he continues, "superior to the prankster and the magician. I'm referring to the semi-god, the angel, through whose works the world is changed. *To annex new provinces to Being*, to conjure up cities and spaces out of shared reality, is a heroic adventure" (*I*, 28, my emphasis).

The poet, then, could create in a literal sense; his invention

could annex new provinces to being. But he could do so only if
he renounced sheer cleverness and used figurative language only
to express intimate feeling. Borges ends "After Images," the essay in which the passages just quoted appear, with an object
lesson directed at avant-garde writers—*creacionistas* and *ultraístas* alike. "It is no longer enough to say," he remonstrates,

> as poets do, that mirrors are like water. Neither is it enough
> to treat this hypothesis as absolute and suppose, as any
> Huidobro does, that a cool breeze blows off their surfaces or
> that thirsty birds drink them up until nothing is left in the
> frame. We must get past such games. One must express
> that fancy by making it seem *the inescapable reality of a
> mind:* one must portray an individual who passes through
> the glass and who persists in his illusory land (where there
> are colors and shapes, but where everything is ruled by a
> motionless silence) and who feels the shame of being only
> a simulacrum that nights blot out and that a glimpse per-
> mits. (*I*, 29, my emphasis)

Here Borges offers his reader what he deems to be a compelling,
because authentically expressive, conceit involving a mirror. Unlike the ingenious but trivial metaphors that precede it, his own
image, Borges claims, captures what is, for him, a powerfully affective inner reality; it conveys, as Borges puts it, the "inescap-
able reality of a mind."

But what is the nature of the intense experiences that Borges,
in his poetry and in this passage as well, endeavors to convey?
I take Borges at his word when he affirms that the image he develops here is one that portrays an intimate and urgent concern
of his; Borges' dread of masks and mirrors is well known.[30]
Dating from his early childhood, it must have had its source in
primitive and powerful conflicts and fears. What might seem an
innocuous fantasy—the idea that someone might pass through a
looking glass—is for Borges charged with fearfulness and shame.
It is impossible to determine with certainty why Borges should
have had this sort of reaction to mirrors and to masks. Without
guessing at its sources, we should take note that the foray into a
shameful "illusory realm," one unnaturally devoid of movement
and sound, resembles greatly what I have provisionally called

the impoverishing journey that Borges' heroes undertake. The "inmóvil silencio" of the looking glass world that Borges imagines probably anticipates the demeaned topography of Borges' narratives. Moreover, the possibility that Borges' imagined creature may altogether disappear, either because he has been effaced by darkness or has left no trace behind in the material world, prefigures the final annihilation of the fictional heroes Borges will later create.

Yet by no means all that suggests irreality in his early texts is colored by fear or shame. Many of his early poems are suffused with a numinous pleasure, another kind of irreality. (*"Numen inest,"* we recall, is the phrase Borges invokes to describe his feeling for the neighborhoods his verses describe.) Now Borges' early poems are so painfully self-conscious that we may wonder whether the mood they convey is anything more than adolescent soulfulness. Borges the poet, during the 1920s, nurtures in himself—one might well say "indulges in"—an elegiac or wistful cast of mind that he must have thought of as a "poetic" mood. He fancies himself in love, but the reader divines that his love is in the service of poetry, not the reverse; Borges enjoys too much the melancholy that his love awakes in him. From the city, too, Borges extracts just the details that induce in him a dreamy serenity. While other *porteño* poets were noisily celebrating in their verse Buenos Aires' modernity—the city bus inspired more than one *Martinfierrista*[31]—Borges turned in reverie from the thriving center of town and extolled instead the sleepy outlying districts of the city. No traffic clogs the streets Borges depicts. No pedestrians jostle him. In fact, no human presence impinges much on Borges as he communes, in the evening hours, with the sunset and with patios and garden walls.

Though we may judge the mannered intimacy of Borges' early poems to be the artifact of youthful self-importance, it is intimacy nonetheless. And the mood Borges often manages to create is one he associates with irreality. Metaphorically, his walking at the close of day through the outskirts of Buenos Aires, as he does in the poems of *Fervor of Buenos Aires* and *Moon Across the Way,* serves to suggest his exploring the periphery of being itself. In the same way that day fades gradually into night and the city becomes more and more sparse as it joins the surrounding plain, Borges' sense of reality, he would have his reader know, becomes attenuated in the experiences he records in these early poems. Again and again he presses to place himself in a liminal state, on the verges of nonbeing. Let us look at an example. In "La Recoleta" Borges describes and—it is to his credit—gently mocks the attempt that he and a friend make to imagine death. Contemplating the marble tombs in the most fashionable cemetery in Buenos Aires, the poet and his companion fall to reflecting on death, and their mood abstracts them from ordinary life. The poem begins:

> Convencidos de caducidad
> vueltos un poco irreales por el morir altivado en tanto
>   sepulcro
> irrealizados por tanta grave certidumbre de muerte
> nos demoramos en las veredas. . . .
> (*FBA*, unnumbered p. 6)

> Convinced we are transitory
> made a little irreal by the haughty death of so many tombs
> derealized by so much somber certainty of death
> we dally along the paths. . . .

Borges finds beautiful not just the well-kept pathways and monuments but the idea of death itself:

> Hermosa es la serena decisión de las tumbas,
> su arquitectura sin rodeos
> y las plazuelas donde hay frescura de patio
> y el aislamiento y la individuación eternales. . . .
> (*FBA*, unnumbered p. 6)

> The calm decisiveness of the tombs is beautiful,
> their plain-dealing architecture
> and the little clearings with the coolness of a patio
> and eternal solitude, eternal individuation. . . .

Still, he is able to smile at his own soulfulness, and recognize that the peace he foresees in nonbeing is really life's peacefulness. He muses:

> Nos place la quietud,
> equivocamos tal paz de vida con el morir

y mientras creemos anhelar el no-ser
lanzamos jaculatorias a la vida apacible.
(*FBA*, unnumbered p. 6)

The quiet pleases us,
we mistake this peace of life with death
and thinking we yearn for non-being
we utter what are really paeans to peaceful life.

It is at this point that Borges perceives that to conceive of
nonbeing is beyond the power of the living, for, he argues:

sólo el vivir existe.
Son aledaños suyos tiempo y espacio, son arrabales del alma
. . . y en desbaratándose esta,
juntamente caducan el espacio, el tiempo, el morir,
como al cesar la luz
se acalla el simulacro de los espejos
que ya la tarde fue entristeciendo.
(*FBA*, unnumbered pp. 6–7)

Only living exists.
Time and space are its outskirts, the far-flung districts of the
  soul
. . . and when the soul expires,
space, time, death all lapse with it
just as, when the light fails,
the simulacrum in the mirrors is put to rest,
that image already saddened by evening's light.

Just as the advent of evening, as the light fails, blots out the
mirror's image, effacing a world that is already unsettlingly irreal, death obliterates utterly even the derealized life that Borges
has conjured up. Death itself must vanish with the consciousness
that stops imagining it.

The poem ends with the same uncomfortable reflection (and
even with almost the same metaphor) that we found in the passage from "After Images." But the peacefulness Borges describes
in the middle of the poem, a serenity the poet and his companion feel as they try to imagine nonbeing, is a second state
that Borges associates with irreality. The text of the 1920s that

most clearly describes this subtly derealized state, and its relationship to utter loss of self, is "Feeling in Death," a confessional prose piece or, as Borges calls it, "emotional anecdote" (*OC*, 766). Borges surely considered it an important text, for after collecting it in *The Language of the Argentines* in 1928, he again reprinted it in 1936 as part of his ambitious essay "A History of Eternity" and returned to it yet once more in 1946, including it as a section of "A New Refutation of Time." In it, Borges recounts that one evening, after having returned home from Barracas, one of the poorer quarters of the city and one he seldom visited, he went for a walk in his own neighborhood. Suspending purposefulness, he lets chance determine his course, and finds himself tending toward the district where he grew up, "sections," he tells us, "that arouse in me a kind of reverence" (*IA*, 148; *OI*, 179). He continues: "I do not mean by this my own neighborhood, the precise environment of my childhood, but rather the still mysterious fringe area beyond it, an area . . . that is at the same time familiar and mythological to me. Those penultimate streets are for me the other face of the known, its far side, almost as completely unknown as the buried foundation of our house or our invisible skeleton" (*IA*, 148; translation adapted from *L*, 225 and *OI*, 179).

In examining this passage it is useful to recall that Freud, in his 1919 essay "The 'Uncanny,'" remarks on the curious double meaning of the German word "Unheimliche," which may mean either "known, familiar" or "concealed and unknown." Freud argues that an experience of the uncanny may entail apprehending at the same time something intimately known and disavowed by consciousness.[32] Emerging, or, more accurately, almost emerging from repression in the unconscious, a thought may produce a feeling of uncanniness. It is interesting, then, that Borges experiences Palermo's back streets as "at the same time familiar and mythological," ("vecino y mitológico a un tiempo") both familiar—"the other face of the known" ("el revés de lo concodio")—and yet strange ("ignoradas"). He seems sensible of the same doubleness in his own perception that Freud remarks, and the mysteriousness Borges feels seems akin to the uncanny feeling for which Freud tries to account.

Having relaxed the thews of conscious will, Borges falls into a peaceful, numinous state:

> I breathed in the night, feeling a peaceful respite from thought. What I saw—it was uncomplicated to be sure—seemed simplified by my fatigue. Its very typicality made it look irreal. The street was lined with low houses, and, although the first impression it created was of poverty, the second was surely of happiness. . . . Above the muddy, chaotic ground a rose-colored wall seemed not to harbor moonlight but to shed an intimate light of its own.
>
> I stood looking at that simplicity. (*IA*, 148–49; translation adapted from *L*, 226 and *OI*, 179)

In the thrice-mentioned simplicity of what Borges contemplates, the poorness of the houses, Borges' weariness, and finally his sense of intimacy, we find portrayed the irreality of impoverishment that so often, in Borges' writing, immediately precedes a more drastic experience of release from self. And here, too, an epiphanic moment is at hand. In a "vertiginous silence" broken only, perhaps, by a bird's song—we think of Keats' nightingale and its immortality—or "the equally intemporal [sound] of the crickets," Borges intuits that time is meaningless. The scene, as he surveys it, is not just similar to but literally the same as it was some twenty years before. The absolute identity of the two moments in time explodes historical temporality, and in "ecstasy" Borges feels his selfhood fall away. He reports: "I felt dead, I felt myself to be an abstract perceiver of the world: that undefined fear imbued with knowledge which is metaphysics' finest clarity. . . . I suspected I possessed the reticent or absent meaning of the inconceivable word *eternity*. Only later was I able to define that fantasy" (*IA*, 150; translation adapted from *L*, 226 and *OI*, 180).

In "Feeling in Death," then, Borges describes an experience of irreality whose two stages correspond rather precisely to the derealized impoverishment and the annihilation that his narrative paradigm depicts. In the first stage of derealization Borges relinquishes volition. He wanders alone, deliberately not choosing his route, through streets that appear to him both intimately known and yet unfamiliar, surroundings that he perceives as impoverished and irreal but that nevertheleses are colored by a sense of happiness. This initial feeling of mysteriousness and well-being gives way to a dizzying moment in which Borges is seized by an ecstatic, although fearsome, certainty. He intuits, in this second and more intense phase of irreal experience, that his personal being is extinct (he "feels dead") but that revealed to his impersonal, abstract consciousness is "the world." Outside time, he apprehends eternity.

In 1980, speaking with Willis Barnstone and Jorge Oclander in one of the many public dialogues in which he has taken part, Borges is quick to declare that he is no mystic. Yet despite his disclaimer he goes on to add: "In my life I only had two mystical experiences and I can't tell them because what happened is not to be put into words, since words, after all, stand for a shared experience. . . . Twice in my life I had a feeling rather agreeable than otherwise. It was astounding, astounding. I was overwhelmed, taken aback. I had the feeling of living not in time but outside time."[33] Speaking again with Barnstone later that year, Borges alludes once more to these two absolute moments, this time supplying a context for one of them that gives a hint of what may have triggered it. "Two timeless moments have geen given me," he says and continues:

> One came through quite an ordinary way. Suddenly I felt somehow I am beyond time. And the other came after a woman had told me that she couldn't love me and I felt very unhappy. I went for a long walk. I went to a railway station in the south of Buenos Aires. Then, suddenly, I got that feeling of timelessness, of eternity. I don't know how long it lasted, since it was timeless. But I felt very grateful for it. Then I wrote a poem on the railway station wall (I shouldn't have done that!)[34]

Borges almost certainly recounts the first of his mystical experiences, the one that "came through quite an ordinary way," in "Feeling in Death." If this is so, then both experiences inspired him to write about them. But what is most striking about Borges' recollection of these events is his linking of a painful experience of loss with the second timeless moment, as though the sentimental reverse he had suffered had made him susceptible of falling out of time. We recall that once before, when parting from a friend, Borges reports having been seized with a similar conviction—that the self does not exist. He describes the experience in "The Nothingness of Personality." Borges' powerful experiences of irreality at these moments of loss are important to understand, for they serve as one model for the irreality of annihilation in his work. It may be that at these moments, assailed by unhappiness, Borges involuntarily warded off painful feelings by experiencing life as irreal. A self that has collapsed into nonbeing cannot, after all, fall prey to dejection, and in a timeless world such as the one Borges intuits, he need never face the end of love.

I shall return in chapter 4 to the notion that an experience of loss may precipitate in Borges a flight toward irreality. For the moment, though, I shall take another tack and ask what sort of pleasure it can be that Borges so often links with the irreality of impoverishment. A passage from *Evaristo Carriego* provides an important clue.

Less a biography of the minor *porteño* poet than an evocation of Buenos Aires at the turn of the century, *Evaristo Carriego* is a puzzling and ambivalent book. Borges began work on it in 1929, so enthusiastic about rescuing from obscurity Carriego and his verse that he was willing to incur his parents' disapproval by writing about a subject they deemed unworthy. But for all his initial eagerness, the volume Borges produced in 1930 talks so little about Carriego, and, when it does examine his poetry, finds such fault with it, that one wonders whether Borges meant after all to immortalize the *criollo* poet with faint praise. Yet the book is of interest to us because in it Borges can be seen to formulate and recast the motif of the duel. In the 1927 text "Men Fought" ("Hombres pelearon"), the first piece of narrative Borges attempted, he had already portrayed a knife fight between two streetwise toughs. He reworks this material several times in *Evaristo Carriego*, generating several variants of the original sequence of events. And once, when he does so, he draws an unexpected connection between the motif of the duel and the peaceful experience of irreality I have noted in his early poems.

Describing, as he does in "Feeling in Death," the peacefulness of his early evening walks, Borges links the tranquil irreality of his reverie with a bit of narrative, a story that, he says, is the emblem of his pleasurable mood. He writes:

> When the impatient October nights drew chairs and people out onto the sidewalks, and you could see all the way into the deepened houses, and the patios were bathed in a yellow light, the street was confidential in its fickleness, and the hollow houses were like lanterns hung in a row. *That impression of irreality and serenity is best recalled by me in a story or symbol, which seems to have been always with me.* It is the shred of a tale that I overheard in a corner store and that was at the same time trivial and complex. Without any claim to being accurate, I set it down here. The hero of that careless Odyssey was the eternal Argentine, pursued by the law, betrayed in this case by a hateful, mis-shapen man who nevertheless was without a match on the guitar. The tale, the snatch of the tale I can salvage, tells how, wandering the moonlit streets the tired wind brought him wafts of the guitar, how he followed that trail among the labyrinths and inconstancies of the wind, how he turned and turned once more Buenos Aires' corners, how he arrived at the out-of-the-way threshold where the traitor played, how, opening a way for himself among the listeners, he lifted him on his knife, how he fled recklessly and escaped, leaving silenced and dead the traitor and his tale-telling guitar. (*OC*, 108–9, my emphasis)

That Borges connects a feeling of peacefulness with so violent a vignette is startling; betrayal and murderous vengeance are curiously at odds with the irreal serenity that, Borges asserts, the story epitomizes and for him represents. One can make sense of this apparent incongruence of content and feeling-tone by subjecting the anecdote to the kind of exegesis appropriate to dreams. This fragment of narrative, of course, is not a dream. Yet Borges presents it as material whose origin is obscure, as if it emerged from the unconscious itself, and he rehearses it mentally in the way that one would a gratifying and soothing fantasy.

Dreams distort their forbidden context in systematic and comprehensive ways to mask raw desire and make it tolerable. A dream's manifest content may condense into a single event more than one element of latent fantasy, and a single dream character may allude to or represent more than one of the dramatis personae of the dreamer's thoughts. In the temporality of a dream, events may occur out of the sequence to which they adhere in the fantasy underlying the dream. And emotional coloration may also undergo distortion. In *The Interpretation of Dreams* Freud notes that the affect that accompanies a dream may be the reverse of the affect proper to the latent dream-thoughts.[35] If one analyzes Borges' anecdote keeping in mind these principles of dream representation, it is possible to interpret the little tale and to explain why Borges finds such pleasure in it. In the betrayal and chastisement that the story recounts we recognize motifs connected, in the *Infamy* texts, with oedipal rivalry and the punishment it incurs. The encounter between the "eternal Argentine" ("eterno criollo") and his foe represents, in a complex way, an oedipal duel, a son's assault on his father that at once succeeds and is put down. For embodied in the hero of the tale are both father and son. The *criollo* has, like an upstart son, affronted the law, or paternal authority, and is being hunted down by the police as the anecdote begins. He is thus in part a filial figure in the tale. At the same time, though, the *criollo* represents aspects of a paternal figure. In that he avenges himself on a traitor, he embodies a father who wreaks retribution on a son. (That the traitor is a masterful guitarist—an artist of sorts—makes him in another way like the filial reprobates Borges will portray in the *Infamy* sketches several years later.)

The story's hero, then, manifests both filial and paternal attributes. Similarly, the plot conflates in a single killing an assault against a paternal figure and the punishment that this assault incurs. We have seen that the knifing of the guitarist may represent a father's punishing of his son's betrayal of him (a betrayal that may take the form of the son's artistic pursuits). But if we disarticulate the temporal sequence of the tale, another way of understanding the story appears. By transposing to the end of the story the *criollo*'s pursuit by the law, it is possible to see that, in part of the fantasy underlying the anecdote, the murder may precede, rather than follow, the *criollo*'s flight from the police. The action of the story condenses into a single event what may, in the original fantasy that the story recasts, be two acts of aggression, one punishing the other.

Interpreted in this way, the vignette that so pleases Borges can be seen to mask the theme of oedipal strife. The reader feels excitement in the story's long last sentence, whose periodic structure sweeps the action headlong toward the murder. Borges makes one share the exhilaration he feels at the fantasy of dispatching his father and getting away with it. Yet enough in the tale disavows this fantasy to render it acceptable to Borges' consciousness. For one thing, the anecdote includes the punishment for this assault, itself adequately disguised. And, what is just as important, the affective coloration of the tale—the irreal serenity that Borges links with it—may serve to disguise from Borges the story's forbidden import. The mood Borges associates with the anecdote may, that is, reverse the affect that the story's events aroused in Borges' unconscious. If irreality, in this passage, serves the end of distancing Borges from oedipal ambition and masking oedipal strife, then the same feeling-tone in his stories may perhaps serve the same function.

Still another mechanism by means of which Borges keeps at a safe remove the story's naked conflict is his ambiguous manner of explaining its source. By telling us that the story "seems to have been always with me," he seems to suggest that it has its origin within his self, and, moreover, that it has the status of a primitive fantasy, one dating from an early stage in his childhood. At the same time, though, Borges disavows authorship of the tale; he says he is merely relating a bit of narrative that he once overheard in an *almacén*. Further, he casts some doubt on his ability to report accurately the "snatch of the tale [he] can salvage"; he demurs, "without any claim to accuracy, I set it down here." The ambiguity about the origin of the anecdote may express Borges' own ambivalent wish to repudiate the psychic material to which the story gives voice. Of course, Borges' claim that he may not accurately recall the story of the *criollo* presages a technique he will later use less naively in his fictional works; many of his narrators protest that, for reasons they cannot help, they have imperfect access to their own sources of information. Thus, to wonder why Borges troubles to tell us at all of the presumed source of the *Evaristo Carriego* vignette is to wonder, as well, why in Borges' later fictional texts his speakers, denied full access to the sources they claim to cite, unwillingly falsify the stories they relate. It may be that this technique, one that Borges comes to exploit consciously, was born of a psychic mechanism by which Borges unconsciously expressed ambivalence toward the unsavory ambitions his stories represent.

The passage from *Evaristo Carriego* is for our purposes an important text. A casual reminiscence buried in a minor work, it allows us to guess that one source of the irreality of impoverishment in Borges' mature tales may be oedipal conflict. Imperfectly repressed, present yet disavowed, Borges' filial strivings may constitute a source of the derealized quality of his finest tales. If this is so, it tends to confirm Freud's view that one source of uncanny feelings may be the arousal of "something familiar and old-established in the mind that has been estranged only by the process of repression."[36] Yet how a writer's scarcely repressed desires and fears work, mediated by his text, to produce in a reader an uncanny or irreal effect is difficult to show. For the moment, we must confront once more the task, a somewhat more manageable one, to be sure, of tracing the thoughts and feelings Borges connects with impoverishment and irreality. We are now in a position to discern that, quite apart from his aesthetics and metaphysical musings, intimate feelings almost certainly underlie Borges' formulations about impoverishment and the irreal. We have traced Borges' conceptualizations about impoverishment—as distinct from his feelings of depersonalization and of personal diminishment—from his early discussions of poetic principle. Let us now examine the essays he produced as he turned from examining the mechanics of prosody to analyzing those of other genres.

During most of the 1920s Borges' principal aesthetic interests revolved around poetry and the possibilities for distilling strong feeling in unsentimental verse. At the same time, in theoretical essays like "The Nothingness of Personality," he intermittently took up metaphysical topics that intrigued him. And in prose works of a frankly confessional cast he began to describe his own experience in metaphysical terms. Already he had begun to integrate into a single system of mind his ideas about aesthetics, his philosophical idealism, and his inner, affective life. This process he will continue but not complete in the essays of *Discussion*. Toward the end of the 1920s Borges' aesthetic interests shift. While he continues to develop the same metaphysical themes, he begins to theorize not so much about poetry as about fiction and film and the modes of presenting the world that their makers employ. In *Discussion*, a volume that contains essays originally published between the middle of 1928 and early 1932, Borges ruminates about the implications of verisimilitude, or the lifelike depiction of an imagined reality.

What unifies the volume is Borges' belief, expressed both in excursus on metaphysical themes and in essays that deal with verisimilitude, that "in the face of an incalculable, enigmatic reality," man must founder, ill equipped as he is to apprehend, with his endowment of mind and sense, "the momentary universe" (*OC*, 198, 200). But this is to intellectualize. It is Borges' vivid and imaginative ways of figuring man's impoverishment that catch one's eye, together with the surprising gratitude he displays for the very limitations at which he ought to chafe. The Borges of these essays regards with positive cheerfulness each new proof of his own incapacities and relative helplessness. He celebrates, in "The Versions of Homer," his innocence of a knowledge of classical Greek, concluding that it has the happy effect of enhancing his pleasure in Homeric translations; relieving him of the obligation to attend to pedantic questions of fidelity, his ignorance renders the *Iliad* and the *Odyssey* potentially infinite texts, each of whose variants may claim a special charm. And in "A Vindication of Basilides the False" he approves the gnostic cosmogony because it views our poor material realm as one among many imperfect worlds, rudely fashioned by a pitiful subaltern god. Concluding his essay rather with smugness than with the resignation one might expect, he asks, "What better gift can we hope for, than to be insignificant?" (*OC*, 216; *BR*, 27).

It is no accident that in both of these examples Borges derives a notion of impoverishment, however benign that impoverishment may be, from the concept of infinity. *Discussion* shows us a Borges who has moved the idea of the infinite to the center of his intellectual field. In many of his previous writings that take up aesthetic themes, Borges does not ground the opposition between "pobreza" and "riqueza"—"impoverishment" and "richness"—in the contrast between the little that man can apprehend or express and the aleph-like infinite of the outer and inner worlds. Instead, we recall, he thought of impoverishment as connected with spareness of diction and the de-emphasizing of personal circumstance. And in his confessional texts he hints at still another kind of psychic structure that may, for him, have to do with impoverishment and the irreal.

Borges' original conviction that in order to convey intense feelings the poet should abstract his emotion from the occasion from which it springs does survive in *Discussion* and in Borges' later works but in a vestigial way. Long after he has given up proselytizing for a particular poetic gospel, he conjoins two attributes that, to his mind, epitomize what he admires in many of the writers and conceptual systems he describes. He judges them to be "passionate," "monumental," or "intense" and, at the same time, "precise," "lucid," "limpid," "rigorous," or "poor." Thus, when writing of Schopenhauer, Borges regularly assigns to him the epithet "apasionado y lúcido" ("passionate and lucid"). And, applauding two of Bertrand Russell's works for their elegant reformulation of Zeno's second paradox, he calls them "books of an inhuman *lucidity*, unsatisfactory and *intense*" (*OC*, 246, my emphasis). In a different sort of context, he describes Josef Von Sternberg's photography in *The Docks of New York*, remembering certain particularly effective shots: "the shot of the already *precise* dawn, the shot of the *monumental* billiard balls waiting for the impact of other balls" (*OC*, 222, my emphasis). Conversely, he damns Charlie Chaplin's *City Lights*, a film that in Borges' view "is nothing more than a *languid* [not intense] anthology of small mishaps, superimposed on a *sentimental* [not rigorous] story line" (*OC*, 223, my emphasis).

As for the constellation of oedipal concerns that Borges has begun to express in writings like "Men Fought" and passages from *Evaristo Carriego*, he does not incorporate this material, or does not, at any rate, in any visible way, in the essays of *Discussion*. He will keep separate a little longer the theme of father-son rivalry and his treatment of aesthetic and metaphysical questions. It is chiefly to narrative—the *Universal History* texts—that he will relegate, during most of the early 1930s, the expression of this side of his inner life.

Borges helped to prepare himself technically for the task of writing narrative by examining closely, in the early 1930s, how various writers and filmmakers go about creating the illusion that the worlds they portray exist. As a poet, Borges had been primarily concerned to express his intimate feeling, not to cajole a reader into imagining with him a fictive time and place. Now, though, he seems intent on studying how to "postulate reality." In June 1931 he published in the literary magazine *Azul* what was to be the first of a number of essays that bear on this subject. As Sylvia Molloy has pointed out, "The Postulation of Reality" is an uncomfortable title, for it implies not that a writer describes an existing world but that he invents the world he offers to the reader.[37] Borges thus premises his study of verisimilitude with the idea that the ulterior existence of an imagined world is beside the point. And, indeed, Borges opens his analysis by examining a historical, not a fictional text. Quoting at length from Gibbon's *Decline and Fall of the Roman Empire*, he anatomizes what he understands to be intricate *rhetorical devices* by means of which Gibbon draws his reader into complicity in accepting the idea that Attila and his Huns and Thuringians did actually engage the Franks in a complex sequence of hostilities. Of course, it is

Borges' own inclination to think that Gibbon's text may *not* correspond to and report "real" events that surprises us here.

In the course of the essay, Borges subjects several other texts to the same sort of scrutiny and identifies three ways a writer can "registrar una realidad," that is, "give an account of an [imagined] reality (*OC*, 218). All three techniques that Borges singles out require that the writer appear to take for granted that his imagined world exists, and that he intimate that it exists in a more complicated way than his account of it details. Paradoxically, it is by seeming to impoverish the presumed reality he describes that a writer creates a feeling of verisimilitude. Borges does not miss the chance explicitly to affiliate his aesthetic observations with his musings on infinity. He ventures the hypothesis that "imprecision is tolerable or plausible in literature because we are always inclined to it in reality." And he follows this observation with an eloquent aside:

> The conceptual simplification of complex states is often an instantaneous operation. The very act of perceiving, of heeding, is of a selective order; every attention, every fixation of our conscience, implies a deliberate omission of that which is uninteresting. We see and hear by means of remembrances, fears, foresight. In all corporal matters, unconsciousness is a necessity of physical acts. Our body knows how to articulate this difficult paragraph; deal with stairs, with knots, with crossings, with cities, with rushing rivers, with dogs; it knows how to cross a street without being obliterated by the traffic; it knows how to procreate; it knows how to breathe; it knows how to sleep; it knows perhaps how to kill: our body, not our intellect. Our lives are a series of adaptations, that is to say, the educating of forgetfulness. (*OC*, 218; *BR*, 31)

Borges continues, both in his film reviews and in a further essay, "Magic and Narrative Art" (published in the summer of 1932), to study the tricks a writer or film director can use to manipulate the response of the reader or moviegoer. In particular, Borges turns his attention to techniques that distort a figured world in a subtle and unsettling way and those that, conversely, dispel what would normally be the reader's disbelief. For example, he praises Charlie Chaplin's early films for their "deliberate irreality." "There are realistic films," he writes, "and there are films that are wilfully irreal." And he continues, "To this second genre Chaplin's primitive beguilements belong, helped along no doubt by superficial photography, by the spectral speed of the action, and by the fraudulent moustaches, outlandish fake chinwhiskers, tousled wigs and portentous frock coats of the actors" (*OC*, 223). Chaplin, notes Borges, turns to excellent effect the very unlifelikeness imposed by an imperfect technology, and, compounding in intended ways the film's quality of artifice, achieves great comic and aesthetic success. In a similar way, he compliments King Vidor's use, in the movie *Street Scene*, of "a glorious, excessive Italian, larger than life, who has in his evident charge the whole comicality of the work, and whose vast irreality rubs off on his normal colleagues" (*OC*, 225). And he notices that by astutely making use of "oblique (and therefore distorting) photography," Russian directors achieve an expressive effect greater than that produced by "a thousand and one Hollywood extras" (*OC*, 224).

"Magic and Narrative Art" begins with a similar kind of analysis. Borges, fascinated with the bewitching power of a writer to conjure away a reader's disbelief, examines William Morris' technique, in his narrative poem *The Life and Death of Jason,* for inducing his reader to accept without marveling the centaurs and mermaids that the poem portrays. An apt student, Borges immediately puts into effect what he has learned. In a long footnote he gives a history of the mermaid's portrayal in literature, in the course of which he himself nudges the reader toward thinking of mermaids as part of the natural world. Consider how craftily Borges shapes the following paragraph:

> In the course of time, mermaids have changed their form. Their first historian, the rhapsodist of the twelfth book of the *Odyssey,* does not tell us what they were like;

> for Ovid, they are birds of reddish plumage and virgin's face; for Apollonius of Rhodes, they are women from the waist up and birds from the waist down; for the master Tirso de Molina (and for heraldry) "half women, fishes half." What nature of creature they are is no less in doubt; Lemprière's classical dictionary takes them to be nymphs, Quicherat's, monsters and Grimal's, demons. They dwell on an island near the setting sun, near Circe's isle, but the corpse of one of them, Parthenope, was found in Campania, and gave its name to the famous city that now is called Naples. (*OC*, 228)

The reader, initially secure in the knowledge that mermaids are imaginary creatures, resists the ambiguousness of the first sentence of Borges' note. If Borges says that mermaids, in the course of time, have changed their form, he must, we infer, really mean that the writers who have depicted them have described them in different ways. The second sentence confirms our understanding of the first; it documents, citing in one case chapter and verse, four literary descriptions of the siren. True, Borges refers to the rhapsodist of the *Odyssey*'s twelfth book as a "historian," but we take this as a graceful figure of speech. The third sentence begins, as the first does, in an ambiguous way. "What nature of creature they are is no less in doubt" hints once again that mermaids may exist and may occasion the same kind of taxonomic debate that any rare and exotic species might arouse. But still we refuse this reading, for immediately following it is a scholarly reference to classical dictionaries. However, Borges has slyly prepared us to give over our scruples and finally acquiesce in the notion that mermaids exist. He can now boldly assert, "They dwell on an island near the setting sun, near Circe's isle." The paragraph's final sentence gives the reader no quarter; he is bound in imaginative collusion with Borges. He must admit that mermaids actually do exist.

Later, in his fiction as well as in half-fanciful, half-learned little books like *The Book of Imaginary Beings* and *The Book of Dreams*, Borges will put to good use the narrative strategies he masters here. But if Borges learns how to demystify the fanciful, he also perceives that a skillful writer can impart to quite ordinary things a certain eeriness. He analyzses what he takes to be Poe's success, in the *Narrative of A. Gordon Pym,* in endowing the glacial runoff of an antarctic land with a disquieting opacity. While I confess that when I read the passage Borges cites, in its original context, my hackles do not rise, Borges makes a case for Poe's ability to create a subtle but sinister—and irreal—effect.

Thus ends the first part of "Magic and Narrative Art." Having explicated these texts, Borges turns to the theoretical part of his argument. "One rightly infers from the foregoing," he reflects, "that the central problem of the novel is causality" (*OC*, 230). Now, despite what Borges says, his essay's second part does not ground itself logically on what has gone before. The question that Borges now proceeds to address is not how to make the marvelous appear real or the quotidian uncanny. It is how to construct a narrative so that a reader will make associative connections among various elements of a text, connections that deepen his experience of the novel or tale in question. As Borges sees it, there are two ways for a writer to preserve the unity of a long text. One, used by psychological novelists, is to "[dream up] or [rig] a concatenation of motives whose aim it is not to differ from those of the real world" (*OC*, 230). A scrupulously detailed and lifelike accounting for the motivation of each character's acts, one that eventually reveals a believable cause for every effect, is one of the two methods that Borges identifies. He discounts it as little used. The other, he says, is to make "ludic and atavistic" use of "the primitive clarity of magic" (*OC*, 230).

By "magic" Borges means the bringing together in a narrative of elements that in no literal way bear on one another, but that the reader links, drawing meaning from their association. To cite one of the examples Borges provides, one of G. K. Chesterton's tales begins with the apparently off-handed mention of an Indian who throws his knife at another man and kills him. The tale goes on to describe a man stabbed with an arrow wielded by his friend. "A flying knife," Borges notes, "an arrow grasped in a fist. The repercussion of words is far-reaching" (*OC*, 232). Narrative, Borges concludes, ought to be mined with symmetries of this sort; it should be "a precise game of alertness, echoes and affinities" (*OC*, 231).

So accustomed are we, as readers, to the premise that our task is to seek out and appreciate symmetries and affinities of just this kind, that we may think Borges' "discovery" here a little naive. So it may be. Two things, however, need to be re-marked. One is that Borges' exploding of logical causality as a feature of narrative suggests Zeno's paradox, which proves that, in a strict sense, nothing can be related to anything else.[38] Thus even in an essay devoted to studying an aesthetic effect, Borges betrays an inclination to be swayed in his thinking by the metaphysical ideas that most attract him. The other feature of interest to us here is that Borges is quite in earnest when he calls the magic of narrative "atavistic" and "primitive." He refers the reader to anthropology that describes the use of sympathetic magic by various "primitive" tribes—the redskins of Nebraska, the medicine men of Central Australia, and Malayan voodoo artists, to name a few. Borges' own depiction of primitive peoples, in his later tales, makes us stop and take note that even at this point in his literary career Borges as-sociates them with practices that mock the predictability of what we accept as real; their magic, he says, "is the crowning glory or nightmare of the causal" (*OC*, 231).

"Nightmare." Here is a new side of irreality, one that arises in tandem with—and perhaps in some part as a consequence of—Borges' study of verisimilitude. The nightmarish, mon-strous, or "atroz" seldom makes its appearance in Borges' very early work, nor is he very much concerned with the portrayal of the uncanny before the essays of *Discussion*. It is here that these preoccupations make their debut. It is primarily in his writing about mirrors that, during the 1920s, he betrays any-thing but pleasurable feelings in connection with the irreal. Certainly, one should not minimize how important is that com-ponent of Borgean irreality that derives from the shame and fear he associates with mirrors. Yet, at the same time, it is important to bear in mind that the Borges who wrote the essays of *Discussion* is a happy Borges, pleased with his own wit and untroubled by many of the anxieties that darken his later work. The permutations of the notion of infinity neither arise from nor prompt in Borges any dread of chaos or insanity, as they will in "Funes the Memorious" or, for that matter, any of a number of Borges' finest tales. Absent, too, from his essays of the early 1930s, is the notion of pantheism that so informs both his mature narratives and many of the later essays he will write.

There is one other discernible and important way in which Borges prepares himself, in the essays he collected in *Discussion* and *A History of Eternity*, to create his greatest stories. In two essays, one of them published in 1929 in the magazine *Síntesis* and the other as the centerpiece of the 1936 collection of essays *A History of Eternity*, Borges explored in scholarly earnest the related histories of hell and eternity as concepts developed by man and fashioned after his need. Tracing in writings drawn from philosophy, theology, and literature the evolution of the two concepts, Borges ends each piece by offering the reader an account of an experience of his own—modest intimations but moving ones nonetheless—that have to do with timelessness and hell.

Both essays discuss the idea of eternity. Borges confesses, in "The Duration of Hell," that what he finds so compelling about the idea of hell—and he says that "no other theological matter holds the same power and fascination for me" (*OC*, 236)—is not the apparatus of torture, luridly portrayed in various ways by writers and Christian theologians. It is, rather, "the strict notion—*place of eternal punishment for the wicked. . . .* The attribute of eternity," Borges affirms, "is the horrifying one" (*OC*, 236, Borges' emphasis). And "A History of Eternity" clearly relates at least one of the conceptions of eternity that Borges describes, Hans Lassen Martensen's formulation of it as *"immediata et lucida fruitio rerum infinitarum,"* to the conception of the aleph that Borges will later invent. Still more interesting for our discussion of Borges' dual conception of the irreal is that both essays oppose and relate two imagined realms, one intolerable by virtue of its infinity or eternity, the other impoverished and phantasmal, sapped of being. Those religious thinkers who argue against the belief that hell is everlasting, Borges notes in "The Duration of Hell," envision immortality as a blessing bestowed on the good, and eventual extinction as the fate of the damned, destined, as this branch of theology has it, to be forgotten by God. Borges, following the Lutheran theologian Richard Rothe, paints for his reader an uncomfortable, slightly uncanny halfway house between life and the cessation of being. Rothe, he says, "favors a dwindling, waning life for reprobates." Borges goes on, "He foresees them, prowling around the edges of Creation, through the emptiness of infinite space, sustaining themselves with leftovers of life." According to Rothe's vision, the governance of hell must fall to the lot of a series of potentates, since all of the demons who occupy the throne of hell "succumb to the ghostliness of their being" (*OC*, 237).[39] They fade, that is, into utter nonexistence.

Borges' interest in an impoverished, empty kind of hell where personal identity languishes or is forfeit, can be seen elsewhere in the essay as well, both in a footnote in which he enumerates various writers' conceptions of hell and in the afterword he appends to the essay. For the Sabians, Borges' note informs us, hell is figured as a place "whose four vestibules, one atop another, let in threads of dirty water onto the floor, but whose principal chamber is vast, dusty, void of anyone." Swedenborg's hell, he continues, is also a dismal place "whose gloom the damned, who have rejected heaven, do not perceive" (*OC*, 236). (Some five years later Borges will return to Swedenborg's conception of hell. He elaborates it in "El teólogo" ["The Theologian"], published in *Crítica* on 23 June 1934 and reprinted under the revised titled "A Theologian in Death" in *A Universal History of Infamy*.) Also exempt from brimstone and engines of torture is the hell that Borges tells us he himself imagines in a dream. He describes it in a personal postscript to his treatise on hell. As he would with Swedenborg's hell, Borges was to return to this postscript, reprinting it under the title "Un infierno" ("One Man's Hell"), together with three other short prose pieces in the 15 September 1934 entertainment section of *Crítica*.[40] Here is his account:

> I dreamed that I was emerging from another [dream]— populous with cataclysms and tumult—and that I awaked in an unrecognizable room. It was getting light: a slow generalized light defined the foot of the iron bedstead, the strict chair, the closed door and windows, the empty table.

> I thought with fear, *Where am I?* and I understood that
> I did not know. I thought, *Who am I?* and could not recog-
> nize myself. Fear welled up in me. I thought: This un-
> solaced wakefulness is already Hell, this fateless wakeful-
> ness will be my eternity. Then I truly woke up: trembling.
> (*OC*, 238)

The irreal quality of this nightmarish text depends partly
on the *mise en abîme* of the idea that dreams may be contained
within dreams; how can Borges be completely sure he is awake
as he records the dream, and how can we, his readers, be entirely sure that we, too, are not on the verge of waking up into
a "more real" world? In part, however, it is the strangeness of
the room, the crepuscular diffusion of the light that suffuses it,
the starkness of its furnishings, and the claustrophobia of its
closed windows and doors that convey the desolateness that
Borges links with a state of diminished, although not wholly
annihilated, being. His fearful disorientation and failure to
know who he is—and the hint that he may not, even when
awake, fully exist—remind us of the shameful divestiture of a
secure sense of self that we have seen Borges express, particularly in passages about mirrors. How different is that state of
enfeebled being from the pleasurable state of numinousness that
Borges describes in happier texts, a state that nevertheless serves
as another precursor of Borges' irreality of impoverishment.
These two currents eventually come to merge in Borges' writings. Yet why Borges conflates them remains for us to see.

In the meantime, we should remark that the first of the
dreams out of which Borges awakes is as "populous with cata-
clysms and tumult" as the second is barren. Borges regularly
opposes two irreal states, one impoverished, the other preternat-
urally replete with things and events. In "A History of Eternity" this opposition reappears as the counterposing of realist
and nominalist belief. In tracing the evolution of the concept
of eternity, Borges opens by giving an account of Plotinus' Neo-
platonist, or realist, conception of eternity. The material world,
according to Plotinus, is not as real as the world of archetypal
forms. These eternally existing forms are prototypes for their
multiple imperfect copies that make up the temporal, material

world. Borges, it is clear, is slightly horrified by this "eternity that is poorer than the world" (*OC*, 358). Our own world, he tells us, is more populous and rich in variety than "the motionless, terrible museum of Platonic archetypes," in which Borges senses something nightmarish; he calls it "quiet, monstrous and classified" (*OC*, 355) and later refer to it as "glacial" (*OC*, 358). Contrasted with the realist view expounded in Plotinus' *Enneads* is the more modern conception of eternity as God's "contemporaneous and total intuition of all the fractions of time" (*OC*, 361), an eternity far more copious than is our world. Moreover, some theologians, Borges notes, expand this conception of eternity to embrace not only the actual past, present and future but infinite virtual ones that might have happened or may yet take place. It is this infinitely more ample eternity whose imagined printed history will fill the shelves of Borges' library of Babel.

These two visions of eternity, one poorer than our world, the other richer, remind us of the two opposed conceptions of poetry, and literature in general, that, a decade before, Borges defended against one another with so much fervor. Borges himself makes this connection explicit. He says of the more copious eternity, "Unlike the Platonic eternities, whose greatest risk is insipidity, this one is in danger of resembling the last pages of *Ulysses*" (*OC*, 363). Consistently, then, in his prose writings of the 1920s and early 1930s, be they discussions of aesthetic principles or confessional texts, Borges entertains, and relates to one another, notions of contrasting states: overabundance and privation, excess and penury. And bringing to bear his metaphysical habits of mind and his understanding of his own affective states on this bipartite conception, he comes to link with each of the two conditions a modality of the irreal. Here, then, are precursors of what I have called the irreality of impoverishment on the one hand and the irreality of annihilation on the other, that all of Borges' mature narratives in one way or another portray.

Yet we may ask how Borges comes to conflate, in his irreality of impoverishment, two separate experiences of derealization, one of the shameful undercutting of his own claim to being, the other of numinous pleasure. That Borges dreams of hell, locus of eternal punishment, as a barren place where his being is at risk may afford a clue. Whatever the conflicts—and I have not ventured to guess what they might be—that Borges associates with mirrors, he understands the ebbing away of selfhood as a form of punishment. So, too, does the filial challenge to paternal sway that the derealized numinousness masks, invite punishment. The intersection of these two constellations of psychic material—his associations with mirrors on the one hand and oedipal strivings on the other—in the idea of punishment and ultimate self-loss may lead Borges to fuse them. (In some of his tales Borges keeps separate these two experiences of irreality. Dr. Yu Tsun, in "The Garden of Forking Paths," passes from a grim sort of experience in his apartment and on the train into a charmed world of labyrinthine country paths and Chinese gardens. And in "The South" Juan Dahlmann's feverish delirium opens out into a pleasurable journey to his family's country home. Indeed, the two-part nature of many of the journeys Borges' heroes undertake may in part reflect the dual origin of this stage of the Borgean irreal.)

It remains for us to ask how Borges comes to portray this twofold conception of irreality in his fiction, and for that matter why he does so. Chapter 2 shows antecedents both of the impoverishment of Borges' later stories and of the annihilating aleph in the narratives of *A Universal History of Infamy*. The frank criminality and perhaps also the very quaintness of Borges' antiheroes, and their sometime links to fetor, drunkenness, and sexual license are early representations of impoverishment. And the mirrors, rings, and coins of these early sketches clearly portend the figurings of infinity of Borges' later fiction. Moreover, it is clear that at about the time Borges composed these early narratives he was studying, in the work of other writers and filmmakers, how to impart to a fictive world a sense of the irreal. Yet for the most part, in *A Universal History* Borges does not endow his narratives with the mystery and sense of weariness that are attributes of the Borgean irreal. What happened that allowed Borges to infuse his fiction with this deepened quality of irreality? Did practice make perfect? Or was Borges' apprenticeship a matter of something more than mastering technique?

Emir Rodríguez Monegal, in his biography of Borges, is sensitive to the role that Borges' reaction to his father's death may have played in his maturation as a literary artist. He offers a rather complex hypothesis that links Borges' recovery from a near-fatal illness he suffered less than a year after his father's death to Borges' rebirth as a writer, a writer of tales. It is no easy matter unequivocally to relate the events in an artist's life to the work he creates. Nor would any thoughtful critic wish to contend that a single event, however portentous, was sufficient in itself to work a change as dramatic as the one that transformed a very clever journalist and man of letters into a writer of genius. Nevertheless, the notion that Borges' mourning may have predisposed him to make certain concrete, discernible changes in his work, felicitous ones, is certainly worth exploring.

IV

Mourning: A Catalyst of Genius?

*Our dead are never dead to us until we have forgotten them: they can
be injured by us, they can be wounded; they know all our penitence,
all our aching sense that their place is empty . . .*
—*George Eliot*, Adam Bede

When a prolific but only moderately accomplished poet and
man of letters—for such Borges was in 1939—begins, when
he is almost forty years old, to produce a spate of short stories
nearly all of which figure among the century's masterworks, one
is entitled to ask what happened that enabled him, at just that
time in his life, to consolidate his talents and to emerge as a
writer of genius. What happy conjunction of sensibility, primed
intelligence and circumstance helped to bring about Borges'
metamorphosis into a writer of irreal tales? For metamorphosis
it was. Borges had experimented, it is true, with composing
narrative and had written one full-fledged tale that he conceived
of as such, "Streetcorner Man." More important even than that
realistic tale, a story hindsight confirms as anomalous among
Borges' early narratives, is "The Approach to Al-Mu'tasim."
This fanciful review of a nonexistent book, published as a
private joke in 1935, is a fully realized Borgean *ficción*. But
when he wrote "Al-Mu'tasim," Borges may not have recognized
in that mock review a backhanded work of fiction.

At any rate he would have us think that he did not. Like his
critics, Borges has felt called upon to account for his apparently
sudden success as a writer of tales. In his "Autobiographical
Essay" he gives this report—it is a highly dramatic one—of

the events that led him to write "Pierre Menard, Author of the Quixote," the tale which, he clearly implies, inaugurates his career as a writer of fiction:

> It was on Christmas Eve of 1938—the same year my father died—that I had a severe accident. I was running up a stairway and suddenly felt something brush my scalp. I had grazed a freshly painted open casement window. In spite of first-aid treatment, the wound became poisoned, and for a period of a week or so I lay sleepless every night and had hallucinations and high fever. One evening, I lost the power of speech and had to be rushed to the hospital for an immediate operation. Septicemia had set in, and for a month I hovered, all unknowingly, between life and death. . . . When I began to recover, I feared for my mental integrity. I remember that my mother wanted to read to me from a book I had just ordered, C. S. Lewis' *Out of the Silent Planet,* but for two or three nights I kept putting her off. At last, she prevailed, and after hearing a page or two I fell to crying. My mother asked me why the tears. "I'm crying because I understand," I said. A bit later, I wondered whether I could ever write again. I had previously written quite a few poems and dozens of short reviews. I thought that if I tried to write a review now and failed, I'd be all through intellectually but that if I tried something I had never really done before and failed at that it wouldn't be so bad and might even prepare me for the final revelation. I decided I would try to write a story. The result was "Pierre Menard, Author of *Don Quixote.*" (*A,* 242–43)

It is easy to credit so moving an account; its very miraculousness persuades us, commensurate as it is with the miraculousness of the genius whose origin Borges explains. Yet examined dispassionately, Borges' tidy anecdote can be seen to rework history. In his biography of Borges, Emir Rodríguez Monegal is doubly astute. He observes that, in shaping his memories, Borges distorts the truth in ways that on the one hand exaggerate the abruptness of his access to artistic power and, on the other, unduly emphasize his passivity and helplessness. And what is equally perceptive, Rodríguez Monegal divines that in linking his terrible accident, as if by the bye, with his father's death—both events, Borges tells us, happen in the same year—Borges provides an important clue to the reasons why he explains his turn to short story writing in the way he does. Borges is essentially, if not factually, right, asserts Rodríguez Monegal, when he regards his accident as implicated in his development as a writer and associates both with the memory of his father's death. "The accident," the biographer suggests, "did bring about a transformation: not as the original cause but as the end product of a complex metamorphosis Borges had undergone since Father's death."[1] Recalling the tutelary role that Jorge Guillermo Borges, himself a poet and novelist of small repute, played in prescribing for his only son a literary career, Rodríguez Monegal suggests that Jorge Luis may have chafed at being required to fulfill his father's ambitions on his behalf. The biographer sees in Borges' accident, illness, and recovery events that Borges himself may have viewed, whether consciously or unconsciously, as a symbolic suicide and rebirth. Rodríguez Monegal further speculates that the self Borges symbolically dispatched in the septicemia incident was that aspect of himself "that was only Father's reflection," while the Borges who recovered "emerged as a different writer, a writer this time engendered by himself."[2]

The way one explains the psychodynamics of the change Borges underwent in the year after his father died depends on the theoretical framework one selects. The present study will offer a slightly different view of Borges' development than the one Rodríguez Monegal provides. Where the biographer sees an authentically Borgean self destroying the golem-like Borges that his father had wrought, I perceive a guilty filial Borges who, by nearly dying, expiates unconscious sins against his father. Nevertheless, Rodríguez Monegal's insight that Borges' relationship to his father was crucial to his literary coming of age allows us to frame useful questions. It encourages us to ask how mourning his father may have shaped the specific changes that Borges, as he turned to fiction, introduced into his work.

To make sense of the particular changes in Borges' fictional texts that his mourning for his father may have helped to inspire, one must first consider the process of mourning itself. What is the nature of the psychic task that someone who is bereaved is forced to confront? What are the functions of mourning? And, as it runs its course, what kinds of behavior does mourning ordinarily cause?

Freud, in his important essay "Mourning and Melancholia" (1917), describes the state of mind of someone caught up in grief and frames terms in which to understand the process of mourning. Struck by the degree to which it isolates the bereaved and preempts his affective energies, Freud provides the following description:

> Profound mourning, the reaction to the loss of a loved person, contains . . . feelings of pain, loss of interest in the outside world—in so far as it does not recall the dead one—loss of capacity to adopt any new object of love, which would mean a replacing of the one mourned, and the same turning from every active effort that is not connected with thoughts of the dead. It is easy to see that this inhibition and circumscription in the ego is the expression of an exclusive devotion to its mourning, which leaves nothing over for other purposes or other interests.[3]

Conceiving of mourning as a pressing psychic task that the mourner must accomplish before he can resume his normal life, Freud defines the nature of "the work which mourning performs":

> The testing of reality, having shown that the loved object no longer exists, requires forthwith that all the libido shall be withdrawn from its attachments to this object. Against this demand a struggle of course arises—it may be universally observed that man never willingly abandons a libido-position, not even when a substitute is already beckoning to him. . . . The task is now carried through bit by bit, under great expense of time and cathectic energy, while all the time the existence of the lost object is continued in the mind.[4]

A mourner, in other words, must slowly and painfully undo the affective ties that bind him to the person who has died. He does this, Freud suggests, by "continuing in the mind" the existence of the deceased, and by gradually modifying his relationship with this inner representation of the dead. Now by "continuing in the mind," Freud means something more than the survivor's remembering of the person who has died. He means that someone who mourns internalizes—takes to himself—aspects of the person over whom he grieves. Withdrawing from the outside world the emotional energy that he has previously committed to the person who has died, the mourner uses this energy, according to Freud, to "establish an *identification* of [his] ego with the abandoned object."[5]

Evidence that a mourner does identify with the person he has lost can be found in behavior common in the bereaved. For example, a mourner very often adopts some attitude or attribute of the person who has died. He may take up some gesture peculiar to the deceased or embrace an idea formerly cherished by him. Some funeral customs, too, can be viewed as ritualized ways of enabling a mourner to express his identification with the dead. The custom of wearing black clothing may, some think, reflect the survivor's identification with the person he has lost.[6] And at least one theorist interprets the funeral feast as the mourners' ritualized and culturally sanctioned ingestion of the dead, a quite literal "incorporation" of the person mourned.[7]

Freud's idea that a mourner sets up within himself a mental substitute for the person he has lost stands at the center of psychoanalytic thinking on the subject of mourning. Otto Fenichel, in his encyclopedic 1945 book *The Psychoanalytic Theory of Neurosis*, paraphrases Freud: "Mourning consists of two acts, the first being the establishment of an introjection, the second the loosening of the [emotional] binding to the introjected lost object."[8] And John Bowlby, writing much more recently in his 1980 work *Loss: Sadness and Depression*, notes that "traditionally, in psychoanalytic writings emphasis has been placed on identification with the lost object as the main process involved in mourning."[9]

However, Bowlby himself, who has devoted exhaustive clinical research to the subject of how people respond to loss, de-emphasizes somewhat the importance of a mourner's identification with the deceased. Without rejecting Freud's ideas, Bowlby argues that a great deal of mourning behavior can be understood as the survivor's unconscious searching for the person who has died. Bowlby reinterprets some of the behavior which Freud viewed as the mourner's psychic assimilation of the dead as a survivor's persistent seeking of the person he has lost. "A mourner is repeatedly seized," Bowlby asserts, "whether he knows it or not, by an urge to call for, to search for and to recover the lost person."[10] This searching for the vanished loved one may take many forms. The survivor may, for an instant, seeing someone in the street, mistake that person for the one he has lost. He may enter into imagined dialogue with the person who has died, summoning him in fantasy in order to solicit his advice, share with him some piece of news or vent recriminations. Or he may contemplate suicide as a possible means of reuniting himself with the dead.

Whether a mourner proceeds chiefly by internalizing his dead or by stubbornly searching for him, both Freud and Bowlby agree that one of the principal aims of the mourner is to preserve his dead loved one and continue a relationship with him. "By taking flight into the ego," Freud movingly writes, "love escapes annihilation."[11] Yet Freud, Bowlby, and others who have studied mourning have been struck with the violent contradictory emotions that the death of a loved one inspires. Bowlby observes: "What is impressive about mourning is not only the number and variety of response systems that are engaged but the way in which they tend to conflict with one another. Loss of a loved person gives rise not only to an intense desire for reunion but to anger at his departure."[12] The anger to which Bowlby alludes may spring from many sources. Frustration at having been helpless to prevent a loved one's death may evoke anger in a survivor. But beyond this, a mourner may be furious with the person who has died. He may feel abandoned and, whether consciously or not, blame the dead for having deserted him. In addition, he may charge the person who has died with having been responsible, entirely or in part, for his own death, with compelling the survivor to assume new obligations formerly discharged by the deceased, or with worsening the survivor's economic lot or position in the community. Moreover, if the bereaved does, as Bowlby suggests all mourners do, engage in symbolic searching behavior, he may be enraged or resentful at what he perceives as the dead person's intransigence in not returning to him. And the disastrous feelings of helplessness that both grief itself and anger may arouse may be further cause for anxiety and therefore rage.[13] In short, strong negative feelings for the dead may vie in the mourner with his feelings of love. Although Freud, in his original comparison of mourning and depression, did not view ambivalence toward the dead as an invariable part of normal mourning, most later theorists agree with Bowlby, who asserts, "there are good grounds for believing that even in healthy mourning a person's anger is often directed towards the person lost."[14]

In addition to resentment aroused by the death itself, a mourner may harbor long-standing ambivalence for the person over whom he grieves. Our relationships with our loved ones are not pure; competitiveness, jealousy, and anger alloy our affections. Consciously or unconsciously, a mourner may, while his loved one still lived, have wished death or some other unpleasantness upon him, and he may enjoy feelings of triumph at having outlived the person he mourns. Such hostile or aggressive feelings do not vanish with the death of their object. On the contrary, compounded with ambivalence occasioned by the death itself, they may revive with particular intensity. And unconscious hostile feelings for the dead complicate mourning, for they often give rise to painful guilt in the bereaved; less tolerant than usual of the hostility he bears his dead—*de mortuis nil nisi bonum,* the saying goes—a mourner may deflect his repressed bitterness for the deceased away from its original target and aim it at himself.

Guilt feelings very commonly afflict the mourner. They may cause a general lowering of self-esteem and give rise as well to remorse and self-reproach. Moreover, the fantasy, common among the bereaved, that the dead person may return to avenge himself, has its origin in the mourner's feelings of responsibility for his loved one's death. Otto Fenichel writes:

The mourner fears that because he has brought about death through the 'omnipotence' of his death wish, the dead per-

> son may seek revenge and return to kill him, the living. This fear of the dead in turn increases the ambivalence. The mourner tries to pacify the dead one . . . as well as to kill him again and more effectively. The pious rituals of holding vigils at the side of the bier and of throwing sand into the grave or of erecting monuments of stone are traceable to archaic measures which are intended to prevent the dead from coming back.[15]

Fenichel points out, in this passage and elsewhere,[16] that the guilt that mourning evokes tends to reinforce itself by spawning renewed hostility in the bereaved. The very acts by which an ambivalent mourner reaffirms his love may take on a double meaning and simultaneously express aggression toward the person who has died. When this happens, the mourner's guilt, rather than being allayed, intensifies, and a cycle of renewed ambivalence leading to increased guilt may aggravate the suffering that mourning inspires.

Despite the self-perpetuating quality of a survivor's ambivalence and guilt, his mourning usually succeeds, at least to a degree. The pain of loss subsides. And the mourning process may even be the cause of a mourner's psychic growth. Many people—Freud among them—testify that their own best work followed on the heels of an experience of mourning. The stories Borges wrote from 1939 on—and particularly those of *Ficciones* and *The Aleph*—give evidence that Borges, too, turned to positive effect the emotions his father's death aroused in him. Not only did Borges' creative power find more unconstrained expression after his father died, but certain specific and felicitous changes he introduced into his work may embody facets of his response to his father's death. In other words, the mourning process itself may have helped to catalyze Borges' transformation into a fiction writer of genius.

By 1936, fully two years before Jorge Guillermo Borges died, Borges had published "The Approach to Al-Mu'tasim," a text that indisputably represents the art of his great period of creative success. A false bibliographic note that describes an imaginary detective novel, "Al-Mu'tasim" not only fuses the essay and short story forms but brings together concerns that, until that time, Borges had relegated to the two separate genres. In his apocryphal book review Borges not only incorporates the idea of infinity but manages to express the irreality with which his essays are taken up, essays, we recall, on topics as diverse as the concept of eternity and verisimilitude. And he successfully integrates with the irreal a version—a denatured one, as we shall see—of the crime and punishment motif visible in his sketches of criminals' lives.

"'The Approach to Al-Mu'tasim" stands as undeniable proof that Borges, somewhat before his father's death, hit upon the hybrid literary form that was to accommodate and express so admirably the several concerns that throughout the 1930s had informed his essays, on the one hand, and his fiction on the other. Yet by the time he composed "Al-Mu'tasim" Borges may already have begun to grapple with strong feelings aroused by his father's decline. Rodríguez Monegal's biography of Borges leaves unclear how early Borges might reasonably have had cause to think his father's death was imminent. "By the beginning of 1937," Rodríguez Monegal writes, "Father was too ill to leave any doubts about the coming end."[17] However, the chronic heart ailment that afflicted the elder Borges may have become quite severe even before that time. The biographer records the reminiscences of José Bianco of his visits to the Borges family, visits that began "in the summer of either 1935 or 1936." Bianco "recalls that Father hardly ever said a word, except to bother about their guest." Rodríguez Monegal comments: "Father's silence, his reticence, was more than justified at the time. He had never been an optimist, and now his health was declining rapidly. Totally blind and suffering from a heart condition, Father was attended with the utmost care by Mother. His will to live had been further undermined by his own mother's recent death [in 1935]."[18]

We shall never be sure at precisely what point Borges started to respond to his father's death. Even if memories were less frail and it were possible accurately to document the date and severity of Jorge Guillermo Borges' final illness, we could not plumb Borges' unconscious. Moreover, other unanswerable questions rear themselves to tease us. Why did Borges apparently not recognize the measure of his success in "Al-Mu'tasim"? For some three years—the two years immediately preceding his father's death and the year following it—Borges produced no work similar to his first fully realized irreal tale, nor is there a record that he was working on drafts of any of his later narratives. Why did he to all appearances give up the project of creating fiction, and in particular, fiction of his own idiosyncratic kind?

Certainly, his time was a good deal occupied with other things. Pressed for the first time in his life to earn money toward his family's household expenses, he had accepted two jobs. Beginning in 1937 he mortgaged his days working as a cataloguer at a neighborhood library. He had already by then undertaken to produce for the high society ladies' magazine *El Hogar* a page devoted to foreign books and authors. Almost every two weeks between 16 October 1936 and 7 July 1939 Borges wrote copy for this literary page that usually included a capsule biography of a writer, a long book review or translation he had done, and several briefer notes on recently published books and on literary life in the non-Spanish-speaking world. In addition to reviewing some several hundred books for the genteel female readers of *El Hogar,* during those years Borges regularly wrote film reviews for the prestigious journal *Sur* and published, in *Sur* and elsewhere, a number of serious essays, studies of writers as diverse as Chesterton and Enrique Banchs, Swinburne and Mark Twain. Among the other literary projects he undertook during this period was the editing, together with his friend Pedro Henríquez Ureña, of an *Antología clásica de la literatura argentina* published in 1937. And, probably in collaboration with his mother, he translated into Spanish André Gide's *Persephone* (1936) and two of Virginia Woolf's books, *A Room of One's Own* and *Orlando* (both published in 1937).[19]

That Borges was busy during these years there is no doubt. Yet one is tempted to wonder whether his turning away from fiction, and turning away at precisely the moment when he had succeeded so well in "Al-Mu'tasim," may have had a cause beyond economic necessity. Narrative, as Borges had practiced it up to that point, was the genre in which he most clearly gave expression to his own oedipal ambitions. How could he persist, faced with his father's very real infirmity, in spinning even the most thoroughly disguised fantasies of triumphing over him? It is not until Borges' own accident and illness help to acquit him of a restraining guilt that he will resume his experiments with fiction.

An examination of the narratives Borges produced in the decade between 1933 and 1943 reveals the important changes Borges made in his fiction as he moved from *A Universal History of Infamy* to "The Approach to Al-Mu'tasim" and at last to the other *Ficciones* texts. In transforming his early fictional prototype into the paradigm that will inform the tales of his maturity, Borges alters his texts in two important ways: he makes changes that tend to disguise the motif of oedipal strife in his narratives and he greatly heightens the irreality of his tales. Let us examine these two kinds of change in more detail, see how they may embody aspects of Borges' mourning, and ask whether they may be related to one another.

As Borges developed as a writer of fiction, he disguised ever more thoroughly the motif of oedipal strife in his narratives. In chapter 2 we noted that, as he crafted the *Infamy* texts, he seems to have shifted his view of what infamy entailed and altered his attitude toward the wickedness he portrayed. The out-and-out, unregenerate villainy that Borges enjoys in the Monk Eastman sketch or the stories of the Tichborne claimant and Billy the Kid appeals to him because in these childlike reprobates the starkest wickedness has an innocent cast. But in many of the late texts of *A Universal History* Borges depicts infamy of a less ingenuous and less wholesome sort. Betrayal that is felt as painful, shamefulness, and serious revenge become components of the *Infamy* tales, and as Borges' view of infamy becomes decreasingly lighthearted, his narratives recount less and less violence. Borges amuses us, in the second and third of his sketches, by detailing the exaggeratedly heinous exploits of Monk Eastman and the Widow Ching, but in his account of the veiled prophet of Khurasan, the tenth of the *Infamy* pieces to see print, he offers us not flagrant and diverting crime but the unsavory—and mysterious—powers of Hákim and, finally, the prophet's degrading leprosy.

The *Ficciones* tales continue Borges' move away from the portrayal of carefree violence. The protagonist of "The Approach to Al-Mu'tasim" may or may not—the reader is left in doubt—be guilty of killing a man, and no character in any of the next six tales Borges published[20] lifts a hand against any other. Avid ambition and shameful degradation are surely to be found in "The Babylon Lottery" and "The Circular Ruins," but these feelings and experiences which, in the early narratives, grow out of the protagonists' acts, are more detached from the argument of the first written of the *Ficciones* tales. It is not, of course, that violence wholly disappears from the tales of Borges' maturity; a number of his heroes are murderers. But the first six stories Borges writes after his father's death do not portray mayhem, and the killers of many of Borges' later stories—Aureliano in "The Theologians," for example, or Otto Dietrich zur Linde in *"Deutsches Requiem"*—commit murderous betrayals that are colored by guilt. Unlike the innocuous misdeeds of Borges' early *infames*, their acts are heavy with moral consequence.

How is one to understand Borges' turning away from happy violence? If one perceives in the crimes of the *Infamy* reprobates the assault by filial figures on paternal authority, then it is possible to account for Borges' change in attitude; his removal of overt violence from his tales—or displacing it from the main plotline to peripheral details of the narrative—may reflect Borges' increasing guilt about his rivalry with his father. As early as 1933, five years before his father died, Borges starts to curtail in his fiction the open expression of his filial ambitions. But in the period between the elder Borges' death in 1938 and the publication of "The Garden of Forking Paths" in 1941, Borges moves to disguise the oedipal motif in his stories by suppressing from them the violence that had embodied it.

This denial of his aggression against his father may express one aspect of Borges' mourning. We have seen that mourners often must contend with intensified ambivalence toward the person they have lost. Just when they wish to preserve within themselves a favorable image of the dead, and just when it seems most unholy to entertain any but the most loving sentiments for the unfortunate deceased, anger and aggression may intrude and arouse guilt in the mourner. Borges' purging of violence from the short stories he wrote in the three years following Jorge Guillermo Borges' death may well reflect his repudiation of hostile feelings for his father during the period when his mourning was most intense.

In addition to Borges' suppression from his tales of carefree violence, three other changes he introduced in the *Infamy* schema around the time of his father's death may well express facets of his mourning. Borges' incorporation in his mature tales of the theme of the double, the changing nature of the journey in his narratives, and the replacement of criminal bands with utopian sects are important changes away from the original *Infamy* pattern, and they are all changes that purge his narrative schema of oedipal strife. But beyond this tendency to mask the rivalry between symbolic fathers and sons, a tendency which itself may reflect Borges' mourning, each of these changes may enact a further mourning response.

The theme of the double is one that scarcely appears in any of the *Infamy* narratives. While in almost every case Borges' filial scoundrel is paired with and matched against an adversary who brings him to heel, there is little evidence that Borges thought of these avengers as his subjects' alter egos. Virgil Stewart, for example, pits himself against Lazarus Morell, Paul Kelly against Monk Eastman, Pat Garrett against Billy the Kid, and Kuranosuké no Suké against Kira Kotsuké no Suké, but except in the last of these cases, where a similarity of names might be thought to suggest an identity between transgressor and justicer, Borges gives no direct indication that we are to think of the two figures as each others' doubles.

In one way, though, Borges does incorporate in his biographies the notion that *infame* and avenger are one. I have suggested that Borges' antiheroes occupy the role of symbolic sons who assail paternal authority and are in the end punished for their oedipal misdeeds. One might suppose, then, that the figures who, in *A Universal History*, subdue the miscreant *infames* would have paternal traits. Curiously, though, most of the characters who redress the wrongs accomplished by the filial upstart act on behalf of paternal interests but are themselves portrayed as filial. Virgil Stewart, Borges embellishes his sources to say, is the nephew of a landowner whose slaves Morell has inveigled away; Stewart betrays Morell in order to come to his uncle's defense. The young Chinese emperor whom Borges invents as a foil for the Widow Ching is portrayed as an inept young pup. And the narrator of "Streetcorner Man" kills Francisco Real out of loyalty to a paternal hero he has learned to despise. All three of these avengers manifest filial traits. Implicit, then, in many of these early figurings of oedipal material is the notion that the son who affronts his father will be curbed and chastised by another incarnation of himself. This avenging—paternal—aspect of the *infame*'s self functions as a sort of internalized father. In developing such an idea, Borges comes very near indeed to portraying the theme of the double in his early sketches. Yet he does not appear to exploit consciously the identity of the pursuer and the pursued in his narratives until "The Approach to Al-Mu'tasim."

Is there any reason to think that Borges' reaction to his father's death influenced his adoption of the theme of the double? His explicit depiction of filial and paternal figures as one anothers' doubles has the effect of masking somewhat the oedipal nature of the conflicts Borges portrays; it is no incarnation of the father, he implies, but the filial self that avenges oedipal crimes. What is more, the configuration the theme of the double affords—self punishing self—is the very type of guilt, and may reflect the intensified self-blame that Borges' mourning probably aroused. But there is another way to interpret Borges' taking up of the theme of the double as part of a mourning response. Psychoanalysts have long believed that people respond to the death of a loved one by identifying with the person they have lost and harboring within themselves internalized representations of the dead. It is intriguing to wonder whether Borges' use of the theme of the double, which begins with "The Approach to Al-Mu'tasim" in 1935, expresses just such a process of identification with or introjection of the father he was soon to lose.

Borges leaves one important hint that the theme of the double expresses this sort of mourning response, and, significantly, it appears in "Al-Mu'tasim," the very text in which Borgean doubles first appear. Borges' speaker closes his fictional book review by pointing out a possible precursor to Mir Bahadur Alí's work: "With due humility, I suggest a distant and possible forerunner, the Jerusalem Kabbalist Isaac Luria, who in the sixteenth century advanced the notion that the soul of an ancestor or a master may, in order to comfort or instruct him, enter into the soul of someone who has suffered misfortune. *Ibbûr* is the name given to this variety of metempsychosis" (*OC*, 418; *A*, 51–52). Thus, at precisely the moment when Borges embraces the theme of the double, he writes of the comforting effect that the soul of a forerunner or teacher can exert when incorporated within the soul of a successor. And, in "The Enigma of Edward Fitzgerald," an essay in which Borges wonders at the mysterious collaboration of Omar Khayyam and his nineteenth century English translator Edward Fitzgerald, he again cites Luria, translating in even more suggestive language: "Isaac Luria of León," he writes, "taught that the soul of *a dead man* can enter into an unhappy soul to comfort or instruct it" (*OC*, 690, my emphasis). Although Borges does not say so in his essay, his father had translated the *Rubáiyát* into Spanish. That Borges inevitably thought of his father in connection with translations of Fitzgerald provides another connection between a suggestive quotation and Jorge Guillermo Borges. It is possible, then, to see Borges' adoption of the theme of the double as in two ways a response to his father's death. It expresses at once an intensification of Borges' guilt and a wish to internalize a benevolent image of his father.

At the same time that Borges, in the "Al-Mu'tasim" review, comes to conceive of the theme of the double in precisely the way that he elaborates it in his most successful tales, he alters his treatment of the pursuit motif. In "Al-Mu'tasim" the question of infamy, and of guilt and retribution, is made very abstract, and in consequence what in Borges' earlier narratives is the chasing down of a criminal change in character. The Bombay law student may or may not have killed a Hindu, may or may not, that is, have cause to flee any further than out of reach of the policemen's whips. Yet flee he does, and there can be no doubt that, guilty of the killing or not, the protagonist is "infamous." Curiously, though, what begins as the law student's flight from the police turns almost at once into a search on the student's part. Borges writes: "The student *flees*, almost under the horses' hooves. He *seeks out* the farthest flung districts. . . . Pursued, he *seeks* refuge in the tower" (*OC*, 415, my emphasis). The student, "threatened by the events of the previous night," decides to flee from the law and lose himself in the subcontinent. Yet even at this point his journey has become a search. Remembering a woman of the thieving caste cursed by the despoiler of corpses he has met in the tower, he resolves to seek her out. And later, after a "pilgrimage" (the word is Borges') in the course of which he exhausts the experiences of man, the fugitive/seeker changes the object of his search and sets out to find the infinitely good al-Mu'tasim.

The sought for has become the seeker. Not only is the student's flight transformed into a search, but al-Mu'tasim, we deduce, is a seeker, as well; al-Mu'tasim's name, the narrator reveals, means "El buscador de amparo"—"The Seeker after Help." The student, who himself "busca amparo" in the tower, is destined, we intuit, to encounter his own face when he at last draws aside the curtain that conceals al-Mu'tasim. He is the "visible protagonist" of the work, while the "no mirado" ("unseen") al-Mu'tasim is his hidden double. In the long footnote with which he ends his tale, Borges elaborates on the idea that seeker and sought are one by summarizing the story of the Simurg. That king of the birds, described in the Persian mystic Attar's poem "Mantiq al-Tayr," is sought by his subjects who, purified by their travail in the course of a long journey, come to realize that they themselves embody their remote monarch. We, as readers, are left to apply this idea to the situation of the speaker of "Al-Mu'tasim" himself. Like the protagonist of Bahadur's novel and the Simurg's followers, Borges' fictional book reviewer is a seeker who must infer from less perfect versions of what he seeks the virtues of a remote original. He cannot lay hands on the *editio princeps* of Bahadur's work which, the speaker confides, "I surmise may be superior" to the edition of the book he has managed to acquire, a reprinting without illustrations of the second edition. Of course, the educated reader is aware that none of the editions exist. The first edition is thus inaccessible in an absolute sense.

The changed nature of the Borgean journey—from an avenger's angry pursuit of the protagonist to the hero's own expiatory or ambivalent search and the narrator's search for documents on which to rely—is further evidence of Borges' mourning for his father. Not only does this reversal of the valence of the Borgean journey purge violence from the *Infamy* schema; it also incorporates a kind of behavior that characterizes mourners. For John Bowlby, no act so typifies the mourner as does his searching in symbolic ways for the person he has lost. This impulse represents an effort on the mourner's part to retrieve and reinstate in his accustomed place the vanished loved one. A noble ambition. Yet Bowlby and others call attention to the ambivalence with which a mourner's search for the dead is regularly charged.

So admirably does Bowlby's description of a search that is colored simultaneously by affection and by hostility seem to apply to Yu Tsun's journey to see Dr. Stephen Albert, or to Emma Zunz's peregrinations after her father's death, that one is tempted to assert at once that the journey we have seen as a part of Borges' narrative paradigm is part and parcel of a mourning response. Yet before we accept this idea, we would do well to examine carefully other antecedents of the Borgean journey that can be found in his early writings.

Chastisement of, and atonement for, oedipal striving is one crucial antedecent of this journey. Both a criminal's flight and the avenging pursuit of *infames* by delegates of those they have wronged serve as figurings of the Borgean journey in *A Universal History of Infamy*. However, it is important to observe that Borges takes few pains in the *Infamy* narratives to represent either atonement or pursuit as a journey. When he happens on a journey in a source that he adapts, as he does in the exemplum that affords the basis for "The Wizard Postponed" and in the episode from *1001 Nights* that he reworks in "Tale of the Two Dreamers," Borges is content to incorporate that journey into his own text. But he seldom, if ever, introduces the motif of a journey into his source material in the course of reshaping it. Indeed, the journeys in the *Infamy* texts seem rather to be part of the complex of material associated with revelation than with the crime and punishment motif. In "The Wizard Postponed" the magical journey the dean takes with his mentor precedes the revelation of his own impotence. And the happy dreamer who, in the other text, journeys from Cairo to Isfahan has revealed to him there the site of a treasure. Similarly, the walk Ebeneezer Bogle takes near the end of the Tom Castro text as, plagued by legal troubles, he seeks the counsel of a visionary god, may be seen as a precursor of journeys in Borges' later tales. In each of these texts Borges' character journeys toward a revelation, and it is with this revelation that traveling seems primarily to be linked.

When, in chapter 3, we discussed "Feeling in Death," the *locus classicus* of the theme of revelation in Borges' early work, we noted that in the moments before Borges is struck with the insight that temporality has fallen away, he has wandered at random through Buenos Aires' back streets. Borges describes this perambulation, in the course of which he abstracts himself from everyday affairs, using many of the terms he associates with the irreality of impoverishment. Here, surely, is another important antecedent of the motif of the journey as it will later appear in Borges' fiction. Yet although sometimes, in Borges' work, the irreality of impoverishment may function to mask oedipal conflict, as I think it does in the passage from *Evaristo Carriego* analyzed in chapter 3, the experience Borges purports to document in "Feeling in Death" may have had other kinds of causes that we cannot guess.

At this point, however, it is germane to recall that twice Borges reports having had an experience of drastic release from self in circumstances that present him with the loss of someone he loves. The parting from a friend which he describes in his early essay "The Nothingness of Personality" precipitated in him an intuition that "there is no composite self," in other words, that the concept of a personal self is meaningless. And some years later, rejection by a woman he loved gave Borges access to a mystical experience. Thus at least some of the models in his own experience for what he portrays in his fiction as the dizzying irreality of annihilation, derive from pain surrounding separation and loss. And the irreality of impoverishment is an invariable precursor to this falling away of self. The death of his father may, like the other two crises of loss Borges describes, have exposed him to similar irreal feeling states.

Yet still we have not examined all the antecedents of the journey motif that one can identify in Borges' early work. In studying Borges' taking up of this motif, one that may ultimately have come to embody a facet of his mourning for his father, one must take into account Borges' fondness for books describing travel to exotic lands. The literary pages he wrote for *El Hogar* between 1936 and 1939 reflect his taste for these explorations-through-literature. Travelogues, such as Julius Meier-Graefe's diary of a trip through Egypt, Greece, and Palestine,[21] attract his notice. And a comment that he makes in an admiring review of C. E. Key's *The Story of Twentieth-Century Exploration* may help to explain why. Key's book, says Borges, serves to reassure the reader that "a more heroic possibility [than that of being a tourist] still exists: that of being an explorer."[22] Borges valued the journey, then, qua heroic exploration. And he may have done so in part out of disillusionment with the state of world affairs. When, in a synoptic biography of Paul Emile Victor, Borges describes that French ethnologist's account of a winter he spent among the Eskimos, it is to observe that implicit in Victor's book is the idea that the primitive Eskimos are more civilized than European men.[23] The worsening political climate is a major concern both of Borges as reviewer and of the authors upon whose works he comments in *El Hogar*.

Borges' embracing of detective fiction and fantastic literature during this period also may reflect his uneasiness with the politics of the time. The rigor and intellectual symmetries he found in these kinds of fiction may have served as fragile intellectual stays against impending chaos in Europe and against the drift toward fascism at home. Both detective fiction, which describes the hunting down of a criminal—and, what is just as important, a pursuit and finally a revelation of hidden truth—and science fiction, which often gives an account of a voyage to other planets or weird dimensions, provided Borges with two other important fictional models of journeys. A devotee of detective stories, science fiction, and fantastic literature, Borges delights, in almost every issue of *El Hogar,* in dissecting the mechanism of these kinds of works. Yet he does not try to work in these genres himself. It will not be until Borges can invest the fantastic or detective models with intimate emotional force that he will attempt them; "The Garden of Forking Paths" and "Death and the Compass" affect us not only (or even primarily) because of their parodic genius or their intellectual elegance, but because Borges instills in them powerful feelings and draws the reader into experiencing them with him.

The motif of the journey, then, as Borges deploys it in his mature tales, compounds many elements that his early writings contain. The way he develops this motif in his greatest tales is consonant with a mourning process, and it may be that his mourning for his father significantly reinforced the direction he took as he altered his *Infamy* schema.

The third of the changes in Borges' narratives that I think a process of mourning may have helped to effect is Borges' altered treatment of the secret society motif. The literary cénacle to which Pierre Menard belongs and the league of scholars who together invent Tlön have precursory analogues in the *Infamy* texts. They are the rather more feisty bands of criminals who disrupt social order, the quasi-Masonic conspirators Morell leads, and the happily iniquitous gangs of Monk Eastman and the Widow Ching. As Borges continues to write, he glories less and less in cutthroat violence, and the seditious alliances that his texts portray become more and more sedate. The forty-seven samurai captains of the ninth of the *Infamy* texts to be published in *Crítica* are a downright decorous lot. As Borges adjusts his notion of what infamy entails, the nature of these delinquent gangs changes somewhat. Beyond this, however, one can see that, at the same time that Borges eliminates the punitive quality from the pursuit of the *infame*, he suppresses to a great degree the criminal nature of the illicit groups he depicts. Tom Castro's conspiracy with Bogle to defraud the Tichborne heirs seems tame beside Monk Eastman's cudgeling of an old man and the streetfighting of his mob war with Paul Kelly.

In making this argument I am generalizing for, to be sure, Borges' movement away from overt and shameless violence in characterizing the unholy fraternities of his narrative texts proceeds in fits and starts. Moreover, I shall not try to correlate with one another what must be seen as several coexisting representations of the secret society motif in the *Infamy* sketches. In particular, Borges' use of religious groups, and of the notion of orthodoxy and apostasy, is a consistent feature of his figuring of ambivalent alliances in these early narratives and will remain a constant in his work throughout the 1940s and 1950s. Neither shall I examine in further detail the relationship between mentors and pupils, which is portrayed in each of the *Infamy* narratives and which is surely another ancillary figuring of the secret society motif. By and large, though, as Borges moves toward his mature fictions, one way in which he masks the curious conspiracy between father and son to overthrow an order that figures paternal authority, is to make of his father-son alliances—be they figured as tutelary relationships or as heretical sects or as carefree criminal bands—more and more the purveyors of mystery, not violence.

Here, too, one must look elsewhere than in the *Infamy* texts to appreciate how Borges' vision of the secret society evolved. An amused Alicia Jurado records that, as a boy on vacation with his family in Adrogué, Borges would play with his sister Norah and their cousin Ester Haedo, imagining that the three of them comprised the "Society of the Three Crosses." This society was "created to defend the male in the group [Borges, that is] from an imaginary enemy who wanted to kill him."[24] Jurado makes it quite clear that the children's fantasy was for them a sustained source of excitement and delight. She writes: "For a whole summer they lived in terror of the product of their imagination, which became so vivid that one day, at the siesta hour, the three of them saw the assassin reflected in one of those terrible wardrobe mirrors. It was, Norah affirms, blurry and green in color."[25] Alive to the charm of Borges' childhood play, Jurado nevertheless pauses to point out the motif of persecution it contains. The function of what may have been Borges' first secret society seems to have been to protect him from dangerous fantasied assault.

Another sort of confraternity in which Borges later took part had the aim of unsettling the world, not of protecting the self. The *ultraístas* who collaborated in *Proa* must have thought of themselves as a privileged fellowship, engaged in purveying artistic heresy. So, too, must the larger *Martín Fierro* group, rebelling against *modernista* orthodoxy, have embraced an iconoclastic credo and regarded themselves as aesthetic evangelists. Among these happy bands of conspirators, who hoped to disrupt with healthy anarchy a set of too long accepted artistic norms, the eccentric Macedonio Fernández achieved prominence. That whimsical idealist at one point conceived a hilarious collective scheme that had much about it of a secret society's plot. He would marshal his disciples in literary collusion to the end of instating himself eventually as president of Argentina. Borges and his friends would together compose a novel, to be called "The Man Who Will Be President," that would insinuate Macedonio's name into the consciousness of the Argentine people. James Irby, quoting from Macedonio's writings, describes the proposed work:

> The obvious plot, relating Macedonio's efforts, all but concealed another, concerning the conspiracy of a group of "neurotic and perhaps insane millionaires" to further the same campaign by undermining people's resistance through the gradual dissemination of "disturbing inventions." These were usually contradictory artefacts whose effect ran counter to their apparent form or function, including very small and disconcertingly heavy objects (like the cone found by Borges and Amorim toward the end of "Tlön, Uqbar, Orbis Tertius"), scrambled passages in detective novels . . . and dadaist creations. The novel's technique and language were meant to enact as well as relate this whole process by introducing more and more such objects in a less and less casual way and by slowly gravitating toward a baroque style of utter delirium.[26]

Some years later—Macedonio conceived his scheme during the 1920s, before the coup that deposed Hipólito Irigoyen—Borges adapted it to his own uses. As Irby suggests, he clearly had it in mind when he thought up Ezra Buckley's society of Tlönists, through whose work "disturbing inventions," harbingers of chaos, would be disseminated throughout our world. The notion of a secret society as implicated in the disruption, not the preservation of order, a sort of reverse utopian dream, will eventually captivate Borges. However, it does not do so immediately.

The notion of utopianism gone awry was in the wind in Argentina by the end of the 1920s. Argentina's first experiment with democracy collapsed in 1930, as the Radical Party, under Irigoyen's leadership, failed to steer the country away from economic ruin. A year earlier, Roberto Arlt had published *Los siete locos,* the first of his trilogy of novels that detail the machinations of a clandestine society, a perverted utopian group that conspires to destroy a fictional Argentina. Yet Borges' own writing in the early 1930s and the material he edits and selects for *Crítica* betray only the beginning of a sense that sinister events, either political or intrapsychic, threaten Borges' well-being. His own attentiveness to the motif of the utopian (or anti-utopian) group that foists itself upon the quotidian world is renewed only in the second half of the decade, as he reviews utopian science fiction and fantastic literature. Then, impatient with the satirical and allegorical bent of Aldous Huxley or H. G. Wells, Borges favors works of disinterested fantasy. He acclaims Olaf Stapledon's "vast prophetic novel" *Last and First Men,* which envisions twenty million centuries of humanity's future, because "It is never, almost never, satirical."[27] And in an adjacent column on the same literary page he takes H. G. Wells to task for moralizing in *The Croquet Player,* a work whose fantastic effect Borges takes to have been spoiled by didacticism.

Borges' comment on *The Croquet Player* appears in a tepid review of Wells' novel *Star Begotten,* one of a number of works Borges reviews on *El Hogar*'s literary page in which utopianism and utopian societies can be glimpsed. The plot of *Star Begotten,* Borges condescends to say, "is not ill-conceived. The inhabitants of a remote planet—Wells irreverently calls them Celestial Uncles, and also Interplanetary Tutors—resolve to perfect humanity by means of emissions of cosmic rays."[28] These Celestial Uncles, with their corrective wizardry, conspire to intervene scientifically in the lives of men, much as their Borgean second cousins the Tlönists will intervene with their contaminating erudition.

The utopian secret society, for Borges, then, is concerned either with protecting its members from peril or, more commonly, with initiating harmful intrusions upon normal life. Since Borges' childhood it had been a staple motif of his imaginative life. Yet the point at which Borges first truly succeeds in making expressive use of the secret society motif is the period in which he makes it a vehicle for his complex feelings in connection with his father's death. The process of mourning his father may have led Borges to conceive of secret societies as implicated in the memorializing of a dead paternal figure. The narrators of "Pierre Menard" and "Funes the Memorious," we recall, join with others to preserve intact the image of a great man who has recently died. And the theme of how adequate or inadequate is memory to the task of fixing and thus retaining realities, informs in several ways the great story "Tlön, Uqbar, Orbis Tertius." At the same time, however, the fictive secret societies Borges depicts in his mature tales design against preserving what is valuable. The inventors of Tlön and Orbis Tertius spread a disorder through the world that obliterates the past.

A review that Borges published in *El Hogar* on 18 November 1938 may shed light on his later use of the secret society motif to express negative as well as positive feelings toward his dead father. *Of Course, Vitelli!*, the book under review, is a fantastical novel by the Englishman Alan Griffith. Its hero is a man who invents a character and inserts him into the world, only to find that first his friends and then the wider world come to insist that the character actually exists. For Borges, who had already convinced many of his own readers that *The Approach to Al-Mu'tasim* was a real book, Griffith's procedure in *Vitelli* must have held great appeal. Yet beyond this, Borges' review of *Of Course, Vitelli!*, published eight months after Jorge Guillermo Borges' death, on the same page as an article in which Borges relates to immortality J. W. Dunne's theory of eternity, is revealing. It is not difficult to see how the ideation of a nonexistent man might have suggested to Borges, at a time when he acutely felt the loss of his father, the reinstatement of a dead person in life. Unexpectedly, though, the last words of Borges' review express an opposite, quite ambivalent fantasy: " 'Each book contains its counterbook,' Novalis has said. This book's counterbook would be cruel and much stranger than it is itself. It would be the story of some conspirators who resolve that someone does not exist or has never existed."[29] In "Tlön, Uqbar, Orbis Tertius" we shall soon see that Borges, in inventing a fictional conspiracy, almost certainly responds to an experience of loss. One should not forget that, combined with an impulse to preserve a departed loved one, Borges figures hostile feelings for the dead. The disruption wrought by the secret societies that Borges creates in many of his mature tales may in part represent the disturbance caused by guilt, the inevitable effect of this hostility.

In the preceding argument I have identified three specific changes Borges introduced into his fiction at about the time of his father's death, changes I think a process of mourning may have helped to bring about. His fusing of father and son figures into fictive doubles, his changing a father's vengeful pursuit of an upstart son into a rather more benign sort of search carried out by the son, and his transmuting the criminal bands of his early texts into mysterious utopian societies are changes Borges makes in his narrative schema that seem to embody aspects of his mourning for his father. In addition to these changes, which work to disguise the oedipal rivalry that underlies his tales, Borges instills in his mature short stories a haunting sense of irreality.

In chapter 2 we examined many of the narrative techniques Borges uses to derealize his finest tales: he places his readers at an unsettling remove from the action his stories describe. Deploying fictional speakers, who are often imperfectly informed about what they relate, he creates in the reader a sense that the "reality" a story reports is irrevocably out of reach, beyond the plae of what is knowable. He has his narrators cite apocryphal sources and presents the action of his tales not as a reporting of events but as a résumé of previous accounts of what has taken place. And in each sentence, by stylistic legerdemain, he creates powerful irreal effects with metonymy, hypallage, and other subtle distortions of syntax.

Borges' mastery of the techniques that derealize his prose was a gradual process whose evolution can be traced in the *Infamy* narratives. But as we have seen in chapter 3, Borgean irreality is not just a matter of technique; it is bound up with content, the empty impoverishment of the paradigm's second phase and the annihilation of the hero that brings the paradigm to a close. As Borges moves from the early narratives of *A Universal History* to the *Ficciones* tales, he comes to figure in a different way both the irreality of impoverishment and the irreality of annihilation.

For the most part, the antecedents of impoverishment to be found in *A Universal History* do not convey irreality. What

Borges has called the "pointedly picturesque" quality of the *In-famy* texts strikes the reader as being quaint and folkloric but in no way imparts a sense of eeriness. Yet if Lazarus Morell's Arkansas haunts and Billy the Kid's Wild West hold no mystery, the grey riparian world of "The Circular Ruins" and the library of Babel are settings whose queerness is disturbing. The filth and primitivism Borges paints in some of the *Infamy* texts, and the ritual decorum of others, may also stand as precursors of the irreality of impoverishment in Borges' mature tales. In *Ficciones,* though, and in his later stories, dirtiness and primitivism change character. The degraded, confusing landscapes of these tales, and the subhuman creatures their heroes come upon, now seem to exteriorize aspects of the protagonists' own inner being.

How can one account for Borges' derealizing of impoverishment and his giving it greater expressive weight in his mature tales? Here, too, it is possible to say that, at least in part, Borges' development may have been influenced by mourning. The impoverishment of the Borgean hero's world as he carries out the journey of the paradigm's second phase may reflect psychic desolation of the sort the bereaved describe. Freud, impressed with the mourner's withdrawal of interest from the outside world, observes in "Mourning and Melancholia" that "[i]n grief the world becomes poor and empty" and, he goes on to say, "in melancholia it is the ego itself."[30] At another point in the essay he compares melancholia, or depression, to an open wound "drawing to itself cathectic energy from all sides . . . and draining the ego until it is utterly depleted."[31] Later theorists, recognizing depression as a part of normal response to loss, have seen ego depletion and a sense of "emotional isolation"[32] as aspects of mourning. Other people than Borges have described the draining of life from their emotional world as a concomitant of mourning. To mention a single example, a psychoanalyst reports that one patient, as he coped with his feelings after his father's death, had dreams that began to lose color. "Grey was the predominant shade, until one day a grey dream was reported as having 'a sprig of green' in it."[33] The faded hues and unnatural soundlessness of the demeaned topography through which Borges' heroes move, and the stunted nature of the creatures he comes upon, may, like the greyness of this patient's dreams, reflect the withdrawn and painfully disordered state of a mourner whose inner life has been made bleak.

Beyond this, it may be appropriate to relate Borges' descriptions of irreal feelings in his own life to the expression of irreality in his fiction. In chapter 3, I suggested that the irreal serenity Borges links with a revealing vignette from *Evaristo Carriego* may result from, and perhaps express, his partial repudiation of the oedipal conflicts that the passage contains. Similarly, Borges' heightening of irreality in the fiction he wrote after his father's death may function to disavow Borges' oedipal striving. Like the suppression from his stories of overt oedipal violence, the heightening of irreality may defend Borges from his feelings of guilt.

But what of the irreality of annihilation? Its early elaborations are to be found not just in the *Infamy* narratives but in Borges' essays as well. The revenge or retribution that the *infames* incur is one key antecedent of the paradigm's fourth phase. But not until "The Approach to Al-Mu'tasim" does Borges add to the punishment motif the hint that the hero must forfeit his individual being and quite literally become one with infinite other selves. The contaminating notion of infinity only slowly comes to be linked, in Borges' fiction, with the punishment of his archvillains. Developed not primarily in *A Universal History* but in essays like "The Duration of Hell" and "A History of Eternity," Borges' fascination with the infinite as implicated in punishment eventually becomes integrated into his mature tales.

As he comes to link punishment with infinity, Borges increasingly imbues with mystery the rings, coins, and mirrors whose early figurings appear in his *Infamy* texts. For the most part, these forerunners of the miraculous aleph are important in Borges' sources as simple lucre. We have seen, though, that from the beginning Borges plays down the mercenary in his notorious crooks and adds touches of the marvelous when he describes the prizes they acquire. By the time he creates "Tlön, Uqbar, Orbis Tertius," he has managed to endow both mirrors and small, circular objects with disquieting powers. The idea of infinity has caught Borges' imagination, and in the stories he writes beginning in 1939 he multiplies epitomes of the universe.

In asking why Borges came to accommodate the idea of infinity within his narrative schema, and to accommodate it in precisely the way he does, one must consider the paradigm's third and fourth phases. The enclaustration of the Borgean hero may to some readers suggest his habitation of a womblike space. Several of Borges' critics, most notably Emir Rodríguez Monegal and Didier Anzieu, have perceived in Borges' labyrinths, his circular ruins, and his city of the immortals, imagery relating to the mother's body and the womb.[34] Certainly, many of the typical attributes of Borges' chambers—low ceilings, dampness, dim lighting, reddish walls, and a single aperture to the outside world—apply equally to the womb. While it would be reductive to view Borges' magical labyrinths as nothing more than uterine symbology, such an interpretation is useful for someone who would make sense of Borges' paradigm. It leads one to see in a new way the imagery Borges links with the paradigm's fourth phase.

When viewed in this context, the particular conjunction at the paradigm's close of the hero's empowering access to the infinite and the dissolving of his self into other selves is very suggestive. Borges seems here to describe a kind of experience that psychologists have ascribed to very young infants. Margaret S. Mahler, a pioneer in the field of infant psychology, has described a child's perceptions during the first several months of life, before he has developed a sense of his own delimited self. Calling this state of psychic undifferentiation from the mother "symbiosis," Mahler writes, "The essential feature of symbiosis is hallucinatory or delusional, somatopsychic, *omnipotent fusion with the representation of the mother* and, in particular, delusion of common boundary of the two actually and physically separate individuals."[35] Borges' description of the annihilation of his heroes has much about it that reminds one of this symbiotic state. His protagonists do not simply die at the hands of paternal avengers. They are suddenly rendered omnipotent and, simultaneously, helpless at a vertiginous moment when their selfhood blends with that of other beings. Emerging from a womblike enclosure (or still confined in it), the Borgean hero attains the psychic state of a child before his ego has begun to be formed.

In one sense, then, it seems possible to view Borges' protagonists as travelers on a regressive *viaje a la semilla*. This additional way of understanding the paradigm is consonant with other interpretations I have offered, for it, too, explains a facet of the paradigm as embodying Borges' response to his father's death; by depicting a son's regression to a stage that antedates his designing against a paternal rival, Borges in one way wards off the guilt his father's death inspired. His filial hero, he implicitly protests, cannot be blamed for conspiring against the father, for he is only an infant as yet unable to sustain a concept of self. Ironically, of course, the self-same regressive journey stands simultaneously in Borges' tales for the continued aggression of the Borgean son against his father, and the paradigm's fourth phase combines the outcome of both processes.

Not only does Borges betray his own mourning in the way he constructs his tales but many of his stories indirectly depict the mourning process. While no story of Borges' can be adequately understood simply as a symbolic portrayal of mourning, several of his tales do capture accurately the psychic dilemma that a mourner's ambivalence creates. "Tlön, Uqbar, Orbis Tertius," for example, movingly treats the theme of loss. Published in May 1940, the third of the *Ficciones* tales to appear in print, it is a text that Borges may have conceived of and contemplated writing for several years. In a review of Adolfo Bioy Casares' *La estatua casera* published in *Sur* in March 1936, he calls for a writer of fantastic literature to "[describe] in detail an imaginary country, with its geography, its history, its religion, its language, its literature, its music, its government, its metaphysical and theological controversy . . . its encyclopedia, in short."[36] This is precisely what Borges undertakes to do in "Tlön." Yet the story is effective not only by dint of its thoroughgoing imaginativeness. It is successful because it manages to convey how disturbing is the narrator's sense of dispossession from what has once been his. Borges himself has recognized in the tale this source of power. In an interview with James Irby he has emphasized what Irby calls the story's "emotional side." Borges explains that he wants his reader to attend to " 'the dismay of the teller, who feels that his

everyday world . . . , his past . . . [and] the past of his forefathers . . . [are] slipping away from him.' "[37]

Borges elaborates this idea of irrevocable loss in such a way
that it seems to arise in the tale not out of a sense of grief, the
narrator's or Borges' own, but rather out of a set of events
that are quite depersonalized. Part I of the story firmly estab-
lishes the idea that between a reality (or a supposed reality)
and an account of it a discrepancy exists, a discrepancy that
is by no means innocuous. The speaker and his friend, a fictional Borges and Bioy Casares, are debating at the opening of
the tale the feasibility of writing a first-person novel of a particular kind. The narrator of this hypothetical work, by omit-
ting or distorting things, would lead a few astute readers to
understand that behind the events of the novel's apparent plot
lurked a different "monstrous or banal" reality. As they argue,
a mirror disturbs the pair of friends. The image it unwaveringly
reflects of the hallway where it hangs is a visual "account"
of their reality. Yet many reproductions of other things prove
mysteriously untrustworthy in the first paragraph of the tale,
and the reader attaches a sense of eeriness to the mirror's reflection. Not only does the book the two friends plan posit two
realities, one slightly but crucially different from the other, but
The Anglo-American Cyclopaedia that Bioy recalls is a "literal
if inadequate reprint" of the 1902 *Britannica;* what is more,
one copy of a volume of the encyclopedia contains the article
on Uqbar while another copy of that same volume does not.
Even the sentence Bioy quotes from memory is not quite the
same as the corresponding sentence in the source.

The discomfiting lack of correspondence between a thing and
an account of it arises in the tale in a context that stresses the
equivocality of memory; it is the issue of Bioy's ability to remember the Uqbar piece that opens Borges' tale. Yet the
second part of the story makes it clear that the memory of a
person who has died is equally difficult to retain. The narrator
begins, "Some small fading memory of Herbert Ashe . . . persists in the hotel in Adrogué" (*OC*, 433; *F*, 20, translation
modified). That self-effacing railroad engineer, whose very
surname connotes the waning of being, "suffered in life, as so
many Englishmen do, from a sense of irreality; dead, he is

not even the ghostly creature he was then" (*OC*, 433; *F*, 20, translation modified). While the narrator does not mourn for Ashe's death, and the story is not "about" mourning in a direct way, the theme of memory may be present in the tale because Borges, at the time he composed the tale, very much wished to preserve the image of his father. (Rodríguez Monegal, by interviewing family friends of the Borgeses, is able to document that the description of Ashe, who in the story is portrayed as a friend of a fictional Borges' father, fits the elder Jorge Borges in real life.)[38]

Several other aspects of the story may have been born of Borges' sadness at the thought of losing touch with the memory of his father. The *hrönir*, objects summoned into being on the planet Tlön through a process of ideation, may elaborate a fantasy on Borges' part of being able to conjure back through his own imaginative power his father's image and reinstate it in the world. In this context it is interesting that in Tlön the deliberate production of *hrönir* first succeeds among a group of children whose school principal has just died, and that among the objects they exhume (their un-burying of things may even suggest the disinterring of the dead) is the "moldered mutilated torso of a king" (*OC*, 439; *F*, 29). The *hrönir*, like memories, exist in differing degrees of likeness to the object they reify.

> The *hrönir* of the second and third degree—that is, the *hrönir* derived from another *hrön*, and the *hrönir* derived from the *hrön* of a *hrön*—exaggerate the flaws of the original; those of the fifth degree are almost uniform; those of the ninth can be confused with those of the second; and those of the eleventh degree have a purity of form which the originals do not possess. The process is a recurrent one; a *hrön* of the twelfth degree begins to deteriorate in quality. Stranger and more perfect than any *hrön* is sometimes the *ur*, which is a thing produced by suggestion, an object brought into being by hope. (*OC*, 440; *F*, 30).

The periodic deterioration and repair that the *hrönir* in their varying degrees of derivativeness undergo reminds us of the fate of memories, which alternately attenuate to an ever greater degree the image of something experiencd in the past and rectify the distortions that earlier memories have introduced.

James Irby has noted that in creating the *hrönir* Borges beautifully recasts a haunting fantasy confided to him by his father.[39] It is a fantasy, a terribly sad one, of being dispossessed, little by little, of one's own experience by gradually losing the true memory of the past. Irby cites the following passage in Borges' remarks to an interviewer, Richard Burgin:

> I remember my father said to me something about memory, a very saddening thing. He said, "I thought I could recall my childhood when we first came to Buenos Aires, but now I know that I can't." I said, "Why?" He said, "Because I think that . . . if I recall something, for example, if today I look back on this morning, then I get an image of what I saw this morning. But if tonight, I'm thinking back on this morning, then what I'm really recalling is not the first image, but the first image in memory. So that every time I recall something, I'm not recalling it really, I'm recalling the last time I recalled it, I'm recalling my last memory of it. So that really," he said, "I have no memories whatever, I have no images whatever, about my childhood, about my youth." And then he illustrated that, with a pile of coins. He piled one coin on top of the other and said, "Well, now this first coin, the bottom coin, this would be the first image, for example, the house of my childhood. Now this second would be a memory I had of that house when I went to Buenos Aires. Then the third one another memory and so on."[40]

Irby surely is right in relating this reminiscence of Borges' to his invention of *hrönir* in his early tale. We may wonder, as well, whether the paradox of the nine coins that Borges' speaker uses to illustrate Tlön's idealist philosophies may derive from the same source in Borges' mental life. I have speculated that the question of whether *hrönir* can retrieve a satisfactory image of something lost may have had special urgency for Borges at a time when he strove to retain through memory— and thereby literally to invest with being—an image of his father. In a similar way the question of whether the coins exist on their own, solid and perduring through time, or instead rely entirely for their being on the people who find them may have had special meaning for Borges. When he conceived of the paradox, he may well have been coming to grips with the fact that his father existed no longer in his own right but as a function of the memories of others. That his father, illustrating man's progressive loss of the past, stacked coins to show the displacement of one memory by others suggests one link between the paradox of the coins as set down in "Tlön" and the reminiscence we have examined above. And here is another: the anecdote of the coins, like the portion of the tale that gives an account of *hrönir*, has indirectly to do with the motif of losing and finding.

This is a motif much repeated in the "Tlön" narrative. In addition to the coins and *hrönir*, objects "found" in the domain of Tlön, Borges' speaker hears of the discovery of, or himself comes upon, a number of things: the encyclopedia article on Uqbar, Ashe's copy of volume II of *A First Encyclopaedia of Tlön*, a letter from Gunnar Erfjord to Herbert Ashe describing the history of the secret society of Tlönists, a small metal compass beneath whose concave top are inscribed letters from one of the Tlönic alphabets, the mysteriously heavy cone whose possession maddens and kills a back-country boy, and the other forty volumes of the encyclopedia of Tlön. Whereas at the beginning of the story the speaker is eager to possess these objects, he eventually learns that they are dangerous and to be shunned, for they imperil the very foundations of his world. Tlön encroaches on and usurps every aspect of earthly life, replacing earth's languages with its *Ursprache* and, what is worse, our history with its history. In the penultimate paragraph of the tale the speaker laments, "already the teaching of its harmonious history, full of stirring episodes, has obliterated the history which dominated my childhood; already, in all memories, a fictitious past occupies the place of any other" (*OC*, 443; *F*, 34, translation modified). Demoralized by what, he foresees, will be the loss of everything that endows his world with sense, the narrator retreats to the hotel in Adrogué where he and his father have vacationed with Herbert Ashe, to perfect a Quevedan translation—into Spanish, not into one of the dialects of Tlön—of Thomas Browne's *Urne-Buriall*. He resolves, that is, to ignore as much as he can the advent of Tlön.

It is interesting, in the context of my reading of the tale, that the work the fictional Borges picks to translate is *Urne-Buriall*. In that treatise, Browne examines in scholarly detail the history of funerary practices throughout the world and meditates on their purpose as a stay against oblivion. "There is no antidote against the opium of time," Browne reflects in a typical aside, "which temporarily considereth all things: Our Fathers finde their graves in our short memories, and sadly tell us how we may be buried in our Survivors."[41] Even Borges' choice of Browne's essay as fit matter for his speaker to render into Spanish may reflect the preoccupation with mourning his father that, I think, informs the tale and gives it force.

If one grants that mourning underlies Borges' account of Tlön and of its creation, it is only one step to identifying, in the chaos the narrator perceives undermining the stability of his earthly world, the emotional havoc into which mourning throws the life of a survivor. Borges tells how the insertion into the world of objects from Tlön contaminates the narrator's sense of well-being. Perhaps, in the fantasy that inspired the tale, the removal of a loved person had the same devastating effect.

"Tlön, Uqbar, Orbis Tertius" is a tale that is noticeably shaped by Borges' own experience of mourning. Yet its immediate subject is not the adjustment of Borges or of one of his characters to the death of someone loved. Mourning, though, does figure as an explicit theme in many of Borges' stories. An astonishing number of Borgean narrators begin by alluding to another character's death, as if the act of storytelling itself grew out of a wish to memorialize the dead. The precious narrator of "Pierre Menard" laments, "It is as if yesterday we were gathered together before the final marble and the fateful cypresses, and already Error is trying to tarnish [Pierre Menard's] Memory" (*OC*, 444; *F*, 45). His note, he informs the reader, will correct the pernicious insinuations others have made about the dead Menard. In a like manner the speaker of "Examination of the Work of Herbert Quain" opens starkly: "Herbert Quain has just died at Roscommon" (*OC*, 461; *F*,

73). Displeased with the qualified and laconic praise accorded Quain in the newspaper obituaries, the narrator sets out to give due honor to the dead writer and his work. And the narrator of "Funes the Memorious" records his reminiscences about the prematurely dead Funes in order to contribute to a *Zeitschrift* for the prodigy. In all three of these works the characters who have died require vindicating. Pierre Menard's "invisible" masterpiece, his independently created chapters of *Don Quixote*, has not been valued enough, his friend asserts. Quain's defender must rescue from critical apathy Quain's experimental novels. And Funes' sedentary life as a paralytic must, his chronicler implies, be shown in its astounding richness. Despite themselves, though, Borges' three defenders of misprized genius convey how second rate or at all events how drastically flawed are the men they make as if to eulogize.

A number of Borges' stories explicitly portray a character's response to the news of another's death. The narrators of the twin stories "The Aleph" and "The Zahir" take up their accounts as they tell of a beloved woman's death. "Emma Zunz" begins as Emma receives word of her father's suicide. And the narrator of "The Other Death" hears, at the opening of that tale, that Pedro Damián has died. Still other of Borges' stories are presented as narrations that can be told because one of the characters involved has finally died. "The Intruder," for example, begins: "People say (but this is unlikely) that the story was first told by Eduardo, the younger of the Nelsons, at the wake of his elder brother Cristián, who died in his sleep sometime back in the nineties out in the district of Morón" (*OC*, 1025; *A*, 161). And the narrator of "The Unworthy Friend," finding an antique store where a bookseller's shop has once been, discovers at the beginning of that tale that Don Santiago Fischbein, the bookseller, has died. Fischbein's death, he informs us, frees him to relate a story the bookseller had confided to him.

Not only do many of Borges' narratives begin with the report of a death, but many of his heroes discernibly manage powerful anger and grief—that is to say, they can be seen to mourn. To perceive these characters as mourners makes one revise one's understanding of a number of Borges' tales. "Juan

Muraña," for example, portrays quite accurately a protagonist caught up with the ambivalence mourning may inspire. The story, published in *Doctor Brodie's Report* in 1970, poses the question of how one copes with disappointment in one's past, and, quite specifically, in one's dead loved ones.

The narrator, a fictional Borges, is the first in the tale to be deflated by having to face the unheroic nature of his past life. He opens the tale with the reflection that his lifelong boast of having been raised in Palermo, the romantic and dangerous haunt "of knife fights and guitar playing," is sadly exaggerated, only literary posturing. The truth, he owns, is that he was brought up in a sheltered home, "in a house with a garden and with my father's and his father's library (*OC*, 1044; *DBR*, 81). A chance encounter with a childhood friend brings home to Borges that his much-vaunted claim to have hobnobbed with glamorous ruffians is, to his shame, ungrounded. His schoolmate Emilio Trápani, when the two meet on a train, scornfully challenges Borges' authority to write about a rough street life he has never known. "Tell me, Borges," Trápani scoffs, "what in the world can you know about hoodlums?" (*OC*, 1044; *DBR*, 82).

Trápani, in his turn, asserts that he in his youth actually lived among the likes of those Borges makes free to glorify in his tales. "I know these people inside out," he would have Borges know. And he goes on to brag, "I'm Juan Muraña's nephew." Having established his own bona fides as a chronicler of Palermo, Trápani goes on to recount to a listening Borges his own experience with Muraña, infamous exemplar of Buenos Aires' turn of the century toughs. Like Borges, Trápani relies on his personal link with the Palermo of legend; it enables him to aggrandize himself through the telling of tales about Muraña. Borges deduces from the polish of Trápani's narrative that he has told it many times before.

But for all Trápani's boasting, his link with the past is as tenuous as Borges'. He retains no memory of his uncle, who vanished from Palermo before Trápani was old enough to remember him. Further damaging his claim to have witnessed directly Palermo's glorious past, Trápani tells Borges that Muraña disappeared in circumstances that were anything but heroic: "Some say that one night when he was dead drunk he tumbled from the seat of his wagon, making the turn around the corner of Coronel, and cracked his skull on the cobblestones. It's also said that the law was on his heels and he ran away to Uruguay" (*OC*, 1044; *DBR*, 82). Whether fugitive or drunk, Muraña figures in Trápani's tale as pathetic rather than glorious. And the *malevo*'s fame loses even more of its lustre when we learn that Muraña, when he disappears, leaves his wife destitute. Trápani's Aunt Florentina closets herself, after her husband dies or disappears, in the attic room upstairs from the flat that Trápani and his mother share. Dressed always in black, grown so timorous that, her nephew reports, she never would go out, Florentina talks to herself and becomes secretive and "a bit queer." The neighbors say that the loss of her husband has left her unbalanced.

By now we have reached the heart of Borges' story, for if the tale's speaker has reason to be disappointed with his past and Trápani with the prowess of his uncle, it is his Aunt Florentina, Juan Muraña's wife, who emerges as the real protagonist of the tale. It is she who, above all others, must come to terms with Muraña's failure both as the man of action she liked to boast that he was and as her provider. In Florentina, Borges portrays the very type of a mourner caught between the need to admit the shortcomings of the person she has lost and the wish to affirm her loyalty to him.

Aunt Florentina's powerful ambivalence toward her vanished husband is played out as she responds to the news that the family's landlord, a certain Luchessi, is preparing to evict them for being in arrears with the rent. As the anxiety and affliction of Trápani's mother grow, Florentina imperturbably insists that her husband will intervene and not allow them to be dispossessed. At the end of the tale we find that she herself coolly murders Luchessi with Muraña's knife. Insisting that Juan Muraña remains with her, embodied in the dagger, she deludes herself into denying the painful fact that he has left her to fend for herself alone. At the same time, though, the murder she commits expresses her rage at Muraña; that Luchessi may be seen as Muraña's surrogate, Borges makes clear in the manner in which he portrays the two.

Trápani, we learn, as the day of the eviction draws near, dreams of his uncle. With Muraña, the boy traverses in the dream a wild landscape that is at the same time the street where Trápani lives. He recalls:

> In the dream, the sun was high overhead. Uncle Juan was dressed in a black suit. He stopped beside a sort of scaffolding in a narrow mountain pass. He held his hand under his jacket, around the level of his heart—not like a person who's about to pull a knife but as though he were keeping the hand hidden. In a very sad voice, he told me, "I've changed a lot." He withdrew the hand, and what I saw was the claw of a vulture. (*OC*, 1045; *DBR*, 84)

The day after his nightmare, Trápani goes with his mother when she visits Luchessi to beg him for extra time to pay the rent. When they reach Luchessi's house, the two of them find that the landlord has been brutally stabbed to death. They remain as the wake commences and overhear the neighbors as they rehearse the account of the crime and talk about Luchessi himself. Luchessi, it seems, lived alone and suffered from rapidly failing sight. When the corpse, fitted out in black, is put on view, the young Trápani at first cannot believe that before him is no wax effigy of the dead, so changed is he, but instead the man himself.

In a tale whose focus is Florentina's reaction to her husband's death, the funeral of a man responsible for her and her family's suffering is curiously fitting. Instead of Muraña's wake, we are given Luchessi's. And in three other ways we are made to see parallels between the two dead men. Muraña, as he appears to Trápani in the dream, is "dressed in a black suit," while Luchessi's corpse is clad in "black clothing." Both of them are "greatly changed" when Trápani encounters them. And we remember the clawlike hand that Muraña reveals to his nephew when we learn of Luchessi's physical impairment, his near blindness.

Seen in this way, Borges' story is one that movingly portrays the hazards of bereavement. It represents a widow who, as mourners often do, takes on a characteristic of the person who has died—in this case it is Juan Muraña's prowess with a knife. In a single, psychologically economical act, Aunt Florentina arrogates to herself and thus preserves what she cherishes in her husband and, what is the obverse of that impulse, avenges herself on him because he has disappointed her.

Having interpreted "Juan Muraña" as a tale that quite accurately depicts powerful and contradictory emotions that may assault someone who mourns, I shall examine two earlier stories that in many ways resemble that tale. "Emma Zunz" offers a very similar sequence of events. Just as Florentina's killing of Luchessi at the same time vindicates her admiration for her husband and symbolically assails him, Emma Zunz's murder of Aarón Loewenthal may be seen as her avenging her father and, simultaneously, as her killing of his surrogate. Borges is reticent and chooses not to spell out too much the reasons Emma might conceive for directing rage at a paternal substitute. But he tells us that her father committed suicide, an act that, even more than simple death, is known to arouse anger in those who survive. And he tells us that Emma thinks, during her deflowering, of her father subjecting her mother to a like degradation. Indeed, what perhaps most bespeaks Emma's anger and her guilt is the masochistic pain she inflicts on herself in engineering her loss of virginity. At any rate, in killing Loewenthal, she kills a man who did not in fact rape her but who in effect has sullied her self-respect. Her father, Loewenthal's former business partner, is another such man.

"Juan Muraña" and "Emma Zunz" are realistic tales, psychological studies. "The Other Death," a fantastic story, can also be seen symbolically to portray the ambivalence with which a survivor remembers the dead. The story recounts the narrator's uncovering of mutually contradictory versions of a piece of history, the account of the death of one Pedro Damián. According to some versions Damián, a soldier who fought in the 1904 battle of Masoller, acquitted himself with glory in combat. Other versions, though, report his quailing under enemy fire. As the story proceeds, Borges' reader becomes convinced that Damián has died in two mutually exclusive ways. The speaker, though, does not readily embrace this particular fantastic interpretation of events. The story portrays the speaker's struggle to reconcile opposing truths about the dead Damián. Like a mourner, he works hard to vindicate the honor of the dead in the face of evidence that cruelly damages it. This evidence, in "The Other Death," does not arise from within the narrator but instead presents itself in the tale's argument. What in a realistic narrative might be cast as the speaker's own ambivalence toward Damián becomes embodied, in this fantastic work, as literal events that make up the plot of the tale.

Though, unlike Aunt Florentina and Emma Zunz, the narrator of "The Other Death" is not next of kin to the person who dies, Borges clearly portrays the speaker of his tale as having a stake in Damián's valor; when the narrator first hears an account of Damián's death that belies the soldier's courage, he feels ashamed. He admits, "I would have preferred things to have happened differently. Without being aware of it, I had made a kind of idol out of old Damián" (*OC*, 572; *A*, 105). Borges' original title for the tale, "The Redemption," may allude to the narrator's wish to redeem Damián from ignominy. In any case, the story may be, among other things, a figuring of a survivor obliged to reconcile both agreeable and unflattering thoughts about someone who has died. A mourner is called upon to do just this.

As does "Tlön, Uqbar, Orbis Tertius," "The Other Death" takes up the larger theme of man's troublesome relationship to the past. The burden of the tale is that man should not conceive of the past as a concatenation of events that have happened and that, to a greater or lesser degree, can be learned about; in remembering things, we actually subject them to change. Yet here as in "Tlön" this idea is charged with force because of the emotional context out of which it grows and because of its disturbing effect on Borges' narrator. We watch as the bewildered speaker of the tale tries again and again— and with less and less success—to establish the facts surrounding Damián's death. At every turn he confronts an elusive past, a past that is in no sense determinate.

The speaker opens the story by telling us that, a couple of years before, he received a letter from a friend named Gannon. In it Gannon promises that he will soon remit a version of a Spanish translation he has done of a poem by Ralph Waldo

Emerson. Suggestively, the poem is titled "The Past." (Later in the tale the speaker will tell us that the Emerson poem "centers around the irrevocability of the past" [(*OC*, 575; *A*, 110–11].)[42] In a postscript, Gannon informs the narrator that Pedro Damián, "of whom I might retain some memory," has died a few days before of pulmonary congestion. The news of Damián's death incites the speaker to try to envision Damián. "When I knew I would never see Damián again, I tried to remember him," he says. But remembering is problematic. The speaker notes, "so poor is my memory for faces that all I could recall was the shapshot Gannon had taken of him" (*OC*, 571; *A*, 104). And he has since lost both the photograph and Gannon's letter, the only documents that link him to Damián.

Another way in which the narrator responds to Damián's death is by setting out to compose a tale, a fantastic one, about the defeat at Masoller. (We have seen that storytelling is a stock response of Borgean characters who react to loss.) Armed with a letter of introduction, he secures an interview with Colonel Dionisio Tabares, a veteran of that campaign. He listens to the colonel's reminiscences of battle and receives the impression that his interlocutor, like Trápani in "Juan Muraña," has told his tale before. "The Colonel's pauses were so effective," he remarks, "and his manner so vivid that I realized he had told and retold these same things many times before, and I feared that behind his words almost no true memories remained" (*OC*, 572; *A*, 105). The colonel's much-rehearsed account may not correspond to his original memory of what took place, much less to what actually happened in that battle.

Both we and the narrator learn that it is naive to presume that any one version of Damián's past "actually happened," to the exclusion of other versions. On the night of the speaker's first visit to the colonel, Tabares recalls the shameful cowardice of Pedro Damián, or Daymán (even his name—it is one that connotes twinship—has more than one variant). When the narrator returns months later to verify several points, he finds Tabares in the company of another veteran of Masoller, Dr. Juan Francisco Amaro. When they fall to telling tales, it comes out that Amaro witnessed Damián's death, a heroic one, in the ranks at Masoller. What is equally strange, Tabares can muster up no memory at all of Damián or of having discussed him before with the speaker. Still another peculiarity of Amaro's account lets us glimpse a further fracturing of history. As he died, Amaro recalls, Damián cried "Long live Urquiza!", shouting the name not of his own commander but of a strongman who some six decades before had fought on behalf of Juan Manuel de Rosas in another war.

By now we are not surprised when, meeting Gannon in the basement of Mitchell's bookstore in Buenos Aires, the speaker finds that his friend has no memory whatever of Damián and that he has never proposed to translate the Emerson poem. Not only Gannon's letter but along with it the events it relates have been lost. When Tabares sends word to the narrator that his memory has cleared and that he can recall that Damián fought bravely and was buried by his men after the battle, the narrator journeys to Entre Ríos, where Damián supposedly had made his home during the thirty-two years after the battle. But his investigation cannot confirm Damián's residence there. No one remembers Damián and the only man who had been witness to his death in 1946 has himself recently died. Even the narrator's own memory of Damián is unsure. When he tries to summon up before him Damián's face, he envisions instead a photograph of the face of a famous singer in the opera *Otelo*. It is not even the actual face of a different man that the speaker conjures up, but a photographic image of that surrogate's face, and the surrogate is playing the role of a fictional character.

The story ends as the speaker tries to account for the inconsistent versions of Damián's fate. He considers the possibility that perhaps, just before he died, Damián begged God to preserve him, but that before God could attend his prayer Damián had been killed. Unable to change the past but capable of changing the images of the past, God may, one hypothesis runs, have intervened to rescue Damián, or at any rate his shade. Unconvinced by this interpretation of events, the speaker is drawn to a centuries-old tract by one Pier Damiani. Damiani claims that "it is within God's power to make what once was into something that has never been," and the speaker divines that Damiani's namesake acted shamefully in battle but that he spent the rest of his life preparing himself for another test of his worth. In the delirium of his final moments, this hypothesis suggests, Damián relived the battle and corrected his weakness of character. Thereupon, all memory of his initial cowardice and of the life that succeeded it was erased and supplanted in others' minds by the memory of his glory.

Does the reader of the story finally endorse this view of events? I think not. He is readily disposed, far more than is the speaker of the tale, to accept the frankly fantastic idea that history has split into two or more simultaneously existing paths. The narrator, lacking the advantage of having read "The Garden of Forking Paths," a tale in which time is shown to fork and contort, appears in a pathetic light at the end of the tale. Not only has he failed to perceive the truth about the double death of Damián, but he has been unable to accommodate in his thinking about that event both positive and negative images of the deceased. In that the story metaphorically depicts mourning, the speaker has failed to accomplish the crucial task of accepting contradictory images of someone who has died.

"The Other Death" quite accurately represents, although it does so in a figurative way, the dilemma of one who survives and has to mourn another, someone who may have been imperfect in life or who by his very death provokes antagonism in the bereaved. Using a device of fantastic literature, Borges makes concrete and plays out in the action of his tale a psychological reality, in this case the ambivalence of the speaker toward Damián. Understood in this way, the bifurcation in history expresses symbolically the contradictory feelings mourning can arouse. The related theme of the untrustworthiness of memory, which Borges often connects with the sadness of loss, corroborates in this tale Borges' abstract depiction of mourning. The narrator in the end finds himself estranged from a past that has become utterly irreal. As in "Tlön," the speaker must ultimately renounce not only someone who has died but the secure memory of the whole of the past. And it is that memory that anchors and defines the self.

The derealization of experience and of the self is the central issue in all of Borges' work. Sometimes, as in his early poetry, irreality is suffused with pleasure. More commonly, though,

Borges' writings communicate a disturbing affective emptiness
that is associated with irreality. His narrative work, in particular, is formed around the story of one who tries, and tries
in vain, to counter this emptiness. The protagonist of each of
his tales struggles to repair an injury that has drastically undercut not just his happiness but his sense of being. Paradoxically—and tragically—the course by which he seeks to recoup
his hold on selfhood has only the effect of further impoverishing
and attenuating his being. I think one model of this experience
that Borges may have encountered in his own life was the
experience of mourning his father.

In this study I have interpreted the Borgean paradigm as a
complex and multiply determined narrative structure to which
Borges insistently returns. He does so, I think, so as to grapple
with and resolve a set of psychic problems, many of which revolve around his relationship with his father. While experiences of loss other than his father's death also precipitated in
Borges the process of derealization he portrays in his paradigm,
it may well have been the final illness and death of his father
that pressed upon him a crucial realignment of his fictional
schema. When one examines the specific changes he introduced in the oedipally charged narrative pattern he had established in *A Universal History of Infamy,* it seems possible to
return to the Borgean paradigm and see how Borges' response
to his father's death is inscribed there. The mishap that motivates the action of Borges' heroes may, for Borges, stand for
the death of a paternal figure. As for the impoverishing journey Borges' protagonists undertake, compounded in it several
mourning responses can be found. The journey may simultaneously represent a symbolic search for the father lost to death
and a continued assault by the filial hero against the father.
At the same time, an analysis of the *Infamy* texts makes clear
that paternal vengeance exacted from an upstart son is another
element subsumed in the Borgean journey. What is more, the
Borgean hero's regression as a means of denying his guilt may
also be embodied in his odyssey toward a symbolic womb.

In chapter 3 I examined the antecedents in Borges' work of
irreality and of the peculiar impoverishment that Borges consistently associates with the more important kind of irreality

in his writings. I concluded that one source of the irreality of impoverishment in Borges' own experience was oedipal fantasy that, satisfactorily disguised, afforded him numinous pleasure. Irreal by virtue of being partially repressed and thus not quite accessible to consciousness, this particularly Borgean modality of experience is, for complex reasons that I have tried to show, also characterized by impoverishment. In some of his early texts Borges relates the subtle devaluation of irreal experience with feelings of shame and diminished self-regard. It seems possible to add that, in his mature narratives, impoverishment may also express the draining away of affective interest in the world that mourning dictates in one who has suffered a loss.

The journey of the Borgean hero ends in an enclosure that, in Borges' unconscious fantasy, may represent the womb. Either confined in this antrum or having just emerged from it, Borges' protagonist experiences omnipotence and, simultaneously, the compenetration of his self with other beings. This final abrogation of selfhood at the same time recalls the symbiotic fusion of mother and child—a defensive position meant to shield the Borgean hero from guilt—and represents a terrible punishment visited upon him at last by the father he has unconsciously wronged.

If one identifies in the death of Borges' father a crucial event that catalyzed Borges' ability to write irreal tales and interprets his paradigmatic narrative as in large part a personal attempt to play out again and again, until they were resolved, the conflicts that mourning may have helped to force on him, it seems necessary to ask why Borges' mourning apparently took so long. I have said that all of the tales that Borges wrote after "The Approach to Al-Mu'tasim" elaborate the Borgean paradigm. Yet normal mourning, psychologists report, seldom persists more than one or two years after a loved one's death.[43] Borges' paradigm, of course, is not one that has exclusively to do with mourning; it centers around a son's ambivalence for his father, ambivalence that assuredly dates from Borges' early childhood and persisted in some measure throughout his life. Yet a number of the stories Borges wrote long after his father's death—"The Other Death" and "Juan Muraña" are just two examples—seem to me to deal specifically with a mourner's response to loss. I cannot account for the unusually extended time during which Borges betrays continued if attenuated mourning in his work. It may be that, having hit on a structuring fantasy that was quite remarkably compelling, Borges exploited it, returning to it again and again as it continued to serve his artistic ends as a writer of fiction.

The fact is, though, that slowly Borges' stories do change. The irreal stories of *Ficciones* and *The Aleph,* written between 1939 and 1953, give way to tales that, although they adhere to the paradigm, are much less interesting—and much less irreal. Even Borges' late fantastic narratives, like "The Other" and "There Are More Things," seem perfunctory and formulaic, not vivified by intense feeling. In *Doctor Brodie's Report* Borges produces a spate of tales—among them "The Duel," "The Other Duel," and "Guayaquil"—that emphasize the hostility of the encounter between adversaries, rivals I have seen as symbolic fathers and sons. "The Disk" and "Avelino Arredondo" in *The Book of Sand* continue this harsh strain. Gradually, though, Borges begins in his late tales to mitigate the antagonism between his fictional doubles. His characters begin to converse with one another; dialogue is much more prevalent in *The Book of Sand* than in his previous four collections of tales. And father figures in tales like "The Book of Sand" and "Utopia of a Tired Man" become less menacing. "Ulrike" even figures the Borgean encounter not as a duel but as an amorous tryst. Little by little, in his own advancing old age, Borges seems, to a degree, to have made peace with the father against whom he continued avidly to compete for some three decades after the elder Borges was in the grave. Borges' narrative work stands as a monument to this reconciliation.

Notes

I   THE BORGEAN PARADIGM

1. "Stories," as Holland uses the word in this sentence, refers not to short stories but to any kind of narration. Norman Holland, *The Dynamics of Literary Response* (New York: W. W. Norton, 1968), 28.
2. Sigmund Freud, *The Complete Psychological Works of Sigmund Freud*, 24 vols., ed. James Strachey and Anna Freud (London: The Hogarth Press, 1953–68), 4:326–30.
3. Ronald Christ, *The Narrow Act: Borges' Art of Allusion* (New York: New York University Press, 1969), 221.
4. Vladimir Propp, in *Morphology of the Folktale*, identifies in Russian fairy tales a basic structure similar in kind to the one I have found in Borges' tales. And he notes that, in a given fairy tale, any component element of the basic schema may appear redundantly. Propp argues that these repetitions, or as he calls them, "moves," are secondary formations and do not constitute variations from a morphological type. See Vladimir Propp, *Morphology of the Folktale*, 1st ed. translated by Laurence Scott, 2d. ed. revised and edited by Louis A. Wagner, American Folklore Society Bibliographical and Special Series (Austin: University of Texas Press, 1968), 59, 96–99.
5. The dates provided are, insofar as I have been able to ascertain, the dates of each story's original publication.
6. In the foregoing analysis of the primary figuring of the Borgean paradigm in "The Approach to Al-Mu'tasim" I have not distinguished between the story itself and the invented novel *The Approach to Al-Mu'tasim* whose plot Borges' narrator describes. A more thorough examination of the tale would locate paradigmatic elements in those parts of the story that fall outside the narrator's précis.

II   ORIGINS OF THE PARADIGM: A UNIVERSAL
HISTORY OF INFAMY

1. Borges' only piece of narrative that antedates these sketches is the anecdote "Leyenda policial" ("Police Legend"), which appeared

in the 26 February 1927 number of *Martín Fierro* and again, with minor revisions, under the title "Hombres pelearon" ("Men Fought") in *The Language of the Argentines* (1928). Borges later reworked this text into his 1933 tale "Hombres de las orillas" ("Men from the Outskirts"), a work he republished in *A Universal History of Infamy* under the title "Hombre de la esquina rosada" ("Streetcorner Man").

2. Borges' early volumes of poetry are *Fervor of Buenos Aires* (1923), *Moon Across the Way* (1925), and *San Martín Copybook* (1929); his collections of essays are *Inquisitions* (1925), *The Extent of My Hope* (1926), *The Language of the Argentines* (1928), and *Discussion* (1932); *Evaristo Carriego*, ostensibly a biography of a minor *porteño* poet, is a set of musings on Buenos Aires.

3. "The Disinterested Killer Bill Harrigan" is the only one of the *A Universal History of Infamy* pieces not to appear in *Crítica*.

4. Roger Caillois, "The Masked Writer," *Review 73* 8 (Spring 1973): 29–32.

5. Emir Rodríguez Monegal, "Borges, Lector Britannicae," *Review 73* 8 (Spring 1973): 33–38.

6. Norman Thomas di Giovanni, "Borges' Infamy: A Chronology and a Guide," *Review 73* 8 (Spring 1973): 6–12.

7. Di Giovanni, "On *A Universal History of Infamy*," privately shared manuscript dated 5 March 1974.

8. Ronald Christ, *The Narrow Act: Borges' Art of Allusion* (New York: New York University Press, 1969), 61.

9. Ibid., 73.

10. David Gallagher, "Evident Words," *Review 73* 8 (Spring 1973): 18–23.

11. Ibid., 18.

12. Sylvia Molloy, *Las letras de Borges* (Buenos Aires: Sudamericana, 1979), 42.

13. Di Giovanni, "On *A Universal History of Infamy*," 5, 8.

14. Christ, *The Narrow Act*, 78.

15. For a detailed analysis of the abstracting elements of Borges' prose, see James E. Irby, "The Structure of the Stories of Jorge Luis Borges" (Ph.D. diss., University of Michigan, 1962), 104–35.

16. For a dissenting view, see Thomas Lyon, "Borges and the (Somewhat) Personal Narrator," *Modern Fiction Studies* 19, no. 3 (Autumn 1973): 363–72.

17. Georges Charbonnier, *Entretiens avec Jorge Luis Borges* (Paris: Gallimard, 1967), 96.

18. Ibid., 98.

19. The sketch was originally published 9 December 1933.

20. Molloy, *Las letras de Borges*, 39.

21. Rodríguez Monegal, "Borges, Lector Britannicae," 38.

22. Emir Rodríguez Monegal, *Jorge Luis Borges: A Literary Biography* (New York: E. P. Dutton, 1978), 264.
23. Frederick Watson, *A Century of Gunmen: A Study in Lawlessness* (London: Ivor Nicholson and Watson, 1931), 79, my emphasis.
24. Walter Noble Burns, *The Saga of Billy the Kid* (Garden City, N.Y.: Garden City Publishing Co., 1925), 56.
25. Burns, *Billy The Kid*, 54.
26. Christ, *The Narrow Act*, 116.
27. Di Giovanni, "Borges' Infamy," 10.
28. Burns, *Billy The Kid*, 57–58.
29. Ibid., 48.
30. Ibid., 51.
31. Ibid.
32. Ibid., 153–54.
33. Ibid., 154.
34. Ibid., 73.
35. Ibid., 75–76.
36. Ibid., 65.
37. Ibid., 73.
38. Mark Twain, *Life on the Mississippi* (Boston: James R. Osgood and Co., 1883), 23.
39. Twain writes of Memphis: "It is a beautiful city, nobly situated on a commanding bluff overlooking the river. The streets are straight and spacious, though not paved in a way to incite distempered admiration. No, the admiration must be reserved for the town's sewerage system, which is called perfect; a recent reform, however, for it was just the other way, up to a few years ago—a reform resulting from the lesson taught by a desolating visitation of the yellow-fever." Ibid., 321.
40. Sigmund Freud, *The Complete Psychological Works of Sigmund Freud*, 24 vols., ed. James Strachey and Anna Freud (London: The Hogarth Press, 1953–68), 9:172.
41. Ibid., 173–75.
42. Richard F. Burton, trans., *The Book of the Thousand Nights and a Night* (London[?]: The Burton Club, 1885), 4:101.
43. Edward William Lane, *The Manners and Customs of the Modern Egyptians* (London: J. M. Dent, 1835), 274.
44. Bernard DeVoto, *Mark Twain's America* (Boston: Little, Brown and Co., 1932), 19.
45. Alicia Jurado, *Genio y figura de Jorge Luis Borges* (Buenos Aires: Editorial universitaria de Buenos Aires, 1964), 16.
46. María Esther Vázquez, *Borges: imágenes, memorias, diálogos* (Caracas: Monte Avila, 1977), 100.
47. Ibid., 114.
48. Ibid., 211.

49. Philip Gosse, *The History of Piracy* (New York: Burt Franklin, 1932), 280.
50. Lane, *Manners and Customs*, 277.
51. Burton, *Thousand Nights*, 4:101.
52. See especially Jaime Alazraki, "Génesis de un estilo: *Historia universal de la infamia*," *Revista Iberoamericana* 49, no. 123–24 (April–September 1983): 247–61.
53. Lane, *Manners and Customs*, 281.
54. It is the detail of leprosy, not attributed to Moqanna in any of the historical or literary accounts of him, that Borges may have found in Schwob's story. Caillois, "The Masked Writer," p. 29.

III   ORIGINS OF THE PARADIGM: IRREALITY

1. Ana María Barrenechea, *La expresión de la irrealidad en la obra de Jorge Luis Borges*, 2d ed. (Buenos Aires: Paidós, 1967), 20.
2. Ibid., 18.
3. René Héctor Lafleur, Sergio D. Provenzano, and Fernando Pedro Alonso, eds., *Las revistas literarias argentinas (1893–1960)* (Buenos Aires: Ediciones Culturales Argentinas, 1962), 145–61.
4. Emir Rodríguez Monegal, *Jorge Luis Borges: A Literary Biography* (New York: E. P. Dutton, 1978), 187–95.
5. Jorge Guillermo Borges, *El Caudillo* (Palma [Majorca]: Privately printed, 1921), 80.
6. Ibid., 193.
7. Ibid., 29.
8. Ibid., 98–101.
9. Ibid., 28, 29, 30.
10. Ibid., 53–54.
11. Brandán Caraffa, "Palabras de Aprendizaje," *Proa* 1, no. 1 (August 1924): 63.
12. Ibid., 60, my emphasis.
13. Ibid., 62.
14. Ibid.
15. See Macedonio Fernández, *Obras completas*, 5 vols. (Buenos Aires: Corregidor, 1974); Jo Anne Englebert, *Macedonio Fernández and the Spanish American New Novel* (New York: New York University Press, 1978); and Naomi Lindstrom, *Macedonio Fernández* (Lincoln, Nebr.: Society of Spanish and Spanish American Studies, 1981).
16. Beatriz Sarlo Sabajanes, comp., *Martín Fierro (1924–1927)* (Buenos Aires: Carlos Pérez Editor, 1969), 69.
17. Ibid.
18. Ibid., 70.
19. Ibid.

20. Macedonio Fernández, "La Mística, Crítica del Ser," *Proa* 1, no. 2 (September 1924) : 33.

21. Ibid., 32.

22. Jorge Luis Borges, "Ultraísmo," *Nosotros* 39 (1921) : 468. Translation adapted from Ronald Christ, *The Narrow Act: Borges' Art of Allusion* (New York: New York University Press, 1969), 3, and Thorpe Running, *Borges' Ultraist Movement and Its Poets* (Lathrup Village, Mich.: International Book Publishers, 1981), 15.

23. The original article appeared in the 29 December 1925 issue of *Martín Fierro* under the title " 'Luna de enfrente' de Jorge Luis Borges." Sarlo Sabajanes, *Martín Fierro*, 128.

24. The original article appeared in the 20 March 1924 issue of *Martín Fierro* under the title " 'El hogar en el campo.' " Ibid., 24–25.

25. The original article appeared in the 4 August 1926 issue of *Martín Fierro* under the title "Filípica a Lugones y a otras especies de anteayer." Ibid., 140.

26. The original article appeared in the 26 June 1925 issue of *Martín Fierro* under the title "Irurtia." Ibid., 89.

27. The original article appeared in the 29 December 1925 issue of *Martín Fierro* under the title "Párrafos sobre la literatura de Boedo." Ibid., 130.

28. Untitled opening statement, *Proa* 1, no. 1 (August 1924) : 6, my emphasis.

29. Those essays from *Inquisitions* that were originally published in *Proa* during its second era are: "Interpretation of Silva Valdés," 1, no. 2 (September 1924); "Ipuche's Americanism," 1, no. 3 (October 1924); "Torres Villarroel," 1, no. 4 (November 1924); "After Images," 1, no. 5 (December 1924); "Joyce's *Ulysses*," 2, no. 6 (January 1925); "Omar Khayyam and Fitzgerald," 2, no. 6 (January 1925); and "Sir Thomas Browne," 2, no. 7 (February 1925).

30. Among the many sources that document this fear are Rodríguez Monegal, *Borges: A Literary Biography*, pp. 29–36; and María Esther Vázquez, *Borges: imágenes, memorias, diálogos* (Caracas: Monte Avila, 1977), 52–53.

31. See, for example, Nicolás Olivari, "En ómnibus de doble piso voy en tu busca," in Sarlo Sabajanes, *Martín Fierro*, 49-51, reprinted from *Martín Fierro* 1, no. 7 (25 July 1924). And Leopoldo Marechal's prose poem "Breve ensayo sobre el ómnibus," reprinted in the same volume, p. 101; the piece first appeared in *Martín Fierro* 2, no. 20 (5 August 1925).

32. Sigmund Freud, *The Complete Psychological Works of Sigmund Freud*, 24 vols., ed. James Strachey and Anna Freud (London: The Hogarth Press, 1953–68), 17:220–26, 241.

33. Willis Barnstone, ed., *Borges at Eighty: Conversations* (Blooming-ton: Indiana University Press, 1982), 11.
34. Ibid., 73.
35. Freud, *Complete Works*, 5:471.
36. Ibid., 17:241.
37. Sylvia Molloy, *Las letras de Borges* (Buenos Aires: Sudamericana, 1979), 110–16.
38. Borges' essay "Avatars of the Tortoise," first published in 1939, develops this idea further.
39. Borges incorporates verbatim into "The Duration of Hell" a long annotation to his poem "El Paseo de Julio" that can be found on page 57 of *Cuaderno San Martín* (Buenos Aires: Cuadernos del Plata, 1929). Both texts were published in 1929.
40. The other texts were "Dreamtigers," "The Veiled Mirrors," and "Fingernails."

IV   MOURNING: A CATALYST OF GENIUS?

1. Emir Rodríguez Monegal, *Jorge Luis Borges: A Literary Biography* (New York: E. P. Dutton, 1978), 326.
2. Ibid.
3. I cite this edition of the essay rather than that contained in *The Complete Psychological Works of Sigmund Freud* because the translation is syntactically better suited to my purposes. Sigmund Freud, *The Collected Papers of Sigmund Freud*, vol. 6, *General Psychological Theory*, ed. Philip Rieff (New York: Collier Books, 1963), 165.
4. Ibid., 165–66.
5. Ibid., 170, Freud's emphasis.
6. Otto Fenichel, *The Psychoanalytic Theory of Neurosis* (New York: W. W. Norton, 1945), 394.
7. Willard Gaylin, ed., *The Meaning of Despair: Psychoanalytic Contributions to the Understanding of Depression* (New York: Science House, 1968), 120.
8. Ibid., 121.
9. John Bowlby, *Loss: Sadness and Depression*, vol. 3 of *Attachment and Loss* (New York: Basic Books, 1980), 26.
10. Ibid., 27–28.
11. Freud, *Collected Papers*, 6:178.
12. Bowlby, *Loss: Sadness and Depression*, 31.
13. George H. Pollock, "Mourning and Adaptation," *International Journal of Psychoanalysis* 42 (1961): 351.
14. Bowlby, *Loss: Sadness and Depression*, 29.
15. Fenichel, *Theory of Neurosis*, 395.
16. Gaylin, *Meaning of Despair*, 121.
17. Rodríguez Monegal, *Borges: A Literary Biography*, 317.

18. Ibid., 205.
19. How much of these translations Borges did himself and how much was his mother's work must remain in doubt. Rodríguez Monegal points out that, in his "Autobiographical Essay," Borges seems to contradict himself, crediting his mother with the translations yet recalling that "On holidays, I translated Faulkner and Virginia Woolf" (ibid., 293). Ronald Christ, in a private communication, has written, "No one I have asked, including [Victoria] Ocampo and Borges, denied that the mother did the job that Ocampo assigned, like the film reviews, to give him some income."
20. The tales to which I refer are "Pierre Menard, Author of the Quixote," "The Library of Babel," "Tlōn, Uqbar, Orbis Tertius," "The Circular Ruins," "The Babylon Lottery," and "Examination of the Work of Herbert Quain."
21. Borges, "Biografías Sintéticas: Julius Meier-Graefe," *El Hogar* (4 March 1938), 24.
22. Borges, review of *The Story of Twentieth Century Exploration* by C. E. Key, *El Hogar* (24 June 1938), 30.
23. Borges, review of *Mi vida esquimal* by Paul Emile Victor, *El Hogar* (10 March 1939), 89.
24. Alicia Jurado, *Genio y figura de Jorge Luis Borges* (Buenos Aires: Editorial Universitaria de Buenos Aires, 1964), 29.
25. Ibid., 29–30.
26. James E. Irby, "Borges and the Idea of Utopia," in *The Cardinal Points of Jorge Luis Borges*, ed. Lowell Dunham and Ivar Ivask (Norman: University of Oklahoma Press, 1971), 41.
27. Borges, review of *Last and First Men* by Olaf Stapledon, *El Hogar* (23 July 1937), 30.
28. Borges, review of *Star Begotten* by H. G. Wells, *El Hogar* (23 July 1937), 30.
29. Borges, review of *Of Course, Vitelli!* by Alan Griffith, *El Hogar* (8 November 1938), 89.
30. Freud, *Collected Papers*, 6:167.
31. Ibid., 174.
32. Bowlby, *Loss: Sadness and Depression*, 102.
33. Pollock, "Mourning," 352.
34. Rodríguez Monegal, *Borges: A Literary Biography*, 68–69; Didier Anzieu, "Le corps et le code dans les contes de J. L. Borges," *Nouvelle Revue de Psychoanalyse* (Paris) (July–August 1971), 186, 198.
35. Margaret S. Mahler, *The Selected Papers of Margaret S. Mahler*, 2 vols. (New York: Jason Aronson, 1979), 2:79, my emphasis.
36. Rodríguez Monegal, *Borges: A Literary Biography*, 334.
37. Dunham and Ivask, *Cardinal Points*, 42–43.
38. Rodríguez Monegal, *Borges: A Literary Biography*, 285.
39. Dunham and Ivask, *Cardinal Points*, 38.

40. Richard Burgin, *Conversations with Jorge Luis Borges* (New York: Avon, 1968), 26.
41. Sir Thomas Browne, *The Works of Sir Thomas Browne*, ed. Geoffrey Keynes (Chicago: University of Chicago Press, 1964), 1:166.
42. The poem to which Borges refers is:

> *The Past*
> The debt is paid
> The verdict said,
> The Furies laid,
> The plague is stayed.
> All fortunes made;
> Turn the key and bolt the door,
> Sweet is death forevermore.
> Nor haughty hope, nor swart chagrin,
> Nor murdering hate, can enter in.
> All is secure and fast;
> Not the gods can shake the Past;
> Flies-to the adamantine door
> Bolted down forevermore.
> None can reenter there,—
> No thief so politic,
> No Satan with a royal trick
> Steal in by window, chink, or hole
> To bind or unbind, add what lacked,
> Insert a leaf, or forge a name,
> New-face or finish what is packed
> Alter or mend eternal Fact.

Ralph Waldo Emerson, *The Complete Works of Ralph Waldo Emerson*, 12 vols., *Poems* (Cambridge, Mass.: Riverside Press, 1904; reprint, New York: AMS Press, 1979), 9:257–58.
43. Bowlby, however, writes: "There is a tendency to underestimate how intensely distressing and disabling loss usually is and for how long the distress, and often the disablement, commonly lasts. Conversely, there is a tendency to suppose that a normal healthy person can and should get over a bereavement not only fairly rapidly but also completely. . . . Throughout this volume I shall be countering those biases." Bowlby, *Loss: Sadness and Depression*, 8.

Bibliography

I   WORKS BY BORGES

"Ultraísmo." *Nosotros* 39 (1921): 466–471.
Fervor de Buenos Aires. Buenos Aires: Privately printed, 1923.
Inquisiciones. Buenos Aires: Editorial Proa, 1925.
Luna de enfrente. Buenos Aires: Editorial Proa, 1925.
El tamaño de mi esperanza. Buenos Aires: Editorial Proa, 1926.
El idioma de los argentinos. Buenos Aires: M. Gleizer, 1928.
Cuaderno San Martín. Buenos Aires: Cuadernos del Plata, 1929.
"Libros y autores extranjeros" pages from *El Hogar* (Buenos Aires).
    Biweekly from 16 October 1936 to 7 July 1939.
Labyrinths. Edited by James E. Irby and Donald A. Yates. New York:
    New Directions, 1962.
Other Inquisitions, 1937–1952. Translated by Ruth L. C. Simms. Aus-
    tin, Texas: University of Texas Press, 1964.
The Aleph and Other Stories, 1933–1969. Edited and translated by
    Norman Thomas di Giovanni in collaboration with the author. New
    York: E. P. Dutton, 1970.
Doctor Brodie's Report. Translated by Norman Thomas di Giovanni in
    collaboration with the author. New York: E. P. Dutton, 1970.
A Universal History of Infamy. Translated by Norman Thomas di
    Giovanni. New York: E. P. Dutton, 1970.
Obras Completas. Buenos Aires: Emecé Editores, 1974.
El libro de arena. Buenos Aires: Emecé Editores, 1975.
Prólogos con un prólogo de prólogos. Buenos Aires: Torres Aguero
    Editor, 1975.
The Book of Sand. Translated by Norman Thomas di Giovanni. New
    York: E. P. Dutton, 1977.
Obras completas en colaboración. Buenos Aires: Emecé Editores, 1979.
Six Problems for Don Isidro Parodi. Translated by Norman Thomas di
    Giovanni. New York: E. P. Dutton, 1980.
Siete noches. Mexico City: Fondo de Cultura Económica, 1980.

Borges, A Reader: A Selection from the Writings of Jorge Luis Borges.
Edited by Emir Rodríguez Monegal and Alastair Reid. New York:
E. P. Dutton, 1981.
Obra poética, 1923–1977. 3d ed. Madrid: Alianza Editorial, 1983.

II WORKS ABOUT BORGES

Alazraki, Jaime. "Génesis de un estilo: *Historica universal de la infamia.*" *Revista Iberoamericana* 49, no. 123–24 (April–September
1983): 247–61.
———, ed. *Jorge Luis Borges.* Madrid: Taurus, 1976.
———. *La prosa narrativa de Jorge Luis Borges.* Madrid: Gredos,
1968.
———. *Versiones, inversiones, reversiones.* Madrid: Gredos, 1977.
Alifano, Roberto, ed. *Twenty-four Conversations with Borges Including
a Selection of Poems.* Translated by Nicomedes Suárez Araúz
et al. Altamira Inter-American Series. Housatonic, Maine: Lascaux
Publishers, 1984.
Anzieu, Didier. "Le corps et le code dans les contes de J. L. Borges."
Nouvelle Revue de Psychoanalyse (Paris) (July–August 1971):
177–210.
Barnstone, Willis, ed. *Borges at Eighty: Conversations.* Bloomington:
Indiana University Press, 1982.
Barrenechea, Ana María. "Borges y la narración que se autoanaliza."
In *Textos Hispanoamericanos: De Sarmiento a Sarduy,* pp. 127–44.
Caracas: Monte Avila, 1978.
———. "Borges y los símbolos." In *Textos Hispanoamericanos: De Sar-
miento a Sarduy,* pp. 145–58. Caracas: Monte Avila, 1978.
———. *La expresión de la irrealidad en la obra Jorge Luis Borges.* 2d
ed. Buenos Aires: Paidós, 1967.
Bastos, María Luisa. *Borges ante la crítica argentina, 1923–1960.*
Buenos Aires: Hispamerica, 1974.
Becco, Horacio Jorge. *Jorge Luis Borges: Bibliografía total, 1923–
1973.* Buenos Aires: Casa Pardo, 1973.
Bell-Villada, Gene H. *Borges and His Fiction: A Guide to His Mind
and Art.* Chapel Hill: University of North Carolina Press, 1981.
Burgin, Richard. *Conversations with Jorge Luis Borges.* New York:
Avon, 1968.
Caillois, Roger. "The Masked Writer." *Review 73* 8 (Spring 1973):
29–32.
Caraffa, Brandán. "Palabras de Aprendizaje." *Proa* 1, no. 1 (August
1924): 59–63.
Carrizo, Antonio, ed. *Borges el memorioso. Conversaciones de Jorge
Luis Borges con Antonio Carrizo.* Mexico City: Fondo de Cultura
Económica, 1982.

Charbonnier, Georges. *Entretiens avec Jorge Luis Borges*. Paris: Gallimard, 1967.

Christ, Ronald. "The Art of Fiction XXXIX: Jorge Luis Borges." *Paris Review* 40 (Winter–Spring 1967): 116–64.

———. *The Narrow Act: Borges' Art of Allusion*. New York: New York University Press, 1969.

Cortínez, Carlos, ed. *Simply a Man of Letters*. Proceedings of a Symposium on Jorge Luis Borges, Orono, Maine, April 1976. Orono, Maine: University of Maine at Orono Press, 1982.

40 Inquisiciones sobre Borges. Special issue of *Revista Iberoamericana* 100–101 (July-December 1977).

de Milleret, Jean. *Entrevistas con Jorge Luis Borges*. Caracas: Monte Avila, 1970.

di Giovanni, Norman Thomas. "Borges' Infamy: A Chronology and a Guide." *Review 73* 8 (Spring 1973): 6–12.

———. "On *A Universal History of Infamy*." Privately shared manuscript dated 5 March 1974.

Dunham, Lowell and Ivar Ivask. *The Cardinal Points of Jorge Luis Borges*. Norman: University of Oklahoma Press, 1971.

Gallagher, David. "Evident Words." *Review 73* 8 (Spring 1973): 18–23.

Irby, James E. "Encuentro con Borges." *Revista de la Universidad de México* 16, no. 10 (June 1962): 4–10.

———. "The Structure of the Stories of Jorge Luis Borges." Ph.D. dissertation, University of Michigan, 1962.

Jorge Luis Borges: L'Herne. Paris, 1964.

Jurado, Alicia. *Genio y figura de Jorge Luis Borges*. Buenos Aires: Editorial Universitaria de Buenos Aires, 1964.

Levine, Suzanne Jill. "A Universal Tradition." *Review 73* 8 (Spring 1973): 24–28.

Lyon, Thomas. "Borges and the (Somewhat) Personal Narrator." *Modern Fiction Studies* 19, no. 3 (Autumn 1973): 363–72.

Matamoro, Blas. *Jorge Luis Borges o el juego trascendente*. Buenos Aires [?]: A. Peña Lillo, 1969.

Molloy, Sylvia. *Las letras de Borges*. Buenos Aires: Sudamericana, 1979.

Newman, Charles and Mary Kinzie, eds. *Prose for Borges*. Evanston: Northwestern University Press, 1974.

Rodríguez Monegal, Emir. "Borges, Lector Britannicae." *Review 73* 8 (Spring 1973): 33–38.

Rodríguez Monegal, Emir. *Jorge Luis Borges: A Literary Biography*. New York: E. P. Dutton, 1978.

Running, Thorpe. *Borges' Ultraist Movement and Its Poets*. Lathrup Village, Mich.: International Book Publishers, 1981.

Sorrentino, Fernando. *Seven Conversations with Jorge Luis Borges*. Translated by Clark M. Zlotchew. Troy, N.Y.: The Whitston Publishing Company, 1982.

Stabb, Martin S. *Jorge Luis Borges.* New York: Twayne Publishers, 1970.

Vázquez, María Esther. *Borges: imágenes, memorias, diálogos.* Caracas: Monte Avila, 1977.

Videla, Gloria. *El ultraísmo: Estudios sobre movimientos poéticos de vanguardia en España.* Madrid: Gredos, 1971.

Yates, Donald A. "Behind 'Borges and I.' " *Modern Fiction Studies* 19, no. 2 (Summer 1973) : 317–24.

III   OTHER WORKS

Arieti, Silvano. *Creativity: The Magic Synthesis.* New York: Basic Books, 1976.

————. "The Loss of Reality." *Psychoanalysis and the Psychoanalytic Review* 43 (1961) : 3–24.

Asbury, Herbert. *The Gangs of New York: An Informal History of the Underworld.* New York: Alfred A. Knopf, 1937.

Barrenechea, Ana María. "Ensayo de una tipología de la Literatura Fantástica." *Revista Iberoamericana* 38 (1971) : 391–403.

Belevan, Harry. *Teoría de lo fantástico.* Barcelona: Editorial Anagrama, 1976.

Bellemin-Noel, Jean. "Des formes fantastiques aux thèmes fantasmatiques." *Littérature* 2 (May 1971) : 103–11.

————. "Notes sur le fantastique (textes de Théophile Gautier)." *Littérature* 8 (1972) : 3–23.

Bessière, Irène. *Le récit fantastique: La poétique de l'incertain.* Paris: Librairie Larousse, 1974.

Blanck, Gertrude and Rubin. *Ego Psychology: Psychoanalytic Developmental Psychology.* 2 vols. New York: Columbia University Press, 1979.

Borges, Jorge Guillermo. *El Caudillo.* Palma (Majorca) : Privately printed, 1921.

Bowlby, John. *Attachment and Loss.* Vol. 3, *Loss: Sadness and Depression.* New York: Basic Books, 1980.

Browne, Sir Thomas. *The Works of Sir Thomas Browne.* Edited by Geoffrey Keynes. Chicago: University of Chicago Press, 1964.

Burns, Walter Noble. *The Saga of Billy the Kid.* Garden City, N.Y.: Garden City Publishing Co., 1925.

Burton, Richard F., trans. *The Book of the Thousand Nights and a Night.* London [?]: The Burton Club, 1885.

Crews, Frederick. *Out of My System: Psychoanalysis, Ideology, and Critical Method.* New York: Oxford University Press, 1975.

Deutsch, Helene. "Absence of Grief." *Psychoanalytic Quarterly* 6 (1937) : 12–22.

DeVoto, Bernard. *Mark Twain's America.* Boston: Little, Brown and Co., 1932.

"Druses." *Encyclopaedia Britannica.* 11th ed. 1910.

Eliade, Mircea. *Le Mythe de l'eternel retour: archétypes et répétition.* Paris: Gallimard, 1949.

Emerson, Ralph Waldo. *The Complete Works of Ralph Waldo Emerson.* 12 vols. Cambridge, Mass.: Riverside Press, 1904; reprint, New York: AMS Press, 1979.

Englebert, Jo Anne. *Macedonio Fernández and the Spanish American New Novel.* New York: New York University Press, 1978.

Falcoff, Mark and Ronald H. Dolkart, eds. *Prologue to Perón: Argentina in Depression and War, 1930–1943.* Berkeley: University of California Press, 1975.

Fenichel, Otto. *The Psychoanalytic Theory of Neurosis.* New York: W. W. Norton, 1945.

Fernández, Macedonio. "La Mística, Crítica del Ser." *Proa* 1, no. 2 (September 1924): 30–34.

————. *Obras completas.* 5 vols. Buenos Aires: Corregidor, 1974.

Freud, Anna. *The Ego and the Mechanisms of Defense.* Rev. ed. New York: International Universities Press, 1966.

Freud, Sigmund. *Collected Papers of Sigmund Freud.* Vol. 6, *General Psychological Theory.* Edited by Philip Rieff. New York: Collier Books, 1963.

————. *The Complete Psychological Works of Sigmund Freud.* 24 vols. Edited by James Strachey and Anna Freud. London: Hogarth Press, 1953–68.

Frye, Richard N. *The History of Bukhara.* Translated by Narshakhi. Cambridge, Mass.: Medieval Academy of America, 1954.

Gardner, Howard. *The Arts and Human Development: A Psychological Study of the Artistic Process.* New York: John Wiley, 1973.

Gaylin, Willard, ed. *The Meaning of Despair: Psychoanalytic Contributions to the Understanding of Depression.* New York: Science House, 1968.

Gordon, David J. *Literary Art and the Unconscious.* Baton Rouge: Louisiana State University Press, 1976.

Gosse, Philip. *The History of Piracy.* New York: Burt Franklin, 1932.

Greenacre, Phyllis. "The Childhood of the Artist. Libidinal Phase Development and Giftedness." *The Psychoanalytic Study of the Child* 12 (1957): 42–72.

Guntrip, Harry. *Schizoid Phenomena: Object Relations and the Self.* London: Hogarth Press and Institute of Psycho-Analysis, 1968.

Hartmann, Heinz. "Notes on the Theory of Sublimation." *The Psychoanalytic Study of the Child* 10 (1955): 9–29.

d'Herbelot de Moulainville, Barthélmy. *Bibliothèque orientale.* Alahaye: J. Neaulme & N. van Daalen, Libraires, 1777.

Holland, Norman. *The Dynamics of Literary Response.* New York: W. W. Norton, 1968.

————. *Poems in Persons: An Introduction to the Psychoanalysis of Literature.* New York: W. W. Norton, 1973.

Huntington, Richard and Peter Metcalf. *Celebrations of Death: The Anthropology of Mortuary Rituals.* Cambridge: Cambridge University Press, 1979.

Jacobson, Edith. *The Self and the Object World.* New York: International Universities Press, 1964.

Kernberg, Otto F. *Borderline Conditions and Pathological Narcissism.* New York: Jason Aronson, 1975.

Klein, Melanie. "Mourning and Its Relation to Manic-Depressive States." *International Journal of Psychoanalysis* 21 (1940): 125–53.

Kris, Ernst. *Psychoanalytic Explorations in Art.* New York: Schocken Books, 1952.

Kurzweil, Edith and William Phillips, eds. *Literature and Psychoanalysis.* New York: Columbia University Press, 1983.

Lacan, Jacques. *Ecrits.* Paris: Editions du Seuil, 1966.

————. *The Language of the Self: The Function of Language in Psychoanalysis.* Translated by Anthony Wilden. Baltimore: Johns Hopkins University Press, 1968.

Lafleur, Héctor René, Sergio D. Provenzano, and Fernando Pedro Alonso, eds. *Las revistas literarias argentinas (1893–1960).* Buenos Aires: Ediciones Culturales Argentinas, 1962.

Lane, Edward William. *The Manners and Customs of the Modern Egyptians.* London: J. M. Dent, 1835.

Lindemann, Erich. *Beyond Grief: Studies in Crisis Intervention.* New York: Jason Aronson, 1979.

Lindstrom, Naomi. *Macedonio Fernández.* Lincoln, Nebr.: Society of Spanish and Spanish American Studies, 1981.

Loewald, Hans W. "Internalization, Separation, Mourning, and the Superego." *The Psychoanalytic Quarterly* 31 (1962): 483–504.

Mahler, Margaret Schoenberger. "On Sadness and Grief in Infancy and Childhood: Loss and Restoration of the Symbiotic Love Object." *The Psychoanalytic Study of the Child* 16 (1961): 332–52.

————. *The Selected Papers of Margaret S. Mahler.* 2 vols. New York: Jason Aronson, 1979.

Manuel, Don Juan. *El Conde Lucanor o Libro de los enxiemplos del Conde Lucanor et de Patronio.* Edited by José Manuel Blecua. Madrid: Castalia, 1969.

Mitford, A. B. *Tales of Old Japan.* London: Macmillan and Co., 1883.

Moore, Thomas. *The Poetical Works of Thomas Moore.* London: Longman, Brown, Green, and Roberts, 1854.

Pollock, George H. "Mourning and Adaptation." *International Journal of Psychoanalysis* 42 (1961): 341–61.

————. "On Mourning, Immortality and Utopia." *Journal of the American Psychoanalytic Association* 23 (1975): 334–62.

Propp, Vladimir. *Morphology of the Folktale.* 1st ed. translated by

Laurence Scott; 2d ed. revised and edited by Louis A. Wagner. American Folklore Society Bibliographical and Special Series. Austin: University of Texas Press, 1968.

Rank, Otto. *The Double: A Psychoanalytic Study.* Translated and edited by Harry Tucker. New York: New American Library, 1971.

Rochlin, Gregory. *Griefs and Discontents.* Boston: Little, Brown and Co., 1965.

Roland, Alan, ed. *Psychoanalysis, Creativity and Literature: A French-American Inquiry.* New York: Columbia University Press, 1978.

Sandler, Joseph and Barnard Rosenblatt. "The Concept of the Representational World." *The Psychoanalytic Study of the Child* 17 (1962): 128–48.

Sarlo Sabajanes, Beatriz, comp. *Martín Fierro (1924–1927).* Buenos Aires: Carlos Pérez Editor, 1969.

Schafer, Roy. *Aspects of Internalization.* New York: International Universities Press, 1969.

Schwob, Marcel. *Le roi au masque d'or.* Paris: Les Editions B. Crès et Cie., 1920.

Scobie, James R. *Argentina. A City and a Nation.* 2d ed. New York: Oxford University Press, 1971.

Secombe, Thomas. "Tichborne Claimant, The." *Encyclopaedia Britannica.* 11th ed. 1910.

Skura, Meredith Anne. *The Literary Use of the Psychoanalytic Process.* New Haven: Yale University Press, 1981.

Smith, Margaret. *The Persian Mystics: 'Attar.* London: John Murray, 1932.

Stoker, Bram. *Famous Impostors.* London: Sidgwick and Jackson, 1910.

Swedenborg, Emanuel. *The True Christian Religion.* New York: American Swedenborg Printing and Publishing Society, 1892.

Sykes, Percy. *A History of Persia.* 3d ed. London: Macmillan and Co., 1930.

Todorov, Tzvetan. *The Fantastic: A Structural Approach to a Literary Genre.* Translated by Richard Howard. Ithaca: Cornell University Press, 1975.

Trilling, Lionel. *The Liberal Imagination: Essays on Society and Literature.* 1950. Reprint. New York: Anchor Books, 1953.

Turner, Victor. *Dramas, Fields and Metaphors. Symbolic Action in Human Societies.* Ithaca: Cornell University Press, 1974.

Twain, Mark. *Life on the Mississippi.* Boston: James R. Osgood and Co., 1883.

Watson, Frederick. *A Century of Gunmen: A Study in Lawlessness.* London: Ivor Nicholson and Watson, 1931.

Weissman, Philip. "Theoretical Considerations of Ego Regression and Ego Functions in Creativity," *Psychoanalytic Quarterly* 36 (1967): 37–50.

About the Author
Mary Lusky Friedman is a faculty member in the Department of Spanish and Portuguese at Rutgers University. She has published articles on Borges, García Márquez, Anderson Imbert, and other Latin American writers and is coeditor of *Homenaje a Jorge Guillén* (1978).

Library of Congress Cataloging-in-Publication Data
Lusky Friedman, Mary 1949–
    The emperor's kites.
    Bibliography: p.
    Includes index.
    1. Borges, Jorge Luis, 1899–   —Criticism and interpretation.   I. Title.
PQ7797.B635Z716   1987   863   86–24139
ISBN 0–8223–0712–x